Religion in the Megacity

Religion in the Megacity

Catholic and Protestant Portraits from Latin America

Phillip Berryman

ORBIS BOOKS
Maryknoll, New York 10545

The Catholic Foreign Mission Society of America (Maryknoll) recruits and trains people for overseas missionary service. Through Orbis Books, Maryknoll aims to foster the international dialogue that is essential to mission. The books published, however, reflect the opinions of their authors and are not meant to represent the official position of the society.

Library of Congress Cataloging in Publication Data

Berryman, Phillip.
    Religion in the megacity : Catholic and Protestant portraits from
Latin America / Phillip Berryman.
        p.   cm.
    Includes index.
    ISBN 1-57075-083-1 (alk. paper)
    1. Catholic Church—Brazil—São Paulo.   2. Catholic Church—
Venezuela—Caracas.   3. Protestant Churches—Brazil—São Paulo.
4. Protestant Churches—Venezuela—Caracas.   5. São Paulo (Brazil)—
Religious life and customs.   6. Caracas (Venezuela)—Religious life
and customs.   I. Title.
    BX1467.S3B47   1996
    278.1'610829—dc20   96-33367
                                                          CIP

Contents

ACROSS THE DIVIDE

Introduction

On a muggy, drizzly Holy Thursday, Father Alfredo Gonçalves described how his viewpoint had evolved. After spending years in the neighborhoods of self-built housing on the outskirts of Sao Paulo, he was now working with the poor who lived in the crowded dark tenements of the downtown area. He acknowledged that he and others had invested heavily in imported socialist ideas, and that their widely shared hope that a worker-led political movement would bring about change in society had been frustrated.

In pastoral matters, he was now raising questions about base communities. Priests or sisters could make impressive advances by working intensively with small groups, an elite of twenty or even fifty people, but such work would have little impact on the many thousands of people whose lives were so precarious that they could not become involved in such a movement.

"Five years ago there were lots of answers and few questions," he noted with a gentle smile, referring to the hopes he and others had up to the late 1980s. "Today it's the other way around: we've got very few answers and lots of questions." He was putting into words the feeling that had gotten me to Brazil and the impulse behind this book.

As early as 1970, many in Latin America had an image of the church of the future. The basic unit would not be the parish in its present form where tens of thousands of people are served by one priest, often foreign. Instead, it would be a smaller face-to-face community, normally presided over by a man of the same social background as the people in the community and hence married (women's ordination was not being raised in Latin America). Parishes would be networks of such communities, possibly coordinated by a figure resembling today's priest, who would function, however, like the *episcopos* ("overseer") of the early church.

This new model of church would exist, it was hoped, in a new kind of society, one in which Latin America was on the way to liberation, that is, free to develop economically in terms of its own needs, and where ordinary people had full rights and participated fully. Although Cuba was not itself a model, by its very existence it proved that a society could be organized along other lines, and that even a poor agroexport Latin American

1

country could ensure that all its citizens enjoyed basic human rights to work, food, shelter, education, health care, and basic human dignity.

How such new models of church and society were to come about was not at all clear; the present was intolerable, and therefore the future had to be different. Pastoral workers and theologians in any case were primarily occupied by more pressing tasks, such as defending elementary human rights, often at considerable risk.

Much had happened in the two or three decades since Vatican Council II (1962–65) and the Latin American Bishops Conference meeting at Medellin (CELAM II - 1968), which had sketched a distinctively Latin American approach to church renewal. Latin American liberation theology had become influential around the world, and had made European and North American theologians aware that theirs was not a universal but a situated theology; the churches had often spearheaded resistance to military dictatorships in Brazil, Chile, and elsewhere; Central America had suffered greatly but had also embodied great hopes; martyrdom was a contemporary reality (Archbishop Romero, the four U.S. church women, the six Jesuits and the two women killed with them, as well as countless other believers and others slain in the struggle for justice, such as Chico Mendes, the leader of the Brazilian rubber tappers).

Despite this undeniably rich and heroic history, the yearned-for liberation seemed nowhere on the horizon, and in fact the very possibility of any genuine alternative to the present order seemed to be ever more firmly closed. Several years ago when I was asked to write a chapter on the Latin American experience for a collection of essays on democratization in the church I had been forced to think about these matters. Rather than meeting the editors' expectations of contrasting the democracy of a "bottom up" base-community model of church to "top down" models old and new, I found myself pondering what had happened to the high hopes for Latin American Catholicism in the previous two decades.

The future now seemed to belong not to Catholic base communities but to evangelical Protestantism, particularly in its pentecostal form.* During the 1980s, Catholics and the Latin American secular left had viewed the advance of Protestant churches in largely political terms. Catholic bish-

---

*Although the term *protestante* exists in both Spanish and Portuguese, the preferred term in Latin America is *evangélico*. Most Latin American Protestants today are far closer to U.S. "evangelicals" (conservative with a tendency toward biblical literalism) than to "liberal" mainstream Protestants. The varieties of Latin American Protestantism are discussed at several points in this book. Both terms— "Protestant" and "evangelical"—will be used to refer to non-Roman Catholic Christians.

ops claimed that these churches were foreign to the "Latin American identity," which they assumed to be Catholic. David Stoll began to change the terms of the debate in *Is Latin America Turning Protestant?* Although he questioned the more extreme claims of the "church growth" proponents who were enthusiastically predicting years when the majority in certain countries would be Protestant, Stoll noted that already the number of church-going Protestants was on a par with that of Catholics in some places.[1]

In *Tongues of Fire* published at the same time, British sociologist David Martin made a more ambitious claim. If Latin America's underdevelopment was largely a product of its Iberian culture, by embracing the "Anglo" values present in pentecostalism (which Martin likened to early Methodism) Latin Americans would acquire the cultural foundation needed for ascending to modernity and development.[2] A writer in the business magazine *Forbes*—which in its pursuit of mammon normally ignores the churches—stated that "Evangelical Protestantism has almost certainly replaced Roman Catholicism as Brazil's most widely practiced faith." A new social atmosphere "more compatible with capitalism and democracy" was coming into being as the "upwardly mobile" urban poor were being encouraged to "change their lives through faith . . . The potential is quite literally revolutionary—more so than Fidel Castro or Che Guevara could ever be." The author concluded that "the growth of Protestantism in Brazil and throughout Latin America offers solid clues to the future—a capitalistic, bourgeois future, not a Marxist or traditional future."[3] In 1993, Caio Fabio d'Araujo, a Presbyterian minister strongly influenced by pentecostalism, told a *New York Times* reporter, "The Catholic church opted for the poor, but the poor opted for the evangelicals."[4] The remark was facile, and perhaps cruel, but contained a nugget of truth.

Like Father Alfredo, many Catholics were struggling to come to terms with events. Liberation theologians were, understandably perhaps, in a defensive mode. Their theology had never depended on "historic socialism," they insisted; its starting point was the poor and the gospel. The emerging post-cold-war world was becoming even harsher on the poor, and hence liberation theology was as relevant as ever—indeed more so.[5] From the perspective of liberation theologians, that was perhaps the point that most needed to be emphasized. Yet I could not but wonder why theologians who claimed to take "reality" as their starting point were not providing greater insight into the changes in society and the churches.

What are the contours of the new situation of the churches in Latin America? What does it mean for the Catholic church to be facing a serious rival in the religious arena? (Is the relationship even best viewed as one of competition?) What does it mean for Protestants to realize that they are no longer a tiny minority but that (at least as measured by church attendance) they are on a par with Catholics? Do evangelical churches view their mission only in terms of converting individuals or are they envisioning a social role for the church? To what extent do new developments in Latin American society require a rethinking of liberation theology and its associated pastoral methods? Who, if anyone, is doing this rethinking?

These questions were primarily qualitative rather than quantitative. I did not set out to measure growth rates of evangelical churches or Catholic church attendance but to assess current trends. Furthermore, I was interested not only in the situations of Catholicism or Protestantism by themselves but in their impact on one another.[6]

My disquietude had arisen in the late 1980s in Central America, but it seemed important to pursue the questions in one or more of the larger Latin American countries and especially in urban environments. Lingering stereotypes notwithstanding, the typical Latin American today is not a peasant but lives in a town or city. Indeed, 72 percent of Latin Americans are urban,[7] and four of the ten largest cities in the world are in Latin America (Mexico City, Sao Paulo, Buenos Aires, Rio de Janeiro). It seemed appropriate to study a city where evangelicals were numerous and another where they were less so.

Through a process both logical and intuitive, I chose Sao Paulo and Caracas. Sao Paulo was the world's largest Catholic archdiocese until 1989, when it was carved up by a Vatican decision. Under the leadership of Cardinal Paulo Evaristo Arns, it had been at the forefront in the implementation of pastoral innovation after Vatican II and Medellin. Part of my reason for choosing Caracas was that, although the numbers of evangelicals were relatively low, mission publications indicated that rapid evangelical church growth might be about to begin.

In 1993, I went to these two cities (and some other sites in Brazil) to pursue these questions. As it happened, both countries were in the midst of a political crisis. Brazil was in the hands of a caretaker government after the forced resignation of President Fernando Collor de Mello as a result of corruption scandals.[8] The former labor union leader Luís Inacio Lula da Silva, head of the leftist Workers Party with strong ties to the progressive wing of the Catholic church, seemed destined to win the next presidential election.[9] As I criss-crossed Caracas looking for churches, I witnessed the final stages of President Carlos Andres Perez's resignation for embezzlement. Although those events were not directly relevant to my research, they were part of a process of questioning taking place in both societies. Neither country had recovered from the economic reverses of the "lost decade" of the 1980s, and neither had yet adopted a clear national strategy for dealing with the increasingly globalized economy of the 1990s.

This book is an effort to distill what I heard, saw, and learned. Writing it has been complicated by the fact that it does not lend itself to easy summary, to catchy new ideas, let alone to a new overarching paradigm. It is a fragmentary record of many partial insights, my own and those of my interlocutors.

Although this is a report on two cities at a particular point in time, I believe it provides a window into the situation of the churches in Latin America more generally. As is frequently pointed out, Latin America has been a "Catholic" continent (and may soon be home to half the world's Catholics) and hence it is obviously important for the whole Catholic church. The voice of its liberation theologians has been heard worldwide. Moreover, the growth of evangelical (primarily pentecostal) churches is also worldwide. Whatever the short-term zigs and zags of United States interest in Latin America, the peoples of the western hemisphere are becoming increasingly intertwined through trade, investment, migration, cultural exchange—and shared faith. For these reasons I hope that this book will offer readers glimpses into recent developments, even (or especially) if—like Father Alfredo—they come away with fewer answers and more questions.

A word on my angle of vision is in order. Although roughly equal amounts of space are devoted to Catholics and Protestants, I inevitably write more as an insider when dealing with Catholics and an outsider when I approach Protestants. The work of academics has been very helpful in my research, but this book does not enter deeply into theoretical matters proper to scholarly disciplines.

An introduction on Sao Paulo and the recent experience of the Catholic church under Cardinal Paulo Evaristo Arns (Chapter 1) is followed by observations on a number of Brazilian evangelical churches and the movement more generally (Chapters 2 and 3). Various aspects of the progressive Catholic church are considered (Chapters 4 to 6), along with the Charismatic Renewal (Chapter 7). Women's voices, Catholic and Protestant, close the section on Brazil (Chapter 8). After an introduction to Caracas (Chapter 9), Catholic pastoral efforts and evangelical churches are portrayed (Chapters 10 and 11). This is followed by observations on the light that these two cities may shed on issues facing the Catholic church (Chapter 12) and evangelical churches (Chapter 13). The conclusion considers—tentatively, to be sure—possibilities for mutual relationships between Latin American Catholicism and evangelical Protestantism (Chapter 14).

The field research was supported by a grant from the Social Science Research Council. Among the many who helped me in Sao Paulo and Caracas, I would like to thank Francisco Weffort, Madalena Freire, Frei Betto, Luis Faria, Ana Flora Anderson, Ricardo Mariano, Luis Gonzaga, Bill Reinhard, and Daniel and Phyllis Levine. I am grateful for detailed suggestions on the manuscript from Paul Freston and Ken Serbin as well as by a number of other readers of the manuscript or portions of it: John Bueno, Samuel Escobar, Ivone Gebara, Mary Hunt, Tom Quigley, and Richard Shaull. For bearing with me during the research and writing, I express my gratitude to my wife, Angela, and our daughters Catherine, Margaret, and Elizabeth. Finally, I dedicate this book to two women of faith, my mother, Katherine Berryman, and my mother-in-law, Catherine Brennan, in whose house the first draft was written.

SAO PAULO

1
A Church for the Megacity

S AO PAULO IS A TRUE MEGACITY—roughly on a par with Mexico City—
but it does not conjure up striking images. It has nothing like the Christ
of Corcovado with his arms outstretched to embrace Rio below, nor the
concrete slabs and circles of Brasilia ambitiously arising out of the plains.

For Brazilians, Sao Paulo is a "New York," a center of business and
banking and a magnet for ambitious people; a "Chicago," an industrial
giant set in an agricultural heartland; a "Detroit" when it was still the auto-
motive center; and a "Los Angeles," a promised land for the poor from
other parts of the country. *Time* rated Sao Paulo second only to Tokyo in its
list of largest cities, although most estimates are somewhat lower and put
the city at third or fourth among the world's megacities.[1] Urban theorists
say that if there is a second tier of "global cities" after London, New York,
and Tokyo, Sao Paulo is among them.

Although the site was settled in the sixteenth century, it remained a
small town for three hundred years. In 1890, when Rio de Janeiro was a
large modern city of over a half-million people, Sao Paulo had only about
sixty-five thousand inhabitants, and served primarily as the regional center
for coffee production in the surrounding state of Sao Paulo. European immigrants around the turn of the century helped spur industrial growth, and
by 1940 the city had 1.6 million inhabitants. In the 1950s it was the fastest
growing city in the world. The 1991 census showed that the city proper
had 9.5 million inhabitants and that greater Sao Paulo had approximately
15.2 million.[2]

Few find the city physically attractive. The sea is only an hour away,
but there is no sign of its presence. The Tietê river winding its way through
town is a polluted canal. The city's colonial past is a only a memory, since
most of the oldest buildings are factories and warehouses dating from the
early decades of this century. Many of these buildings are now abandoned.
No grand design is evident in the city layout, as the various districts run
into each other at angles, reflecting the chaotic, unregulated way the population has expanded during this century.

Jorge Wilhelm, the city's leading urbanist, has written that people's "basic loyalty to Sao Paulo, rather than coming from love for the city, comes from the challenge of conquering it. As in many large cities, the aggression needed for survival in a highly competitive environment has generated an atmosphere of restlessness, determination and admiration for those that are successful."[3] That assertiveness is the image other Brazilians carry of the *paulista* (resident of the city or state of Sao Paulo) as an ambitious, aggressive person who arrives in other parts of Brazil claiming to be the owner of a piece of land or wielding a chain saw to cut down trees.

There is of course no single Sao Paulo; people experience the city from the perspective of their own circumstances. Perhaps half the city lives comfortably, traveling primarily by car over freeways and broad avenues (there are almost 2 million automobiles in greater Sao Paulo).[4] Many in the middle class commute between their twenty-story apartment houses or private homes and ever more decentralized work sites. On the other hand, a priest in the eastern part of the city told me that people in his parish could not afford to go even to shopping centers a half-hour bus ride away, let alone to downtown Sao Paulo. Those living in dark one-room apartments with common bathrooms in tenement buildings near the city center experience the city in yet another way.

"Dom Paulo"

Sao Paulo was the largest Catholic archdiocese in the world until it was subdivided by a Vatican decision in 1989. It may also be the large archdiocese that has made the most systematic effort within its own institutional structures to implement the spirit of Vatican II and its particular Latin American and Brazilian embodiment. That has been the work of Dom Paulo Evaristo Arns who has guided the archdiocese since 1970, through the worst periods of military dictatorship into the present. Two constants throughout his leadership have been a concern: to devise a corporate pastoral response to the vast complex reality of Sao Paulo and a vigorous defense of human rights.

On Ash Wednesday—which for most of Brazil meant little more than the conclusion of the five-day Carnival holiday—I was in the cathedral for the launching of the annual Brotherhood Campaign. Because the 1993 theme was housing, spokespersons for housing movements and organizations for the homeless stood with priests in the sanctuary. Some took the microphone to address the congregation, many of whom were standing in the aisles. During his sermon, "Dom Paulo" (the title "Dom" given to Brazilian bishops is both honorific and familiar) had the congregation repeat after him several times: "All Brazilians have a right to housing." It seemed a little heavy-handedly didactic, but I was assured that people were used to this longstanding practice of his.

Such combining of a "secular" matter like housing with the liturgical action of receiving ashes symbolized not only Dom Paulo's personal bent, but what had become the trademark of post-Vatican II Catholicism in this megacity. "Housing" was one of the three priorities of the 1991–1994 archdiocesan pastoral plan, and also one of the numerous officially recognized *pastorais* (ministries).

For many years Arns taught patristics at the Franciscan seminary in Petropolis (where his fellow Franciscan Leonardo Boff, who is also from Arns's native region of Santa Catarina in southern Brazil, taught theology). In 1966 Arns was ordained a bishop and assigned to help Cardinal Agnelo Rossi, partly, it is said, because other bishops felt the need for a bishop of Arns's intellectual caliber to defend the church in the wake of the 1964 military coup.

Assigned to the region of Santa Ana in the northern part of the city, Arns set out to implement the conciliar reforms by assembling a team of priests, sisters, married couples, and dedicated women from what were then called secular institutes. As part of a program called "Mission to the People of God," they organized week-long visits to each of the fifty parishes in the district. In their follow-up, Arns and the team conceived of a way of extending or "multiplying" the work begun in the mission by preparing people from the parishes and subdivisions of parishes to do outreach within their own sectors. Each sector of several parishes provided training courses in scripture for lay leaders who then held meetings in their neighborhoods or their churches, thus eventually giving rise to some Christian base communities. This organizational approach, which exemplified what Latin American pastoral specialists call *pastoral de conjunto* (jointly planned and executed pastoral work), has been a characteristic feature of Cardinal Arns's tenure in Sao Paulo.

While he was still an auxiliary, Arns had his first clashes with the military dictatorship. Although the jailings and exile of labor and student leaders began with the coup itself, repression became harsher after the promulgation of Institutional Act No. 5 in 1968. Some Dominicans had been secretly helping activists make their way south through Brazil and eventually out of the country. In 1969 the police broke into the Dominican convent in Sao Paulo and arrested all present. Although they gradually released those whom they deemed uninvolved, they continued to hold at least twenty in an undisclosed location. Frei Gorgulho, the scripture scholar, went to ask Cardinal Rossi for help and, after some initial resistance and hesitation, it was decided that Bishop Arns would go with

Gorgulho, partly because most of the military bases where the students were apparently being held were in Arns's area of the city.

In the process of trying to locate the Dominican students, he had contact with the other political prisoners and saw their torture marks. He also encountered a sister who had been imprisoned and so tortured that she had almost gone out of her mind. "Don Paulo was so scandalized that it was like one of those rude awakenings that turns into a conversion," says Ana Flora Anderson, an American biblical scholar and theologian who has worked in Sao Paulo for over thirty years.[5]

Made archbishop of Sao Paulo in 1970, Arns extended what he had been doing by sponsoring courses to update priests, sisters, and lay people. Noting that the church's personnel and resources were disproportionately concentrated in the schools and parishes of the central portion of the city while vast numbers of the poor in the outlying areas had little attention from the church, Arns and his collaborators launched "Operation Periphery." The idea was simple: the church's resources should go to where the people were, and that meant the *favelas* (shanty towns) springing up on the city outskirts. Religious orders were encouraged to free personnel from their schools and other institutions to go to live in these areas. A major emphasis was on the construction of chapels or multipurpose community centers. Within a few years, fifteen hundred such centers had been erected.

Arns brought people together to reflect on the theological understanding of the "local church" and its pastoral consequences for how the archdiocese should be organized. Sao Paulo was too large for the archbishop to know the clergy personally, let alone the parishes and people. Yet the people of Sao Paulo experienced the city as a single vast unit that they traversed in the course of their work and other activities. Hence, carving it up into separate dioceses would be inappropriate. The solution was to divide the diocese into episcopal regions, which were further subdivided into sectors, each composed typically of several parishes. With encouragement from Pope Paul VI, in the mid-1970s Arns was able to assemble a team of a half-dozen pastorally minded bishops who shared his vision to head the episcopal regions. (None of them would be made a bishop today, a chancery official told me.) The bishops of each region handled most routine ecclesiastical and pastoral affairs and dealt with local clergy. The structure seemed to keep ordinary administration on a manageable scale while retaining a "local church" structure suited to the situation of the large city. However, it did not really fit canon law, which regards individual bishops as sovereign in their own territory and has them relate directly to Rome (rather like feudal lords under a monarch). Under Paul VI, the Sao Paulo approach found a favorable hearing from some sectors of the Vatican, but that support proved temporary.

In 1975, after an extensive consultation process, the diocese published its first pastoral plan. Defined in that process were four priorities: Christian base communities, the periphery, the world of labor, and human rights. Thereafter, the plans were prepared at three- or four-year intervals. The sixth such plan, "Mission in the City 1991–1994" was the fruit of almost two years of consultation culminating in a large assembly of delegates chosen by the parishes or movements (including for example, the Catholic Charismatic Renewal). Based on what I had seen elsewhere, I was skeptical of such planning because the documents produced could easily be ignored at the parish level, but I was told that in Sao Paulo participation had been high, at least for a period of years. The plans embodied ongoing serious reflection on the response of the church to the needs of this massive city.

Resistance to human rights violations brought further confrontation with the military. In March 1973, as troops menacingly surrounded the cathedral, Arns celebrated a funeral for Alexandre Vannucchi Leme, a university student who had been tortured to death; Arns assured the congregation that Christ's resurrection meant victory over the forces of death. When the journalist Wladimir Herzog was tortured to death in 1975, Arns, in defiance of government orders, joined Rabbi Henry Sobel and Presbyterian minister Jaime Wright in an ecumenical service. Troops again impeded movement toward the cathedral. Still, eight thousand people managed to attend, despite the military photographers snapping photos in a blatant attempt to intimidate. Although the first hints of a loosening of military control had appeared in 1974, many later regarded Herzog's funeral as the moment when people began to corporately resist the worst crimes of the dictatorship. The media that generally had supported the military reacted to the murder of one of their own. That Herzog was a Jew and a Communist proved that Arns's concern for human rights went beyond his flock.

Under Arns, the archdiocese utilized its resources to defend human rights. Although the military had closed the church radio station in 1973 and subjected the archdiocesan paper to direct censorship, archdiocesan offices continued to document human rights violations and to offer services to victims and their families. One office published a detailed account of human rights violations in Argentina, to the dismay of some Argentine bishops. Arns defended the human rights of Brazilians and others in Chile, Uruguay, and Paraguay.[6]

In 1977 Arns took advantage of a visit to Brazil by President Jimmy Carter (whom he had recently met at the University of Notre Dame when both had received honorary doctorates) to hand him a list of twenty-three of the "disappeared," which the media also then published. Santo Dias, a lay leader active in archdiocesan-level activities, was shot point-blank during a 1979 strike and became a martyr of the archdiocese. The following year, Dalmo Dallari, a leading jurist who had been chosen to be a reader at an outdoor mass celebrated by Pope John Paul II, was abducted and beaten the day before the mass and had to be lifted into the podium.[7]

In early 1979, as the power of the dictatorship began to wane, Arns and others discovered that military archives contained testimony relating to torture, testimony given by courageous people to military courts themselves. Realizing the value of the material, Cardinal Arns, the Presbyterian pastor Jaime Wright, and their collaborators engaged in a highly secretive operation: over a period of years documents were checked out of the archives overnight (ostensibly for use by lawyers on individual cases), photocopied, and returned the following day. With funding primarily from the World Council of Churches, the group compiled a million pages covering 707 trials, from which they published a twelve-volume collection that Wright called an "encyclopedia of torture." Excerpts from that collection were published as *Torture in Brazil*.[8] The aim was to create a climate of public opinion that would serve as a deterrent to such actions in the future. The fact that over two hundred thousand copies were sold in the following years attests to a public yearning for the record to be revealed.

Meanwhile, the city had continued to grow and the archdiocese seemed to be reaching an unmanageable size, even with a half-dozen like-minded auxiliary bishops. Arns and others had continued to think about the matter and had studied plans implemented in other large archdioceses, including Detroit and Paris. On the basis of his ongoing consultations with the pope and Vatican officials, Arns believed that while some new dioceses would be created, something of the pastoral collaboration achieved over the years would be preserved. In 1989, shortly after he had described these discussions to a gathering of eight hundred clergy, news reports from Rome revealed that four new dioceses were to be created, reducing the Sao Paulo archdiocese by half—to 7 million people. The humiliating manner in which the action was taken perhaps reflected longstanding Roman pique at Arns's international reputation. The divisions of the new dioceses cut through the city of Sao Paulo arbitrarily and made no pastoral sense. Among the areas cut off were those in the industrial south and in the east, where labor and popular organizing and Christian base communities had been most vigorous.

This action, it should be noted, was part of a consistent Vatican policy of making episcopal appointments based more on loyalty to Rome than on proven pastoral concern and ability. Brazil's leading dailies and news magazines interpreted the move as a "serious defeat" for Arns's pastoral approach and as a Roman action to bring the local church back into line.[9] Their reaction reflected an opinion widely shared among business people and the upper middle class that under Arns the clergy had become politicized (that is, pro-Workers Party) and that Arns was "defending the human rights of criminals" (by insisting that even prisoners have rights).

By the early 1990s, bishops in some of the new dioceses were dismantling the work done earlier and setting a different tone. Discouraged church workers, some sisters in particular, had moved to other dioceses to work under more progressive bishops. I was told that clergy were reverting to traditional activities and authoritarian ways of working, although I was unable to verify this observation systematically. Even in 1993, it was assumed that when Arns resigned in 1996, his successor would probably dismantle his work. It would be wiser, I was told, to do the dismantling slowly, by attrition, although a more rapid clean sweep, such as had been carried out by Archbishop Helder Camara's successor in Recife, could not be ruled out.

Not all the difficulties of the progressive wing of the Catholic church can be attributed to the Vatican. The world itself has changed in ways not anticipated during the heroic days of resistance to the military dictatorship. Furthermore, the church may be discovering some important facts belatedly. During the 1980s even social scientists were surprised to discover the intensification of a new kind of poverty in Sao Paulo: more and more people were living in the tenements of the central region of Sao Paulo, where older houses had been subdivided and were being rented out. Unlike the *favelas* which are visible to anyone willing to venture to the outskirts of the city and are familiar from decades of journalistic photos, the *cortiços* (lit. beehives), as these tenements are known, are hidden behind facades. Three million people were estimated to be living in approximately ninety thousand *cortiços*. On a visit to these areas Arns admitted (referring to the thrust of the archdiocese that he had encouraged), "The periphery is now in the center." No "Operation Center" was launched, however, and relatively few church workers were active there; those who were, like Father Alfredo, readily admitted that they had no adequate pastoral response.

Despite the end of repressive military dictatorship and the return of elected civilian government, the world of the 1990s seemed far less clear than it had in the days of Operation Periphery and face-to-face confrontation with the torturers and murderers. "Really, I think that the church as such does not have an answer for the city," said Bishop Decio Pereira, whose area of responsibility was an arbitrary portion of the city running from close to downtown in a southeasterly direction. "The church is used to working in a rural setting...In the village the church is the center of everything. We transferred the rural parish to the city, [but] it is not a sufficient instrument." With refreshing candor, the bishop admitted that "we don't have very strong or clear models of what a ministry for the city itself would be."[10]

Although the Catholic church was beginning to acknowledge that it had no model for its approach to the city, under the leadership of Cardinal Arns, those involved in the archdiocese—sisters, priests, active lay people—were now stating that the church exists *for* the city. In their 1995–1998 pastoral plan, the object of the church's pastoral action was defined as:

> evangelizing the city of San Paulo by means of urban ministry, by renewing the life of ecclesial communities, hearing the cries of the people, especially those who are excluded from the world of work, health, housing, and education, and responding with action in solidarity.[11]

Drawn up with the full awareness that Cardinal Arns almost certainly would not see the end of the period since he would reach the age of seventy-five in late 1996, the plan sought to articulate the understanding of the church's mission that had developed under Arns's leadership. Rather than a conventional division between internal (biblical, liturgical, sacramental) and external (social action) activities, the plan reflected, in theory at least, a high degree of interpenetration. Thus in the passage above, hearing and responding to the cry of the people in their need is itself viewed as evangelization. At various points the document invoked the term "inculturation," one of the clearest innovations to come from the documents of the bishops' meeting at Santo Domingo (1992). In a city such as Sao Paulo, the church had to seek inculturation as surely as it did among indigenous tribes in the Amazon.

In short, after two and a half decades of innovative—and often heroic—pastoral work, Catholics were acknowledging that in some respects they were just beginning to face the challenge of the large modern Latin American city.

Their tentative and exploratory attitude stood in sharp contrast to that of evangelicals who seldom paused to ask questions as they confidently strode forward.

2

Windows into the Evangelical World

E VEN AS I LEFT THE METRO STATION I began to spot them: poor mulatto or black men in suits and ties, obviously evangelical ministers. In twos or threes they were moving down the streets of the Belém district east of downtown Sao Paulo on a Monday night. By the time I arrived at the headquarters church of the Assemblies of God (Belem Ministry), the buzz of a hundred conversations filled the air.

Taking a seat in the back of the church, I soon saw that many pastors were kneeling and praying with their eyes closed. Their backs were to the sanctuary and their elbows were resting on the benches. Some moaned out loud, shouted, gesticulated. Others, meanwhile, continued to wave to one another, shake hands, and converse. In the sanctuary, the major ministers surrounding Jose Wellington, the head of this ministry,[1] also knelt down and prayed, facing their chairs. At the sound of the bell, individual prayer ceased, and Pastor Wellington began the evening's proceedings. This was the regular monthly meeting of ministers.

The jeans and short-sleeve shirt that had made me inconspicuous on the metro made me an obvious outsider here: quite literally 99 percent of these men were wearing suits and ties. Seeing about twelve hundred pastors from one denomination under one roof was an impressive sight. The number of pastors equaled the number of Catholic priests in the area.[2] Other comparisons came to mind. Most of these men were mulatto; some were black, but few were white. A Catholic clergy gathering would be made up of Europeans and Brazilians disproportionately from southern Brazil, which is mainly white. From the looks of these men it was clear that they were from the poor strata, although not the most desperate. The intense outpouring of prayer and hearty singing also set them apart from a group of Catholic clergy. In one respect, however, they were similar: there were no women in the group, although one woman stood in the doorway for some time, and at one point Wellington mentioned "our wives," some of whom were evidently occupied elsewhere on the premises.

A major agenda item was the presentation of plans for an evangelistic crusade planned for Holy Week. Wellington insisted that all weeks are holy for evangelicals; he was referring to what the "world" calls Holy Week. Since the gym they had used last year was too small, they were now going to hold the meeting in the heart of the city at a large plaza that could hold thousands. This army of pastors obviously offered a good starting point for assembling a critical mass of people.

That evening provided me with a revealing window into the dynamics of the evangelical world. This chapter will present a further series of such windows. Broader questions, especially about evangelical growth, are taken up in Chapter 3.

First, however, it is well to make some brief observations on the Protestant field as a whole.[3] In Brazil, the most obvious dividing line is between what may be called the "historic churches," which correspond to mainstream denominations in the United States, and pentecostal churches. Some of the historic churches arrived with national groups, most notably the Lutherans in southern Brazil who remain largely identified with the descendants of German immigrants. The major historic churches include Presbyterians, Methodists, and Baptists, whose arrival reflected the missionary effort from the United States in the late nineteenth century.

Pentecostal churches now make up the majority, and they are by far the fastest growing. A 1992 study in Rio de Janeiro classified 39 percent of churches as historic and 61 percent as pentecostal. Even more significant was the fact that 91 percent (648 of the 710) of the new churches in Rio established during the 1990–1992 period were pentecostal.[4]

It should be noted that the division into historic and pentecostal churches is an oversimplification, since some churches are neither. In particular, churches deriving from the turn-of-the-century faith missions, unlike the historic churches, profess biblical inerrancy, but they are focused on biblical preaching and do not accept the pentecostal conviction that the gifts of the Holy Spirit are available now and manifest in healing and exorcism. Such churches had only a relatively minor presence in Sao Paulo, however.

Moreover, these boundaries are fluid. Many churches from historical traditions—Baptists and Presbyterians, for example—are far more conservative than their counterparts elsewhere. Further, pentecostal practices have been making advances in historic churches, where they are usually referred to as charismatic.

A relatively small circle of churches (Lutheran, Methodist, Episcopal, one branch of Presbyterians) has formed a Council of Churches (CONIC), which includes the Roman Catholic and Syrian Orthodox churches. The largest groups of historic churches—several bodies of Presbyterians, for example—do not belong to CONIC, and thus it is fair to say that the vast majority of Brazilian Protestant churches are not ecumenical as understood in the liberal mainline churches in the United States and Europe.

Among pentecostal churches, a half-dozen stand above the rest. Paul Freston has pointed out that they were founded at three distinct moments: 1910–1911 (the Assemblies of God and the Christian Congregation), the 1950s and 1960s (Foursquare Gospel, Brazil for Christ, and God is Love), and the 1970s–1980s (best typified by the Universal Church of the Kingdom of God).[5] After some initial observations on the Baptist church, this chapter will focus primarily on these churches, and will conclude with glances into other evangelical groups.

Being Baptist at Mid-Century

My first formal interview was with Plinio Moreira da Silva, a Baptist minister now in retirement after forty-five years in the ministry. I was thus reminded that Protestantism has well over a century of history in Brazil and Latin America, a fact often ignored or forgotten by those who concentrate only on its current manifestations. Moreira was raised conventionally Catholic, but by adolescence he had little use for religion. Then in the mid-1940s he was attracted to Marxism, joined the Communist Party, and became party secretary in the town of Jundiaí, not far from Sao Paulo.

His conversion came through a young woman who introduced him to the bible. He became "fascinated by the person and the teachings of Jesus" and by the fact that church members actually sought to live by those teachings. He concluded that "Jesus was what was missing in my life, and so I then gave up communism and embraced Jesus Christ." (Like all conversion stories, his may have taken on added sharpness over the years.) The young woman became his wife, but when she died shortly after their marriage, he decided to go to the seminary to study for the ministry. He had held various positions in the interior of Sao Paulo state and then in the city.

Wasn't it difficult to be a Baptist minister in the 1950s? I asked. "In the 1930s, that was true," he responded. "People faced persecution and were separated from their families, and there was a great deal of pressure from society. The priest was very influential and could prohibit, persecute, burn bibles. All of those kinds of things happened, even the burning of churches. But by the 1950s that had changed; society had evolved after World War II. Advances had been made in the spirit of democracy and of respect for other people's opinions.

"So I never suffered any limitation for being a Christian or a pastor. On the contrary, I was admired, respected, and praised. I never suffered any persecution from Catholics—never." Such things might happen elsewhere in Brazil, where religious or family traditions might be stronger, but not in Sao Paulo.

He described his everyday routine in the town of Araraquara. "From 8 A.M. to noon, I worked in the church office with a secretary. I studied, prepared sermons, did church administration, and was thère to receive people and provide help for those in need. After lunch I spent part of the afternoon visiting the homes of people who were interested in getting to know the Christian message. Or I visited members of the church who were having health problems, or I gave family counseling. At night I had bible study, or church meetings, or further visits with people who were not home during the day, or I met with people in my office." Under his leadership the church grew from 70 adult members to 120 or 140. He later pastored other churches, served as state secretary of the Baptist Convention, and taught in the seminary.

The Baptist church, he explained, had come to Brazil when some families had fled the American South during and after the Civil War. "They were slaveholders and preferred to emigrate to Brazil rather than live in a country where they no longer had cheap slave labor." Some of them sent back requests for missionaries to come and evangelize Brazilians. The first church was officially set up in Bahia in 1882. The missionaries were welcomed by the emperor, Dom Pedro II (1840–1889) who was interested in all forms of modernization.

Whereas Presbyterian missionaries emphasized education and evangelized the elite, "the Baptists evangelized the poor classes, the working classes." They and their children prospered, however, and today Baptist congregations include doctors, engineers, and university professors. The four or five hundred Baptist churches that existed in Brazil when he was ordained had grown to two thousand.

After his conversion, Moreira turned anti-communist, so much so that he justified the actions of the military under the post-1964 dictatorship. "It was war—the universities were nests of subversion." The military was "the only force able to bring order to the country." He called pastor Jaime Wright (who had worked with Cardinal Arns on human rights) a Marxist. His animosity extended to the Workers Party. Although the Baptist church had not endorsed Fernando Collor in the 1989 election, as some evangelicals had done, few Baptists had voted for Lula, he said. His distrust of the Workers Party was only aggravated by its ties to the progressive sector of the Catholic church (he was sympathetic toward Catholic charismatics).

Moreira was more sanguine than some other Baptist ministers over the success of pentecostals. As the Baptists became middle class, "The Assemblies of God came in to fill the void." The Assemblies of God and other pentecostals had been very successful in evangelizing low-income people. They were also rising socially as the Baptists had before them, and were in turn ceding territory to the newer pentecostal churches.

Some Baptists, like those in other historic churches, feel threatened by the fast growing pentecostals. Ed Kivitz,[6] a young pastor of one of the older churches in the city, observed, "The Baptists have been in Brazil for over a hundred years, and there still aren't a million Baptists. The Universal Church of the Kingdom of God is only ten years old and only God knows how many millions it has." His own congregation was looking for new methods. It had lightened the traditional Sunday schedule of services that would have members in church most of the day and was trying innovations such as organizing small groups that would meet in homes.

Assemblies of God

"The Assemblies of God is the largest Protestant church in any Catholic country," said Paul Freston, who was completing his dissertation on Protestants in Brazilian politics. "At a conservative estimate—not their own—I would say that a reasonable figure is 7 million—four times the number of adherents of the Church of England in England." Freston had been in Brazil since 1976, when he began to work with university students in the Evangelical Biblical Alliance, and, like others whom I encountered, he was fascinated by the Assemblies of God.

The church was founded by two Swedish workers, Daniel Berg and Gunnar Vingren, who arrived in Brazil in 1911. They had been members of a pentecostal congregation in Chicago. When Vingren was shown in a dream that the two of them were to do missionary work in a place called "Pará," they had to go to the City Library in Chicago to learn that it was in northern Brazil. Berg and Vingren did not live permanently in Brazil, and hence the Assemblies of God quickly became Brazilian, growing steadily over the decades.[7]

My first contact with the Assemblies was at a Sunday night service in the church headed by Jose Wellington, the site of the pastors' meeting described at the beginning of this chapter. Three separate choirs were on hand and, in addition to the several hundred or perhaps a thousand people in the body of the church, about one hundred and fifty were seated around the main platform. A preacher extolled God's wonders: a woman who had heard doctors tell her that she had a week to live was still alive twenty years later. "God saves, God cures." Another preacher ridiculed the oncoming Carnival as the work of the devil. Wellington's own sermon was a rather methodical exposition of Isaiah 6:1-8. Much of the music was in a pop idiom. The climax of the service was the call to accept Christ. With some coaxing, a half-dozen individuals came forward, each accompanied by a member of the congregation. They gave their names and were told to come on the last Sunday of the month wearing clothes that could get wet.

Although there was nothing elegant about his office—it was situated under the church on one side of a space that was partly a garage—the half-dozen or so pastors milling about as I waited for Wellington reminded me of a Catholic chancery office. After I had been ushered into his office, Wellington talked for a moment about Panama where he had preached and said his son pastors a church in Arcadia, California. I was struck by his self-confidence.

Why was the Assemblies of God the largest denomination in Brazil? I asked. "I think it is first because of a more effective, more communicative, clearer message." He reminded me of how the church had spread throughout Brazil from its origins in the far north. "The message of the Assemblies of God is very identified with our people, the Brazilian people."

Aware that I was Catholic, he added that in the last twenty years the Brazilian Catholic church had come very close to partisan political involvement on the left. Alluding to the many ministries to the poor that are especially characteristic of the Sao Paulo archdiocese, he said, "They went down a political road and forgot the spiritual. In abandoning the spiritual, they left a vacuum for the people. We preached and we were concerned about the spiritual side ... we sought to preach the gospel of Jesus Christ in its essence, at the very heart of biblical teaching: the doctrine of salvation, the doctrine of the complete transformation of man, not just in his spiritual life but also in the moral life; we also preached God's power, God's power that blesses, which not only protects and guides but also cures illnesses. We preach, we believe in, we seek, baptism in the Holy Spirit, which is the essential thing, the secret, the number one thing in the everyday activity of the Assemblies of God, the operation and baptism of the Holy Spirit ... the Holy Spirit is the third person of the Trinity given to the church to be in the churches ... He is the power of God ... Each believer in the Assemblies of God enjoys sharing with someone else what he has received; so the person speaks of 'what God is doing in my heart.' That is why the Assemblies of God are growing, because each believer is an evangelizer."

Jose Wellington, who had been president of the national convention for some years and was now vice-president, said that their own last census taken in 1989 gave them a figure of 11,800,000 baptized members (over twelve years old) and indicated that they were growing at between 700,000 and 1,000,000 people a year. These figures were considerably higher than Freston's 7,000,000, but in a nation of 150,000,000 either one is impressive. Sao Paulo had a thousand Assemblies churches.

The Sunday night service that I attended was the more public worship in which preaching is aimed at visitors. Other types of meetings exist for the training and formation of congregation members. Like most Protestant churches, the Brazilian Assemblies have dress and behavior codes (women's dresses are supposed to have sleeves, for example), although Wellington chuckled and seemed to acknowledge that they are not all fully observed in everyday life.

When I mentioned the Assemblies church in Vila Cisper, a poor area in the east that I had gotten to know, he said that during the 1960s this same site had been used for *macumba* (the designation for one form of Afro-Brazilian religion). Most of those attending had been converted, and then the Assemblies had bought the site and turned it into a church. I had no way of verifying the story, but the fact that it could buy the property is indicative of the economic clout of the church, whose finances are centrally administered. Pastors are authorized to pay water and electric bills and maintenance, but otherwise funds go to church headquarters and are administered for all of Sao Paulo. One effect is that the pastor is not dependent on the week-to-week contributions of the local congregation. The pastor "is always linked to headquarters; we are a collegial body; there is no top figure—here the big figure is Jesus," he said, theologically downplaying his own obvious power. Asked about the church's social work, he stressed, "We don't get a cent from the government." Their social projects included a senior citizens' home and a $120,000 drug rehabilitation center that they were about to open.

Several people recommended that I contact Ricardo Gondim Gonçalves for a critical perspective on the Assemblies of God from within. The small Bethesda church of which he was pastor was situated on a residential lot in a middle-class area about a half-hour south of downtown by car. A thin and intense man, perhaps in his late-thirties, he was from Fortaleza, a northern city where the Assemblies had arrived with Swedish missionaries around 1914. A great-aunt had been a Catholic sister and a great-uncle a priest, but Gondim had been raised only nominally Catholic. His father was a leftist who had been jailed for a year after the 1964 coup. Bible reading led Gondim first into the Presbyterian church. Then, at the age of twenty, he had a pentecostal experience and found his way to the Assemblies of God. When the pastor of the church was killed in an auto accident, he became pastor in March 1982. Initially there were only about fifteen people in the church, but it "grew explosively for nine years until it had more than four thousand members and we had started thirty-two churches." He came to Sao Paulo to start a mission church, and a year and a half later, three hundred people were participating. He consciously saw his own approach as an alternative to that of most Assemblies churches.

The strength of the Assemblies of God is that it has "an extremely simple message" and a simple preaching "made by people who are equal, lay persons preaching to lay persons, on the basis of an experience that they have had of God." The Assemblies have their own ethics and their own culture that differs from that of other churches, such as the Four-square Gospel church with its openness to the world. Until recently, advanced studies were regarded as "worldly" within the Assemblies of God. Even today it is "traumatic" for members to have a TV set because it introduces evil influences.

His own church was striving for a more "contextualized theological reflection." He said that they were trying to re-read church doctrine, e.g., regarding the fall, and to see "how we can interrelate with the various strata of society." He used the term "co-belligerence" to define their stance: the idea was that church members should be struggling alongside others. "We want to be a counterculture but not outside of the culture. We want to exercise a prophetic role within our culture. We want to reach a segment that the Assemblies of God themselves have had a hard time reaching, the thinking classes in society, the opinion shapers."

The Bethesda church was "a cross section of society. We have everything in our church, poor people and professors, intellectuals, university students, business people. But I would say that the great appeal of our church is precisely the appeal of bringing the pentecostal message, the charismatic message, and the message of access to God through Christ, without any need to commit intellectual suicide. You can think, and you can experience God simultaneously. The two things aren't mutually exclusive."

That combination was what made Gondim intriguing. He did not water down his pentecostalism. "We are charismatics. I believe that the spiritual gifts are with us today, gifts such as speaking in foreign tongues and prophesying. I believe in the gifts of healing. I believe in exorcism of devils. Our church is a pentecostal church and it looks pentecostal. But we want our struggle here, our pentecostal practice, to be balanced with reflection and with exposition of the scriptures. We have a community here, and we want to be holistic in our mission with the church." That mission included political involvement. Gondim had recently become notorious in church circles by publicly joining the Workers Party. He regarded the Lausanne statement (a 1974 document of evangelical churches that acknowledged a social and political dimension to the gospel) as important. The actual social projects of his church, however, were rather conventional: schools (with over two thousand students), a shelter for street children, and an old people's home.

The three-day Holy Week crusade announced at the pastors' meeting was held at the Vale de Anhagabau (An-ya-ga-ba-ú), a plaza sunk below street level and a logical place to try to hold a large rally in Sao Paulo (it was where perhaps one hundred thousand Brazilian soccer fans had gathered to watch a giant TV screen when their team won the 1994 World Cup in the United States). On Good Friday night I calculated the crowd to be five or six thousand, mainly evangelicals.[8] The number looked small given the announced intention of the major preacher, Bernhard Johnson, an American who had grown up in Brazil, to bring six to ten thousand people to Christ.

In a raspy voice Johnson launched into his topic. Of all the divisions in the world, those based on nation and race and so forth, the deepest is the division between those who love Jesus and those who hate him. The latter turned out to be an amalgam of Communists (who were certainly scarce by 1993) and an array of others including clergy who deny some basic Christian beliefs. Why is Jesus hated? Because he's alive—you can't hate a dead man! Johnson then developed at some length the three proofs that Jesus is alive: his effect in us, in the church, and in the word. As always, the high point of the service was the invitation to come forward to accept Christ. People in the audience were asked to encourage those alongside them to come forward and to accompany them if necessary; those who did so were to receive a copy of the gospel of John. The numbers could be counted by dozens rather than hundreds.

The crowd at the third and last gathering on Easter Sunday afternoon seemed to be about the same size. Johnson told those gathered that the Holy Spirit had told him to change the text on which he was to speak and he had done so (rather like a politician adjusting one of his stump speeches, I thought). Although there was a good deal of shouting "Gloria a Deus!" and enthusiastic singing from within the crowd, around the fringes things were more casual: vendors were selling popcorn, and adolescents were milling about and socializing. At the meeting of pastors, Wellington had said that this gathering would not be a celebration of the Assemblies of God. However, in view of the meager numbers of those who came forward at the call, it was hard not to conclude that the gathering served primarily as an opportunity for the Assemblies to assert themselves in a public space. Johnson himself boasted, "This space is ours!" and "We've expelled the devil from this space."

The Christian Congregation

Having passed the large rough concrete church of the Congregação Cristã or Christian Congregation on the metro numerous times, I finally decided to attend a Wednesday-night service. Located in the Bras district neighborhood where it had been founded by Italian immigrants in 1910, the church is shaped like huge half barrel on its side. Seen from inside, the white walls curving toward the ceiling appeared even taller than they had seemed outside and felt uncanny—reminding me of a mosque.

Several hundred people—perhaps a thousand—filled the pews; the women were on the left, wearing veils on their heads and net scarves, and an almost equal number of men were on the right, perhaps half of them in suits and ties. A woman was telling of an experience with illness; then came a man, and then a woman—all of them giving testimony, not preaching. At the next hymn I was startled to hear horns and strings from an orchestra seated up front that I had not seen from my position in the rear.

The sermon began with a long reading from Joshua, in which the accent was on God's sovereignty, submission to God—here called "Jehovah" —and the need for humility. There was no collection. Toward the end some announcements were made, a hymn was sung, and then—another surprise—people turned to one another and kissed on the lips, men with men and women with women. They obviously took literally the scriptural injunction, "Greet one another with a holy kiss." (Rom. 16:16, 1 Cor. 16:20). Although some aspects of the worship were similar to those of other pentecostal churches, the strong sense of decorum gave the service a very distinct feel.

Worshippers streamed out of the church, some to cars, and others toward the metro station several hundred yards away. Partly in order to start a conversation, I told an older man that I was impressed by the number of males present and asked him if he could explain why so many men attended. Paying no attention to my question, he said that God had chosen this moment to prompt me to ask him this question—God has my name in a book—and that I should keep returning to the church. He went out of his way to stress certain observances that the church regards as important (women covering their heads in church, for example).

Unlike other churches, the Christian congregation does not proselytize —no crusades, no leafleting, no door-to-door visiting—because it is God who calls. Its theology is thus quite predestinarian and its public stance quietist. There is no clergy: the various officers such as elder, assistant, deacon, and porter, are all lay. The church has no strong visible leader even like Jose Wellington, let alone the preacher-founders of the more flamboyant churches, such as God is Love and the Universal Church (discussed below). The church publishes no magazines or books and indeed its most important piece of writing is only twenty pages long. Oral transmission is crucial to the church's tradition.

In regarding itself as the only true church, the Christian Congregation again differs from most other pentecostal churches which at least recognize other similar churches. Yet it does not take a combative stance toward Catholicism or Afro-Brazilian religions. It does not pressure its members to tithe; in fact, contributions are voluntary and are handed discreetly to the porter. Its strong if unwritten behavior codes depart sharply from usual evangelical practice on one point: moderate use of alcoholic beverages is allowed.

The acceptable beverage is wine with meals. This is a custom which is, of course, found in the scriptures. It may also reflect the background of the founder of the church, Luigi Francescon, who was an Italian immigrant. Francescon was first a Presbyterian and had a pentecostal experience in Chicago shortly after the first ripples of pentecostalism radiated out from Azuza Street in Los Angeles. Francescon came to Sao Paulo and, initially disappointed there, went to a rural area in the state where he founded a congregation. He then returned to Sao Paulo and founded a church in the Bras neighborhood together with some Presbyterians, who then split away. The hymnal remained in Italian for the first twenty years, but the church is quite Brazilian and has never had ties with other overseas churches.[9]

Despite its size, the Christian Congregation does not have a bureaucracy—no ministers, no paid staff, no offices. One writer suggests that the basic organizational model is the family, and that people are drawn into the church largely through family ties.[10] One important practice is that of journeying to visit other congregations both nearby and distant. At the teeming bus terminal in Sao Paulo, I saw delegations waiting to receive visitors. The church also is said to have a thriving social program which is, however, limited to its own "brothers and sisters."

Although it began among poor immigrants, the Christian Congregation has to some degree risen socially in recent decades, as evidenced by the cars outside the main church. How was it possible for well-educated people to adhere to a church that was so rigid and apparently so closed off from the world? The question was uppermost on my mind as I talked to Iara Monteiro, a historian who was working on her dissertation at the University of Sao Paulo, and who was well known in ecumenical church circles. Acknowledging that her church "speaks more of heaven than of earth," and that this was quite different from Catholic base communities, for example, she said that it satisfied her own "spiritual yearnings." Her scholarly work as a historian and her life as a believer (very connected to family) seemed to take place in separate spheres. The fact that her church did not accept scientific evolution did not trouble her. Her position reminded me of the kind of "concordism" that finds rough parallels between the "days" of Genesis and the unimaginably vast periods of the scientific view of the world.

After our interview, as I stood waiting for a bus among crowds of students and professors, the grass and flowers freshly soaked by a thunderstorm, it occurred to me that Iara Monteiro's theological position was rather like that of Catholics at mid-century: Tridentine Catholicism was a closed religious system whose literalism was centered on the magisterium rather than on scripture. In other words, my not-quite-articulated question to her, "How can an otherwise intelligent and sophisticated person like you continue to believe in a closed literalistic type of theology?" could have been posed to most Catholics before Vatican II.

The Christian Congregation does not publish its growth figures. Nevertheless, its battleship-gray churches were prominent in the Sao Paulo area and on highways leading in all directions. Building projects, plans, money—even paint—were centralized at church headquarters. Monteiro's father served on a committee that was overseeing the construction of an average of a church and a half a month.

As I approached the hilltop site of the local Christian Congregation church in Vila Cisper on a Sunday night, I could see much of eastern Sao Paulo spread below. The church was filled well in advance of the service; there were about 350 people by my calculation, all clearly content to be present. The sounds of the opening hymn by the small orchestra would have delighted Charles Ives: the elders must have learned to play their instruments solely for use in church. Periodically, an elder said it was time for a hymn, another person chose the hymn on the spot, and the music would start; in keeping with the church's reliance on the Spirit, music was not scheduled beforehand.

During the testimony period, a widow spoke of God's work in her life, particularly her impending marriage. Several times the congregation prayed out loud with obvious intensity. At another moment, a man who had wandered in, either drunk or mentally unstable, rose to speak. Whereas in another church ushers might have pulled him away by force, here an elder gently sought to dissuade him, while urging others to be tolerant with him.

Topics in the sermon on Jacob (Gen. 28) included the church as God's abode like Bethel and the prosperity promised to Jacob. Sermons are not prepared in the Christian Congregation, since to prepare a sermon would be a failure to trust in the Holy Spirit. Before the close of the service, a man urged the congregation to send or bring young people for bible class, since it would be a shame if they were to drift away. "If they should get to be eighteen or so and drift away, that's another matter." Consistent predestinationism was plainly not easy.

Writing in the mid-1980s, Reed Elliot Nelson noted that the Christian Congregation, then estimated to number 2 million members, not only had impressive growth but seemed to contradict organizational theory, which postulates that as organizations become larger, they must become more complex and bureaucratic, particularly in a country as "highly bureaucratized" as Brazil. Among the strengths of the church for attracting members ("inputs" in organizational theory) he noted its family ties, the location of churches, the conservative image (including the architecture), and the oral transmission of information. He pointed to the church's "principle of non-accounting," that is, its refusal to count members, or to register what individuals contribute to the church. Such a practice is at

odds with modern society, and particularly capitalism, in which everything is counted. But, he says "it is the lower classes that understand accounting the least and suffer most from it, so people on the outskirts do
not look on it favorably." By rejecting accounting and relying on family
ties, the Christian Congregation "provides a convincing explanation for
the problems that traditional people have in dealing with the semi-modern
state: the world is a fallen place that is heading day by day toward the
abyss and only by renouncing the world and embracing the faith can a
person find relief and salvation."[11]

Foursquare Gospel Church

In 1952, at the invitation of the Independent Presbyterian church, two faith
healing preachers from the Foursquare Gospel church in the United States
came to churches in both the city and state of Sao Paulo. "The movement
spread with tents put up on vacant lots as if for the circus," writes Protestant scholar Antônio Gouvêa Mendonça with evident distaste. The Foursquare Gospel church in Brazil was then launched in 1953. The faith healing movement swept through Brazilian Protestantism and led to the
formation of other churches such as Brazil for Christ, the Pentecostal
Church of Christ, and the Evangelical Biblical Revival Church. "The National Evangelization Crusade of the Foursquare Gospel Church was what
set off the pentecostal explosion in Brazil," says Mendonça.[12]

The main distinguishing feature of the church, said Waldir Agnello,
the director of the church's publishing house, "is that we don't preach
'customs,'" referring to the strict behavior codes, common in many
churches, prohibiting dancing, movies, TV, popular music, and so forth.
"We think it's a matter of each person's decency, not whether or not
women cut their hair, wear long sleeves, or use makeup." Consuming alcohol and tobacco are ruled out because the body is a temple of the Holy
Spirit. Unlike the Assemblies of God, however, the Foursquare Gospel
church encourages sports and has no problem with dancing—it even holds
a kind of debutante ball for fifteen-year-old girls in the congregation. A re-

markable feature of this church founded by a woman is that 35 percent of the pastors in Brazil are women.

Agnello reeled off some figures: there are 4,500 persons who are active in the ministry; 13,000 active lay leaders; 3,711 congregations; and 6,141 preaching points (congregations in formation). From 1987 to 1992 the church grew 50 percent, from 338,000 to 510,000 members. The previous year, 70,000 people had been baptized with water. The Foursquare Gospel church now had more members in Brazil than in the United States. Later in the year the church was planning to hold a four-day seminar for 5,000 church leaders, including some from other churches, such as the Assemblies of God. Missionaries had been sent from Brazil to Portugal, Switzerland, Italy, and Paraguay and the hope was to send more in the future.

Brazil for Christ

Brazil for Christ is inevitably associated with the career of its founder Manoel de Mello, who worked for the Crusade in the early 1950s and then broke away from the Assemblies of God to form Brazil for Christ in 1956. The nationalistic name was not an accident; that very year President Juselino Kubitschek had announced that a boldly modern new capital to be called Brasilia was to be built from the ground up in the interior of the country.

De Mello was the first Protestant church leader to actively encourage members to become involved in electoral politics, and some church members were elected as legislators. Unlike other pentecostal leaders, he cultivated good relations with the historic Protestant churches, and Brazil for Christ became one of the few pentecostal churches in the World Council of Churches. Brazil for Christ thereby gained status, and the generally liberal W.C.C. could appear somewhat more inclusive. De Mello was a dominant presence in the church until his death in 1991.

From the outside, the central church and offices in the Pompeia district of Sao Paulo have the look of a sports arena. At a Wednesday evening service I observed about six hundred people in a rectangular space with the sanctuary in the middle. As people shook hands and women kissed one another before the service, it was clear that this was a congregation in which people knew one another. Worshippers carried well-worn bibles. The band consisted of three guitarists and musicians playing an electronic keyboard, a saxophone, and a trumpet. The music began with what was clearly a blues pattern, at first slowly and then in faster tempos. People clapped on the off beat to what was something like a rock and roll tune. The preacher (Manoel de Mello's son, I was later told) was applauded when he appeared, and he led more singing. At one point he took over the drums, while the drummer led the singing. At another point, while everyone prayed aloud, the lights were dimmed and the preacher came offstage to walk amid the congregation, apparently to indicate that the congregation did not need the preacher in order to have direct communication with God. A woman came forward, and the congregation prayed that the lump in her breast not be malignant; the pastor repeatedly affirmed that "cures and transformations take place here."

My impression at this service was similar to what I had felt at a Foursquare Gospel service. Brazil for Christ, like the Assemblies and the Foursquare Gospel church, was a pentecostal church that had moved beyond its youth and was now an established church. Unlike the other two churches, however, Brazil for Christ was not experiencing rapid growth.

God Is Love

"Deus é Amor" (God is Love) proclaim red letters over the powder blue and white complex that occupies a whole city block one metro stop east of downtown. Most of the space consists of two adjoining areas that still look largely like the factories or warehouses that they once were; they now accommodate hundreds of people at services held several times a day, every day of the week. The central figure in the church is David Miranda, who started the church in 1962, at the age of twenty-six.

To my eyes, the most striking feature of this church was that those attending were uniformly poor. They were dark, many of them immigrants from the Northeast, their clothes were worn and perhaps dirty, and they seemed to be in this church seeking solace or relief from the pain that was visible on their faces.

At my first visit, which happened to be during Carnival time, a yellow "on-the-air" light behind the minister's platform indicated that the service was being broadcast by radio. The church boasts that it broadcasts hundreds of hours weekly throughout Brazil. After the worship leader announced that there would be ten minutes of prayer, people began wailing, "God, O my God, alleluia, Glory to God," while two ministers in front writhed spasmodically. The intensity of prayer was apparently measured by decibel level.

A striking feature of the church is its highly regimented nature. One day in the church I noticed a sign on the wall indicating that any minister who failed to show up for his turn to lead worship would be suspended for a month. An official regulation book contains detailed prohibitions, each listing the date the rule was made, the biblical verses invoked, and the punishment for infractions. "Going to the beach or a public pool—Meeting August 11, 1986. It was approved that: Going to a beach or a public pool, being semi-naked and bathing; going to a beach or a public pool and merely being near the bathers and remaining in one's street clothes observing the sin. It is prohibited according to the Bible: Ps. 1:1, Rom. 6:12-13, 1 Cor. 5:8 and 8, Rev. 16:15." Varying lengths of suspension were listed, depending on whether one was a member or a "worker" and whether one bathed or merely observed. Dozens of such detailed prescriptions are set down for gambling, reading immoral books (including westerns), watching television, betting on lotteries, and so forth. Having a TV in the house is forbidden unless it belongs to a non-believing spouse or children. Men are not to let their hair grow (to where it begins to cover the ears), whereas women are not to cut theirs. Separate rules define what constitutes "vain" eyeglasses for men and for women. Members are not allowed to work selling cigarettes, alcohol, lottery tickets, makeup, jewelry; they are not to repair TVs, work in motels or drive-ins, or sell lunches at the beach or at soccer fields, and so forth. Should they do so, they are to be excommunicated from the church until they find permitted (honest) work.

Other pentecostal churches certainly observe similar rules. What is distinct about God is Love is the high degree of detail and the prescribed punishment, generally some form of temporary exclusion. This church does not accept the legitimacy of other churches—only its own members will be saved. One mark of its literalism is that it obeys the scriptural injunction to "pray always" by maintaining a "ministry of prayer" organized in such a way that at any moment of the day or night some members are praying. Full members are expected to bring their tithe to a central office and have their identity card stamped. At one point in the worship service I attended, people held above their heads the money that they planned to contribute.

My efforts to interview leaders were unsuccessful. All my requests were met with vague statements that the authorized person was not available, although it was clear to me that numerous church personnel were always on hand. It was my impression that these church officials were instinctively employing the longstanding practice of the poor of staving off someone from another class (in this case a foreigner claiming to be a writer) with vague statements. The culture of the leadership (perhaps up to Miranda himself) was very much from the poor and thus well suited to the uniformly poor people who made up the congregations. Not surprisingly, the church does not maintain seminaries and does not encourage its ministers to receive seminary training.

The very features that keep middle-class people away—the poverty of the adherents and the unschooled nature of the leadership—partially help explain the church's success (together with the charismatic nature of the leader and the practices of divine healing and exorcism). Deus é Amor has five thousand churches in Brazil and throughout Latin America (and some in the U.S.). The church newspaper included photos of thousands of people being baptized at a river and a report on caravans of buses from Peru to Sao Paulo, in what must be an arduous journey, much of it on unpaved roads.

Universal Church of the Kingdom of God

On my second day in Sao Paulo, I went to an evening service at the Universal Church of the Kingdom of God (Igreja Universal do Reino de Deus), which in the eyes of many Brazilians epitomizes the new pentecostalism. The site looked like it had once been a showroom for appliances or perhaps adjoining retail stores with one or more walls removed. "Jesus Christ is the Lord" read the sign on the back wall. About two hundred people were present, primarily women. Distinctively attired church workers circulated through the church.

The young preacher dominated the proceedings. At one point he spoke of expensive rent payments and urged people to come forward and make donations. He began by asking for donations of an astronomical number of cruzeiros and, since there were no volunteers, he began to lower the sum. When he reached the equivalent of a few dollars people began to come forward, and eventually those who did so included a good portion of the audience.

That last word, "audience," is itself significant. Worship at the Universal Church feels much like a performance, and the ministers have more than a hint of television host about them. Those outside the church, and especially other evangelicals, doubt whether the Universal Church is indeed a church. "It seems more like a business to me," said more than one pastor.

Like Brazil for Christ and God is Love, the Universal Church revolves around its founder, Edir Macedo, who was for some years a minister of the Casa de Benção (House of Blessing) before founding the Universal Church in 1977. By 1990, the organization had seven hundred churches and claimed five hundred thousand members, and that year it bought a TV station in Sao Paulo for 45 million dollars. One indication of its almost instant notoriety is that this church is not mentioned in Antonio Gouvêa Mendonça's article "Panorama of Contemporary Brazilian Protestantism," which was published in 1989.[14]

Macedo obviously has mass appeal. One morning in September 1990 he drew one hundred and fifty thousand people to a stadium in Rio and then jetted to Sao Paulo where he addressed fifty thousand. Like soccer fans, some carried banners including one that read, "Pele, the king of soccer, has gone, and Jesus, the king of kings, has come in." Journalists eagerly reported bizarre and disturbing events at these mass gatherings. On one occasion Macedo promised to heal people's eyesight and asked those attending to hand over their glasses. Hundreds of pairs of glasses were brought forward where he trampled on them. One woman died at a stadium while Macedo was preaching, allegedly because his followers refused to send for a doctor when she had a stroke; they told her that she must have faith. After a pastor defied warnings and baptized five thousand people at two dangerous beaches in Salvador, two people were drowned and eight others were reported missing.[15]

Macedo was accused of being a charlatan and swindler who was getting rich by taking advantage of the faith of believers. Ricardo Mariano, a young researcher, said that the image of the Protestant "used to be of someone who was honest, a good worker, a good employee, upright, truthful, poor, someone who is proper...That image has completely changed with Edir Macedo. The image of the pastor is now that of a thief, someone who misleads people, who fakes miracles." Those who most wanted to get their distance from Macedo were the historic churches, said Mariano, "the churches that have sought respectability in Brazil, churches that have celebrated their hundredth birthday, and have theological institutes, schools, and universities. With Edir Macedo things have gotten difficult, because a lot of other people, and especially Catholics, don't make distinctions: Protestants are Protestants and that's all there is to it."[16] Members of other churches were concerned about the effect of the Universal Church's image on the whole Protestant community.

Double standards seem to have been applied in the case of Macedo. Police once humiliated him by hauling him away as he was returning home from a church service. If his crime was that of making money from religion, why were the same standards not applied to the figures in Afro-Brazilian religions who were given money for their services? Why not against the Redemptorist priests who ran the shrine of Our Lady of Aparecida, (Chapter 12), the pilgrimage destination of millions of Catholics every year who also contributed money? Setting aside their personal distaste and concern over a rival, some evangelical church leaders banded together to protest discrimination against Macedo. On the occasion of the 1992 Earth Summit in Rio, evangelical churches organized a large rally and Macedo addressed an assembly of major Protestant leaders. The Dominican theologian Frei Gorgulho rankled some Catholics by drawing attention to the media's portrayal of Macedo. He singled out their habit of using quotation marks ("Bishop" Macedo), and said it was not up to the media to determine the legitimacy of any religious leader.[17] After years of seemingly endless lawsuits, Macedo had not been convicted of any wrongdoing.

The Universal Church's rapid expansion may be partly due to Macedo's reversal of the normal evangelical method of expansion in which individual congregations grow and sometimes split, or they establish mission fields and slowly develop new congregations. Building a new church comes only at the end of a long process, and in fact may be delayed years while land is located and funds raised. The Universal Church, in contrast, locates a suitable site, very often a commercial property, and often leases it. After modifying the site to serve as a church, it then assigns a minister who is responsible for developing the church and making it self-sustaining. As with a business, traffic is slow when the doors first open, but soon people begin to arrive and within months the church may be thriving. This method of operation requires a cadre of ministers available to be sent out to open new churches.

A researcher reported how one person described the process of becoming a church "worker" or volunteer. "Ah, that is the Holy Spirit moving you." You know that such is the case when "you see that you are more aware of others, you begin to talk to the person next to you on the bus about Jesus Christ; you try to help people, you feel a joy, a peace." The uniformed volunteers feel that they have been helped and want to help others. The Universal Church requires that full time ministers be married, and they must be willing to be sent to any church as a husband-and-wife team. No minister remains at any post longer than two years, and hence believers remain loyal to the Universal Church rather than to particular ministers. Macedo is evidently aware of and guarding against the process whereby strong pastors break off to start their own churches—as he himself had done. All the ministers I observed seemed to be in their thirties, and looked like they could easily be selling appliances or automobiles. They appeared well suited to their target audience, the lower middle class (just as the Deus é Amor ministers are suited to their target population, the very poor).

Churches in the larger cities tend to have four services a day (typically 10:00 A.M., 12:00 noon, 3:00 P.M. and 7:00 P.M.), seven days a week. Each day has a theme:

Monday	–	Prosperity
Tuesday	–	Praise and Imposition of Hands
Wednesday	–	Health
Thursday	–	Family
Friday	–	Liberation
Saturday	–	Prosperity[18]

Attending a Saturday evening service at a relatively small site on Avenida Consolaçao I found perhaps 100 people when I arrived and around 120 by the time the service ended. The preacher was slightly self-deprecating with little jokes. For this night's prosperity-oriented sermon, he was insisting that believers have to act. "God does his part and you have to do yours. It's fifty-fifty: God has done his part and now it's up to you." Taken literally, this statement is highly unorthodox, since all classical theologies insist that human activity is fully God's, and still fully the responsibility of the individual human being. Universal Church preachers are trained in-house, and do not receive anything approaching a seminary education, plainly reflecting Macedo's own view that theology is worse than useless.

This preacher stressed the importance of planning one's activities. "When unbelievers get up in the morning they complain, but we believers do not. We have something to do. The second Commandment of Prosperity is: Never get up in the morning without having a plan for the day." Such advice—redolent of motivation seminars for business people—was applicable to all: if you are a domestic, think of the day when you'll have domestics under you.

At one point people made requests and took their money up to the front where they trampled upon it: the more they offered, the stronger would be their battle sword. Money and money talk do not embarrass the Universal Church. Macedo insists that the bible sees money as a tool and that it uses the term "offering" 640 times. When a journalist objected that Jesus was poor, he replied, "That is an enormous misrepresentation. Jesus was never poor, He said, 'I am the Lord of lords, the king of kings.' A king is never poor, unless he is unseated. As king of kings, Jesus was rich." He came into the world in poverty and felt what it meant to be poor, but Jesus was never poor.[19]

One of Macedo's little books, *Life with Abundance,* is full of statements like, "God wants you to prosper in three aspects, according to the apostle John: 1) financially, 2) physically, 3) spiritually. Total prosperity for your life." In the closing chapter, on the "miracle of the tithe," Macedo quotes Malachi—"Test me on this says the Lord of hosts, whether I will open the gates of heaven"— and says that believers are to test God. He goes on to cite famous people who paid tithes and became millionaires: "Senhor Colgate, Senhor Ford, and Senhor Caterpilar" [*sic*].[20]

The "liberation" practiced on Fridays is not from oppression but from devils; this is often understood to be liberation from Afro-Brazilian religions. After introductory hymn singing and prayers, people at the service I attended were invited to come forward to find relief. Although three or four dozen came forward to be prayed over, only about eight people (mainly women, one a teenager) showed physical signs of possession. Seemingly in a trance, they writhed and sometimes wrestled their way out of the control of the "workers" (mainly women) who were handling them; sometimes they broke out in violent fits. The preacher went up to one of the women who was grunting and making heavy breathing sounds and read the gospel account of the expulsion of the demon from the man in the land of the Gerasenes. He then ordered the devils to leave. The whole procedure lasted an hour. The preacher insisted that the demons were being cast out in the name of Jesus Christ—not that of the pope or Edir Macedo, nor of the Catholic or the Universal Church. He was supremely confident throughout the process. While the shrieking and writhing were at their highest pitch on the platform, I noticed two women workers in one corner smiling and conversing—obviously about something else. (They observe this every Friday, I realized, perhaps more than once.) The "liberation" ended gradually as the women drifted away, apparently at peace, and the preacher made a smooth transition into the collections.

"My first impression when I began to visit the Universal Church of the Kingdom of God," said a researcher who was herself Catholic, "was that they said, 'We're doing what Jesus Christ did.'"[21] That simple observation may help explain the appeal of the church: in the instance cited, the preacher read the account from the gospel of Mark and then proceeded to expel the devils.

In *The Liberation of Theology* (ironically also the title of a book by the Uruguayan Jesuit theologian Juan Luis Segundo in the mid-1970s) Macedo argues that theology has divided the churches when it should unite them, and that it has failed to deal with a whole series of -isms: agnosticism, asceticism, atheism, deism, dualism, and so forth in alphabetical order up to universalism. Macedo's book attacks all forms of theology, which he accuses of confusing and dividing people, and contrasts them with the simple message of Jesus.[22]

When I asked a Pastor Alfredo what made the Universal Church different, he said that it accepted everyone. This open door expresses the meaning of "universal" in the church's name. The church is a place "where one can find the solution in a person whose name is Jesus." The church does not prescribe explicit behavior codes but simply describes the "two ways" and leaves it to individuals to decide. "We don't force anybody," he said.

Wasn't that rather simplistic (meaning, in my mind, "primitive," I suppose) I asked, and he replied, "Well, Jesus was simple, wasn't he?" True enough, I thought, and easy to forget; Macedo and the Universal Church had a point. On the other hand, Macedo did not take a "birds of the air" approach to managing his rapidly expanding economic empire.

Business People and Youth Accepting Christ

ADHONEP (pronounced *ahh do NEH pi* by Brazilians) is the abbreviation for the international Full Gospel Businessmen's Association. My first surprise as I entered the reserved meeting room in the prestigious National Club in a well-to-do section of the city was that a lot of the businessmen were women, and not all were spouses. About ninety people were crowded into a conference room which became uncomfortably warm.

After a moderately charismatic opening prayer, with discreet "Amens" from those assembled, the president began with a thumbnail sketch of the organization which was founded in Los Angeles in the 1950s and now has chapters in 126 countries. The Brazilian branch dates from the fifties when a businessman was introduced to the founder, Demos Shakarian, on a TWA Constellation flight in the United States. Recently 700 members had met in Minas Gerais and a large number of people had accepted Christ, including the mayor. The fact that the mayor was a member of the Workers Party (PT) prompted a buzz of amusement and disbelief, since most of those attending no doubt regarded the PT as a threat to their way of life.

A layman then gave an exposition on the universality of salvation that turned out to be rather sophisticated theologically, if somewhat long. It was not unlike the scriptural and doctrinal section of a Catholic pastoral letter, and stood in sharp contrast to the absence of sustained theological reasoning in the pentecostal worship sessions that I had been attending.

At about 10:30 P.M., people rose to give testimonies about God's presence in their lives. A young woman and her husband had been on the brink of despair as they were house hunting, and then they found a house in the very neighborhood where they had hoped to live; she interpreted their various problems as evidence that the devil is ever at work. (In passing she mentioned her earlier use of drugs and so forth.) Things had been going badly for another woman and her husband—both of whom have businesses—but now their businesses were doing well and they were in good health. The most interesting story was that of an attractive young couple who had been drifting apart: the man put his business first, and on weekends rode off on his motorcycle. They attended an ADHONEP supper, found Christ, repaired their marriage—and sold the motorcycle. Written prayer petitions from those present were passed forward to be prayed over (with insistence that there was nothing magic about this) and were then torn up. As at a church, there was a moment in which people were invited to come forward to accept Christ. After more prayer, the session ended at 11:20 P.M., about two hours later than would be customary in poor neighborhoods.

Sao Paulo had ten ADHONEP chapters, each of which organized activities, such as this one. The basic mechanism seemed to be social events at which people testify to God in their life: sharing with people of one's own class was part of the attraction, as was the relatively restrained worship style.

ADHONEP is not a church, and the vast majority of participants at the meeting I attended were lay. They readily incorporated their marriage relationships into their prayer. Participants were expected to testify to Christ at their businesses; the president described how he had recently counseled an employee about her boyfriend and the two had ended up praying together. There was no sense that such testimony would go beyond being willing to testify to one's faith in Jesus and to be personally honorable. That is, ADHONEP did not encourage its members to challenge prevailing business practices on ethical grounds, let alone to question the extremely unequal distribution of income and wealth in Brazil. The ADHONEP God seemed quite well adapted to life along Avenida Paulista with its banks, stores, and businesses.

THE GRACE OF GOD PENTECOSTAL CHURCH, situated a block from Avenida Paulista had a similar feel to it, pentecostal in a genteel way. During an orderly exposition on scripture texts the preacher used an overhead projector so that people could follow his outline. In the course of emphasizing God's closeness, he ridiculed the Big Bang theory and evolution—it was as improbable as a dictionary resulting from the explosion of a print shop (a kind of apologetic argument heard in Catholic circles before Vatican II). The congregation prayed that upon awakening the next morning members might offer up to God their day, their household tasks, the decisions they would have to make (this echoed the "Morning Offering" of the not-too-distant Catholic past). Despite its location near the center of financial power, those attending seemed to occupy modest stations in life.

THE RENASCER ("TO BE REBORN" OR "REBIRTH") CHURCH was a reconverted theater, and as I entered for the Monday night youth service, I observed seats in jumbled piles along the side and perhaps two or three thousand young people standing and filling most of the gently sloping concrete floor. In one of its first numbers the rock band on stage went through a catalogue of words intended to evoke the last three decades of international youth culture: beatnik, drugs, yoga, natural foods, politics, punk, violence ("Do we have to kill?")—to finally discover that, "The revolution is God the Father and his Son Jesus Christ."

The musical language was rock but the pedestrian words in this and other songs had no hint of rock anarchy. The other music did not have such an overt (anti-) political message (although a book in the display window outside was an attack on the Christology of liberation theologians). The audience, mainly adolescent but with a sprinkling of thirtyish parents and some pre-teens, was having a good time. Some couples half-embraced, many swayed, but none were actually dancing. The band occasionally stopped abruptly, allowing those present to continue a cappella, sometimes with complicated rhythms. A number were wearing T-shirts with messages, often in English: "Be Cool—Jesus Loves You."

At about 9 P.M. the crowd sat on the floor while a man still in his twenties began a sermon with a personal experience familiar to his listeners: that day he had had to take an exam for which he had not studied. With references to eighteenth-century deism, death-of-God theologians, and so forth, he contrasted a distant (for practical purposes, dead) God with the living God. "Jesus Christ wants to become part of your life, folks." At the end they closed their eyes while he prayed for God to change their lives. As at virtually all pentecostal services, there was an invitation to come forward and accept Christ, although not exactly in those terms. The preacher supplied the words for a prayer which all repeated (as at AD-HONEP) and those who had accepted Christ were taken backstage (presumably to be welcomed, fill out a card, and be given further instructions).

The music recommenced as an Argentine with shoulder-length hair and a white suit (the jacket soon came off) did a blues arrangement. A guitarist, billed as one Brazil's best, had accepted Christ and now performed a simple song based on Psalm 22. The Argentine said, "The devil uses soccer to divide Brazil and Argentina, but God uses music to unite them."

Founded in 1986, Renascer now had eleven churches (including one in Madrid). It did not impose behavior codes, but claimed to follow only the bible. It did not preach an angry, punishing God. All forms of music can be used to praise God. I was told that twenty classes made up of thirty to thirty-five people each were attending "prophet schools."

Was I seeing the future? Was Renascer the harbinger of a post-modern form of worship? The presence of several thousand young people (they were holding two such sessions each Monday) suggested Renascer's power. Luiz, with whom I was sharing an apartment, dismissed it contemptuously as a middle-class foreign import. Could it not just as easily be seen as an adaptation of the international youth culture? Might it provide a way for youth who might otherwise be drawn to drugs, alcohol, and heedless sex to come together in a wholesome way? Or was it a raucous but ultimately vacuous equivalent of a "smile" button?

These glimpses into the evangelical world of Sao Paulo raise questions, at least some of which are addressed in the following chapter.

3
Effectiveness and Authenticity

Facts and Questions about Evangelical Growth

·

T HE EVANGELICAL MOVEMENT stood at a "crossroads," said Ricardo
Gondim, the Assemblies of God pastor who was questioning his own
tradition. At stake was nothing less than "the relevance of what was
historic... in our Protestant heritage and of the sixteenth-century concept
of *sola scriptura*." Unlike the reformers, who had made scriptural exposition the center of worship, evangelical churches were now in danger of
abandoning that tradition, especially in syncretistic practices that incorpo-
rate aspects of the very popular religiosity that evangelical churches used
to combat. Whereas the churches once denounced the use of medals and
other objects, now radio preachers told listeners to place a glass of water
on their radio. Gondim regarded prayer practices, like the "twenty-one
days of Daniel" in order to obtain a blessing, as similar to Catholic novenas and other devotions. The bible itself was being made a holy object instead of an authoritative text. In turning a blind eye to the growing tenden-
cies toward practices such as those of encouraging and paying heed to
prophets (primarily women) who have visions of the future through a "direct channel to God," Assemblies of God leaders were behaving like
Catholic priests and bishops who ignore popular religion. They might be
vigilant in keeping their members from going to soccer stadiums or watching TV, but church leaders were ignoring practices that were shaping the
"true theology of the church."[1]

Pastors from other traditions voiced different concerns. At a Saturday
afternoon workshop on church growth, about fifteen Baptist ministers,
most between thirty and fifty years of age, were discussing their own work
as compared to that of the faster growing pentecostal churches, especially
the Assemblies of God. Without the suit and tie "uniform" of pentecostal
preachers, they looked like school teachers or engineers. One of the pastors spoke of being caught between generations: older traditionalists and
young people. Another spoke of the need for an "urban theology" that

would not begin with the doctrine of sin as does a traditional Baptist presentation, but would adopt an anthropological approach and take human yearning and aspiration as its starting point. To me they looked and sounded rather like Catholic priests.

The reactions of Gondim and these pastors indicate that evangelical growth raised questions from within the evangelical camp itself. As much as Protestants might look alike to Catholics and secularists, they had significant differences—so much so that it was at least open to question whether any single all-encompassing Protestant or evangelical movement even existed.

This chapter therefore takes up several issues that run across the evangelical churches of Sao Paulo, beginning with that of recent church growth and what it means.

Numbers and Growth

In early 1993 many evangelical pastors were convinced that data gathered during the 1991 census had revealed that Protestants numbered 35 million. If that figure were true, almost 22 percent of Brazilians would be Protestant, up from 8 percent in the 1980 census. The census agency (IBGE— Brazilian Institute of Geography and Statistics), however, had released no figures. A church leader assured me that an evangelical employee of IBGE had seen the figures and that the Catholic church was using its influence to keep them suppressed; the high figure seemed to be making the rounds in evangelical circles.

Although IBGE had not published statistics on religious affiliation even in early 1996, an electoral opinion survey taken by the polling company Datafolha indicated that 13.3 percent of electors identified themselves as Protestants. Paul Freston observed that it is reasonable to regard the Brazilian population as approximately 15 percent Protestant since nonelectors such as children, old people, and illiterates are more heavily represented among Protestants.[2]

The research institute ISER (Institute for Research on Religion) had recently completed a census of churches and other evangelical institutions in greater Rio. Of the 3,477 churches, 2,122 (61 percent) were pentecostal. The most dramatic finding was that 710 new churches had been formed (91 percent of them pentecostal) in the 1990-1992 period; the authors pointed out that the rate was five new churches a week. To drive home the point they noted that only one new Catholic parish had been created during the period.[3] Rubem Cesar Fernandes commented that the growing visibility of these churches stood in contrast to the "lack of broader research on the issue." He added his opinion that "the evangelical movement today has a symbolic weight equal to what liberation theology (and its ecclesial expressions) had in the seventies." If social scientists had been drawn to study base communities and other forms of popular pastoral work in the 1970s, now they should learn something about evangelicals, which elsewhere (and again implicitly chiding his fellow social scientists) he called "the most significant movement for changing ways of thinking in contemporary Brazilian society, especially at the poorest urban strata."[4]

Despite the lack of accurate statistics, there was considerable reflection on reasons for growth. Ed Kivitz, the young Baptist pastor, had recently participated in a conference on church growth, and his notes comparing the fast and slow growing churches expressed uncomfortable dilemmas if not paradoxes: "Churches that grow don't know much, those that know much don't grow" (the knowledge in question was no doubt of the bible and theology). The "enthusiastic" were not deep; the deeper churches were not enthusiastic. "Those who do faith healing are ill in the soul" (referring to Bishop Macedo?); "those who are healthy in the soul, don't do faith healing." "Those who are democratic are slow; those who are growing explosively are not democratic and are even tyrannical" (Baptists are proud of being democratic).

The fast-growing churches, continued his notes, "ask for money; use the media; have simple structures—leadership comes by performance, everyone is active." He noted two other features: they have declared a "holy war" (against Afro-Brazilian religion), and their architecture is secular. The description of those churches that were not growing was largely the reverse: they emphasize doctrine and the institution; "their leaders are chosen for doctrinal fidelity, not their passion"; they are awkward about money; their decision-making is bureaucratic and often far removed from the grassroots; "communication is from the pulpit and church bulletin, and in a sacred language distant from everyday life." In Kivitz's notes, the characteristics of respectability that the Baptists had achieved over decades had become a series of negative features when held up against the newer and fast-growing churches.[5]

Donald Price, a professor at the Baptist seminary, was beginning a comparative study of the Baptists and the Assemblies of God (the latter organization chosen because it was moderate and closer to Baptists than, for example, the Universal Church). "My hunch is that the Assemblies of God do a better job in the urban environment than we. We are doing a good job in some places where our ethos more closely approaches the pentecostal ethos. And in some of the places where our ethos is more traditional and staid, we haven't done as well." He wanted to understand how pentecostal churches establish and use networks and he intended to pursue his hypothesis that they were better adapted to the urban environment than the Baptist church, whose roots are rural. Although he acknowledged that growth was not the only criterion for a church, "all things being equal, a congregation that is expanding means that people are finding Christ and meaning in their lives."

Price also believed that pentecostal churches had taken better advantage of the need that people (especially migrants experiencing for the first time the pressures of the city) feel to establish connections. People had told him that they had attended one church, "and then another, and then another and then I went to a church where they prepared beans the way we did back home and that's the church where I stayed." He understood such people to be saying, "these are my kind of people and I can again become part of a community in this dehumanizing environment."

Price was not looking simply for techniques, and he was aware of a possible tension between effectiveness and authenticity. In his view, redemption involved the whole person, the community (even the cosmos). Believers should be involved in community struggles, such as those of *favelas* controlled by drug lords. This was not an imaginary case; as we were talking, a fellow seminary professor came by and said that he was sheltering in his house a young man who was in danger of being killed because power had shifted from one gang to another in the *favela* (the police had become irrelevant and real local power was in the hands of gangs).

Another foreign missionary, Christine Kraft, said that the faster growing churches "satisfy the need for a mystical experience with God in a way that Catholics don't and traditional Protestants (Baptists, Methodists, Presbyterians) don't either: the need to see God active in your life. This is especially true of the poor, with their need for healing because medicine is often inaccessible. When you go to these churches you see a strong emphasis on giving to God so you'll receive what you need." This experience "touches your daily life; it can heal your marriage, help your children in their relationships, help you pay your bills." These churches do not address problems in a physical way, as Catholics and traditional Protestants have tried to do. "The more indigenous Protestant denomination addresses [problems] in a mystical way that feels very right for Brazilians because it's coming directly from God's hands. That's why those churches work, because they address Brazilian problems in a way that feels comfortable to Brazilians."

Another reason that conservative churches were growing was that with their dress codes and behavior, "they clearly define belonging, who's in and who's out." In a world that is so unstable and uncertain, with continuing inflation, for example, conservative churches provide "the rules and stability that the more liberal and more flexible and more tolerant churches, both Catholic and Protestant, don't provide. The edges are too fuzzy in those churches."[6]

Such broad generalizations should not obscure the significant differences among the churches, for example, between the detailed prescriptions and punishments of God is Love and the policies of Foursquare, Universal, and Renascer churches based on the view that such matters cannot be prescribed in detail. Ricardo Mariano noted the Universal Church's emphasis on those places in the bible where "there is a relationship between a biblical figure and God—an exchange relationship, one in which God gives the person something and the person gives something to God." They do not speak about salvation after death, but everyday problems. "You're worried about your wife? Jesus has the answer. You need a job? Jesus has the answer. You're afraid to die? Jesus also has the answer." Such focus was distinct from that of the Assemblies of God which preaches salvation after death. Only God is Love linked salvation here and now and eternal salvation. The churches that emphasized problems of the here and now tended to grow faster, said Mariano.[7]

Bibles, Books, and Theological Education: Parachurch Agencies

It had been suggested to me that the staff at the Bible Society often has a good overview of the evangelical churches, and so early in my stay I sought out the Sociedade Biblica. The Brazilian program is one of the largest of the more than one hundred around the world. It was distributing more than 1.2 million bibles a year, over half a million of them from the Sao Paulo office, primarily through subsidized sales. The Bible Society also published small flyers with bible verses, which evangelicals distributed free in public places. A cover story featured in one issue of the organization's magazine was "Bible Distribution Increases 50 Percent in Year of Crisis" (referring to the 1992 impeachment of President Fernando Collor).

The Bible Society is one example of efforts linking evangelical efforts. The Bible Society and its staff span the various gaps separating individual churches, pentecostal and non-pentecostal, those with strict behavior codes and those with looser interpretations.

Another such effort is that of the vigorous publication of evangelical literature. Eudes Martins, the editor of a publishing house and the director of the Brazilian Association of Christian Publishing Houses, explained to me that there were about forty-five evangelical publishing houses in Brazil and 1,800 evangelical book stores. In 1991, the most recent year for which figures were available, 666 evangelical books had been published (over 2 million copies). Seventy percent were by non-Brazilian authors, however, as could be seen in the bookstore just outside his office as well as in other bookstores I had visited. Martins said that the disproportion reflected not only the greater prestige of foreign authors or the relative ease of translat-

ing existing works, but also the lack of good writing by Brazilian evangelicals. To remedy that problem, the association was organizing a series of
workshops in various parts in the country. Their aim was to discover people who had a "calling" to write, those able to think and connect ideas, and
for whom they could provide training. Such people he expected to be lay
rather than pastors (many pastors are preachers rather than writers, he
said).[8] It may be noted that the Assemblies of God have their own publishing house, and that most of their titles are by Brazilian authors.

One of the major concerns of those who view the Protestant field as
a whole is training for the ministry. In 1985, according to one study, there
were 27,100 ordained ministers (almost all Brazilians) for 9.4 million
communicant church members. Note that the Catholic church then had
13,153 priests for over 115 million Catholics.[9] The same study indicated
that there were 321 bible institutes and seminaries in Brazil (up from 80 in
1970). Such institutions, it should be noted, are often very small, as the
study itself indicates when it says that "Half a dozen pastors with a couple
of hundred books between them is sufficient to start another school."

Emphasis on formal training varies widely. Formal training is required for the ministry in the historic churches and the Foursquare
churches, and is increasingly common in the Assemblies of God; God is
Love and the Universal Church, on the other hand, provide only a minimum of training and do so in-house. In three seminaries (including the one
in Sao Paulo where Donald Price was teaching) the Baptist church was
training 1,751 seminarians in 1989.

The tensions outlined by the Baptist pastor Ed Kivitz earlier in this
chapter reflect some of the problems of churches that emphasize ministerial preparation. Numerical growth may be fastest among churches that are
least encumbered by theology. Ministers of the Universal Church, for example, show no evidence of having systematically studied the scriptures,
much less church history or systematic theology. For churches striving to
grow at any cost, theological education is probably a hindrance. If, however, growth is understood in qualitative as well as quantitative terms, and
if understanding the bible in its original context is important, further education is essential.

Christine Kraft, who worked with SEPAL (Evangelization Service
for Latin America), a non-denominational parachurch agency, took a larger
view of the cycles of church growth, somewhat reminiscent of that of the
Baptist pastor Plinio Moreira da Silva. Churches begin with enthusiasm
and spread with lay preachers whose credentials come from their work itself. As church members start to rise out of poverty, they take on more orderly habits of life, and they begin to look for better training and greater
knowledge of the bible in their pastors. "It's my observation that as they
become more biblical, as their pastors are better trained, they lose some of

the fire that ignited the initial growth. I don't necessarily see that as bad, as long as there continues to be this continual new influx of new expressions of the church. Maybe it's an expected life cycle. Poorly trained but with lots of zeal, they go through this refining process. Social action and social awareness also seem to slow down the growth of the churches here."

Kraft's viewpoint is common in members of parachurch agencies, who tend to be non-pentecostal, theological conservatives who are socially non-left. They often speak of "holistic" mission. While they accept the basic validity of personal conversion, they do not see it identified with one church, and they are familiar with the history of Christian missions. The organization with which Kraft and her husband were working, SEPAL, [Servicio y Educación Para America Latina] has been active since 1963 when it was formed in the wake of the Billy Graham Crusade in Brazil. In its early years it organized *Vencedores para Cristo* (Victors for Christ), singing groups formed for evangelization. An inactive Baptist woman whom I got to know told me with some pride that she had sung with the Vencedores as a teenager.

My impression was that parachurch agencies tended to take a long-range view of church growth, and regarded themselves as aiding local churches. Typically they provided services—training, consultation—for those churches interested in collaborating, which were typically not the fastest growing churches. The presence of a number of such agencies, mostly from the United States, sometimes fuels the notion that Protestant growth is the result of a massive campaign supported by foreign resources. The fastest growing churches, however, are entirely Brazilian (e.g., the Universal Church) and entirely independent of outside resources. Moreover, the generally non-pentecostal staff members of parachurch agencies tend to play a supplementary role, as media consultants, seminary teachers, or trainers. Far from being the explanation for rapid growth, these agencies might find it beneficial to hitch their wagons to the fast-growing churches, not least because demonstrable success aids fundraising back home.

An Ecumenical Conviction

The word "ecumenism" has a pejorative sound to most Brazilian Protestants, if they understand it at all. Although the advocates of ecumenism are striving to overcome the scandal of division between Christians and to communicate a God who is larger than human divisions, conservative Christians identify ecumenism with churches that do not accept biblical inerrancy, and hence see it as incompatible with basic Christian faith.

During the late 1950s and early 1960s, a number of Protestants from the historic churches, notably Presbyterians, were involved in struggles for change. Young church people in Sao Paulo associated with Richard Shaull were in dialogue with Catholics, especially with members of the Dominican order, and were exploring the connections between revolution and Christian faith. In the wake of the 1964 military coup, church organizations did their own purging, and a number of these people found themselves marginalized from their religious communities. A well-known example is the theologian Rubem Alves who was forced out of the Presbyterian church.[10]

Many of these church figures came together in ecumenical agencies, sometimes after a period of exile. Although they were a minority in their churches, they maintained good contacts in Europe and the United States, where they were often regarded as spokespersons for Protestantism. Their influence in seminaries and universities was strong. ISER (Instituto Superior de Estudos Religiosos) which functions as a research agency independent of church organizations (and carried out the study of pentecostal church growth in Rio cited earlier), is staffed by such people and draws on them in its network throughout Brazil.

Jaime Wright, who grew up in Brazil as the son of missionaries, is one of the most well known advocates of ecumenism. His brother, Paulo Wright, was abducted by security forces in 1973 and never seen again. Over the years Jaime Wright worked closely with Cardinal Arns in defending human rights. He bluntly expressed his own conviction that "Protestant churches can be relevant today in Brazil only if they are ecumenical. Churches that have no ecumenical concern have nothing to say to society."

The institutional expression of ecumenism in Brazil is CONIC (National Council of Christian Churches), which was founded in 1982 and is composed of several historic Protestant denominations along with the Catholic church and the Syrian Orthodox church. More than a decade before CONIC, leaders from these churches "decided to set aside their long-standing differences in order to meet the emergency situation in the country." In the 1970s, members of the various churches met to consider how they should respond to the repression of the military dictatorship, which was then at its height, calling themselves the Ecumenical Coordinating Body (CESE).

One of CESE's early projects was to prepare a pamphlet combining the thirty articles of the U.N. Universal Declaration of Human Rights (1948) with biblical quotes and citations from Christian tradition for each right. "It was a risky thing to do in those days, to take a stand." Practically no organizations in civil society were willing to speak out (one exception was the Organization of Lawyers of Brazil). Working in a quasi-clandestine way, the group prepared a large number of the flyers for simultaneous distribution. The idea was that once the information was public the military would find it difficult to suppress the U.N. Declaration and the bible. The flyer touched a nerve and stimulated so much demand that eventually over a million were distributed, primarily through Catholic church channels.

Wright joined Cardinal Arns and Rabbi Sobel for the funeral of Wladimir Herzog in 1975 (Chapter 1). He was also central to the courageous photocopying and documentation project that resulted in the publication of *Torture in Brazil* (Chapter 1). Some of Wright's fellow Presbyterians regarded Cardinal Arns as "Public Enemy Number One," and "had no qualms about denouncing a fellow Presbyterian to the military." Wright felt more support during those years from Arns than from his own denomination. "That's what ecumenism means in Brazil."

Although struggling for human rights was no longer so dangerous, in some respects it was more difficult. "When the churches were denouncing torture and so forth up to 1978 we had society's support because most of the victims were sons and daughters of middle class people... 89 percent of the torture victims during the dictatorship were university students, and so by definition middle class.

"Torture continues in Brazil. It is no longer described as political or politically motivated. It is endemic. It existed before the dictatorship, during it, and now. It's a way of life for the police. They use it as the first step of intimidation to get a quick confession so they can be promoted. Torture is used in practically every political precinct in the country... The newspapers, radio, and TV describe Cardinal Arns, myself, and others as 'defenders of the human rights of bandits, of killers,'" he said, because they had criticized the police attack on the Carandiru prison near Sao Paulo in which 111 prisoners were killed.

With pain and consternation in his voice, Wright said that defenders of human rights now found practically no support from society for the simple reason that the victims are poor and usually black.[11] "Torture continues today and the victims are always the poor. They have no way of contacting lawyers or of finding people who will help them." The Fundação Samuel, a foundation that he had helped create, was planning to help poor people get legal help. "So the church has had to become creative to meet human rights needs which today are not necessarily individual violations." This is the "institutionalized violence" that Archbishop Helder Camara had been talking about for decades. "It's very difficult for the church to meet these needs today because—if you'll pardon the expression—it's more difficult now to identify who's the enemy. During the dictatorship it was easy to identify and to denounce. Today it may be the mayor; it may be the entire police force. It's hard to work in this direction, and the church has suffered tremendous opposition because of this." He had in mind Christians doing advocacy for the poor in this more ambiguous time, typically in the official *pastorais* or ministries of the Sao Paulo archdiocese.

His own experience colored how Wright viewed the rapidly growing churches. Just as when seeing a film or play one should look for the socially redeeming factor, so too with the churches. "Where is the socially redeeming factor or concern of their preaching, their prophetic message? What risks are Christians called upon to bear or take on in these churches? You have to listen long and hard to hear anything. That's why I would say they are really irrelevant." He said this fully aware that his own breakaway Presbyterian church had been formed in the late 1970s like the Universal Church, and had only fifty-three congregations in the country, as opposed to the thousands of the Universal Church.

Although Wright acknowledged the effectiveness of evangelical churches in helping people to overcome personal vices, he insisted that Christian ethics entails much more. At a time when many Brazilians seemed to be pursuing their own interests in an unprincipled and heedless way, the evangelical churches were tending to do the same. He cited the example of evangelical members of congress who had cut a deal with ex-president José Sarney (1985-89), agreeing to vote to allow him an extra year as president in return for radio and TV licenses for their churches.

Paul Freston pointedly said that it was unrealistic to have expected the pentecostal churches to have acted like the Catholic church and Wright. "They are churches made up of poor people. They have no protection whatsoever. They would have been crushed in the repression." Jaime Wright could defend human rights only by working with Catholics, that is, by "allying himself with the only religious institution that could provide coverage for that type of situation." The only other church that raised its voice—timidly—was the Lutheran church, which sociologically tends to be more like a "church" in the Weberian sense, and hence was similar to the Catholic church.

CONIC, he said, was dominated by the Catholic church, and most of its other member churches were small or had strong immigrant roots (Lutherans). It was an elite of established churches that sought to base their legitimacy on "criteria that the pentecostal churches cannot attain." His comments were not so much a criticism of what Wright had done as a reminder of certain sociological realities. Freston repeatedly insisted that when considering Brazilian Protestantism, it was essential not to repeat broad generalities but to pay attention to the particulars of individual churches.

On a number of grounds, Freston insisted that it should not be assumed that Brazilian Protestants would inevitably be politically conservative. The pentecostal churches were not right-wing in principle. The behavior of the evangelical members of the Brazilian congress was driven not so much by ideology as by a desire to gain ground for their churches.

Nor should one assume that the people in the pews always shared the political viewpoints of their leaders. Just as research had shown that grassroots pentecostals in Chile had been more to the left than the general population (even though their leaders were quite willing to publicly support General Pinochet), in Brazil one should not assume that the members of pentecostal churches reflected the sentiments of their leaders. By the same token, the people in the pews in the historic churches were generally more conservative than their liberal leaders and did not necessarily share their public political stances.

In an essay on the political potential of evangelicals,[12] Freston begins by insisting that they are gradually becoming a significant social force. Their image as a conservative bloc must be relativized. Leaving language aside, pentecostals and members of Catholic base communities are surprisingly similar. He suggested that the political parties of the left, which were largely based on labor unions, and hence on workplace issues, could learn from evangelical churches, which are rooted in communities where people live. An effort to relate to the evangelical church environment would likewise bring such parties closer to the experience of women and their constant struggle for survival.

Urging the need to learn from history, Freston warned against repeating the experience of the 1960s, when the more progressive Protestants had been forced out of their churches and into ecumenical spaces, while the fast-growing Protestant churches were deprived of critical leadership. The implications were that with humility and openness, the historic and pentecostal churches could learn from one another and together be a force for progressive change.

4

Contending with Dragons

Progressive Catholics in a Time of Uncertainty

I BELONG TO THE GENERATION that went through the whole process of the late 1970s and early 1980s." Father Luiz Carlos Marques was thinking out loud. "We were carrying around lots of truths from grand systems," such as Marxism and liberation theology. On the basis of such convictions, he and people like him had "wagered" on the leaders they were training and on political strategies. "We thought things were going to change quickly. Today we're left with a lot of questions."

Based on recent discussions with other pastoral workers, he was hopeful that the "anxiety" they were feeling would ultimately "open up new paths." While not denying the validity of their previous efforts, he said that it was now important to give more attention to Brazilian culture. He recalled an earlier experience of celebrating mass on the traditional feast of St. John with a small base community, while ignoring the crowds of people lighting the "fires of St. John" and celebrating outside. He now believed that by concentrating on a small elite he and others had been "going against the traffic." Which is better, he asked, moving forward seven steps with one person or taking seven people one step forward? Instead of wagering on organizations (presumably meaning labor unions and the Workers Party) it was time to return to the gospel and to "wager on the unpredictability of the poor."

He was articulating sentiments common to a generation of Catholic church activists who, after a heady period of heroic struggle for the rights of the poor in the 1970s and into the 1980s, now found themselves in a changing context. Although the military dictatorship was gone, the liberation for which the activists had yearned seemed to have receded over the horizon.

This and the two following chapters consider the situation of what is often called the progressive church in Sao Paulo, primarily through portraits of a number of people whom I found to be struggling to come to terms with a changing world.

Ana Dias

Ana Dias dated her commitment to a weekend church gathering in her parish in November 1970 during one of the worst periods of the dictatorship. Previously she had been active in church activities but from that moment on "we began to live more committed to the gospel," striving to serve all their brothers and sisters, especially the poorest and most persecuted. The church, they learned, was not a building but persons. "It was a kind of school, a school of life."[1]

Ana Dias and I were talking at a day care center that had grown out of that parish work and had now been operating for twenty years. She and other women from the parish core group had begun to visit this neighborhood and to work with the people. They had first built a shed and then the two or three small classrooms and kitchen, whose floors were still hard dirt. "All this here is the result of joint struggle, church and people. Through this work the people have gained these victories." The project was similar to hundreds, even thousands, of similar initiatives in Brazil and elsewhere.

From the outset I had a sense of melancholy, pain, frustration, and perplexity in Ana Dias, a slight dark-haired woman of around forty, who had been suggested to me as an outstanding lay Catholic from the *igreja popular* ("church of the people"). Her husband, Santo Dias, had been a metal worker and union leader, a man who had been active as a church leader even at the archdiocesan level. At a 1979 strike, the police were menacing and provoking a picket line when a conflict broke out between two workers. Dias moved in to try to break it up when a policeman—who had earlier asked him if he was Santo Dias—shot him point blank through the stomach. He bled to death in less than a half-hour, while police kept the area cordoned off and prevented him from being taken for emergency treatment. When the police drove him away, no doubt intending to dispose of him, as they had others, they were followed by both a priest and a sister, making a coverup more difficult. Santo Dias became the leading martyr of the base communities of Sao Paulo.

"Look, Felipe," Ana Dias said to me, "Santos was always one of those people with faith—I am too, but he had a thousand times more. His faith was beautiful." Now, more than thirteen years later, the pain was still present. Why did a man who never hurt anyone have to die? "People remember Santo. They talk about him, but it doesn't bring him back to life. It's been very difficult for us, for our children; it's marked their whole lives. I've had to go through something very difficult. To this day I ask, 'My God, why does it have to be this way if you're struggling for justice?'" She repeated her husband's wonderful qualities: he never missed mass, he read the bible, he took communion to the sick, he visited families. "Do you understand?" She was further pained by the continuing lack of appreciation for their struggle. "All the movements, all the improvements"—getting electricity, schools, health care, transportation—"arose out of our work, out of the church's work," she emphasized. While they still had these needs people were involved, but once they had their houses and a few basic city services, people closed their doors to the outside world. The leaders were still involved, but the masses were not.

Her church was a further source of pain. This area in the south had been cut off from the Sao Paulo archdiocese and the bishop now sympathized with the charismatics. She believed that the new pastor had been appointed to weaken their work, which was now viewed with suspicion. Some priests from outside the parish still offered them support, and their work with women, labor, housing, and the day care center continued, but it was no longer recognized by the local bishop.

Resistance came from the community as well, since people were used to looking to religion for consolation, not for inspiration to involve themselves in social struggles. Many people were now turning to evangelical churches; these churches seemed to be on every corner, as common as bars. Ana Dias regarded evangelicals as ignorant and apt to be manipulated, but acknowledged that they warmly welcome people at church, and, unlike Catholics, they visited those who failed to attend. Their pastors were just like everyone else, and hence did not have the same barriers as Catholic priests. In their preaching, they knew "what people want and what they need." By paying attention to social issues, "our church...created a lot of conflict in people." Noting the way evangelicals put on their best clothes to go to church, she said, "People may not be eating, but if they're well dressed they think they've changed their lives." Although evangelicals' understanding of Christian faith seemed diametrically opposed to her own, she could not but express admiration for some of their qualities and practices.

That ambivalence continued in her evaluation of where their own work, almost entirely being done by women, now stood. "Our work is very slow and requires a great deal of responsibility. You're not just a Catholic; you are a person who is involved and committed—not just in words but in actions. I think it's a lot easier to stay inside the church or at home because our work means struggling with the Dragon—and not just one dragon but a number of dragons" (Rev. 12). "But people are not going to look kindly on you—look at what happened with my husband. Even in your family they're going to look askance at you." The same was true of "the church, and politicians, and your boss, and society. You are rejected, you're persecuted, you're isolated, you're mistreated. Things seem so difficult. People have sacrificed so much. It's easier to give up. If you look back over twenty years, you can see that the results have been meager in relation to the hardship you've endured. Why?"

Rather to my surprise, Ana Dias had expressed a deeply felt pain. I was grateful that this outstanding figure of church renewal in Sao Paulo and widow of one of its martyrs had not only given voice to her own feelings but had articulated some of the perplexity facing those who had wagered most on that renewal and on the popular struggle. Whatever her frustrations, she was nevertheless persevering at the day care center and in her organizing.

Upon reflection, however, it is not so surprising that the number of activists has declined sharply. People are willing to attend meetings and march in demonstrations while they are struggling for their most basic needs and they have a reasonable hope that some of those needs will be met. After they have electricity, water, bus service, schools, and perhaps a clinic, people may still be poor, but they understandably pursue their ends as households. The "root cause" of their poverty may be an economic system that excludes masses of people but, for many individuals and households, looking for work or finding a form of self-employment appears to be the most rational course of action.

Moreover, the heroic moments in which Ana Dias, Santo Dias, and many others had struggled against a military dictatorship that violated human rights with impunity were now a receding memory. The ideals might be still alive in the Workers Party and in Lula, then the most important opposition political figure, but the end of such a heroic age brings a letdown.

The carving up of the archdiocese and the general climate in the Catholic church had left people like Ana Dias feeling abandoned by the church itself. She recognized that many ordinary Catholics had never accepted the direction given by Cardinal Arns and his team. Her pain—even though her husband's murder made it especially sharp—was not hers alone, but expressed the frustration and perplexity of a generation of people who had wagered their lives for an ideal of faith.

A Day with Frei Betto

To the Brazilian public, Frei Betto symbolizes the progressive church as much as Leonardo Boff or Cardinal Arns. Curly-haired and boyishly energetic, he is a Dominican friar and an indefatigable activist constantly sought after throughout Brazil. By 1993 he had written over twenty-five books, including drama, fiction, pastoral works, theological reflections, catechetics, biography.[2] Although I was living in an apartment that he maintains a block from the LeCorbusier-style religious house where he lives, I rarely saw Betto. The many phone calls that came to the apartment from all parts of Brazil and other countries indicated how greatly he was in demand.

In the late 1960s, Betto and other young Dominicans were helping activists escape from the increasing military repression. In 1969 the police broke into their house in Sao Paulo and arrested all present (Betto was arrested farther south). Some were released while others were held incommunicado. Betto spent four years in prison; his letters from jail were published in several languages before he was released. In *Batismo de Sangue,*[3] which tells the Dominicans' side of the story, he did not hide his admiration for the Communist and urban guerilla leader, Carlos Marighella, and made it clear that the Dominicans had nothing to do with his assassination.[4] The book gave a chilling inside account of the activities of interrogators, especially the notorious inspector Sergio Fleury. The final section is a haunting coda on Frei Tito de Alencar Lima, a Dominican whose prison experience drove him to madness and then to suicide as an exile in Paris. When *Batismo de Sangue* was published in 1982, while the country was still under direct military rule, the book's daring revelations about repression made it a best seller in Brazil.

After his release from prison, Betto worked with the poor in the diocese of Vitoria do Espirito Santo, where he played a crucial role in shaping pastoral ministry around the base-community model of work. Betto was closely involved in the labor struggles that led to the founding of the Workers Party. He was part of Lula's inner circle and wrote a short biography of him. In 1985 Betto published *Fidel and Religion,* a transcript of his 1983 discussions with Fidel Castro, which was translated into several languages.[5]

As we headed south on the city's freeway system one Sunday morning Betto explained to me that the ABC region (so called from the names of the municipalities of Santo André, Sao Bernardo, and Sao Caetano) is the most industrialized area in Latin America. Its labor movement had been crucial in ending the dictatorship, bringing back civilian rule, and creating the Workers Party. For many years, a skilled factory worker in this area could earn the equivalent of $500 a month (double or triple the amount that factory workers were paid elsewhere in Brazil) and, until the economic crisis of the early 1980s, might own a modest house and even a car.

Once a month, Betto came to meet with this group as part of the *pastoral operaria* (labor ministry). Arriving at the parish hall we found about thirty men and women, each a leader of a local group in a social movement or labor union. A woman in her thirties named Dulce, who was finishing two years as coordinator of the group, led the meeting. Three people were brought forward to taste vinegar, coffee, and salt to alert the group to the gospel passage on the "salt of the earth."

After a scripture discussion that I found listless, the meeting moved on to a discussion of the coming plebiscite regarding what form of government Brazil should have.[6] On one level, it seemed wonderful that Brazilians were being given a chance to debate their form of government. In the actual circumstances of 1993, however, the debate seemed far from most people's concerns, especially the ongoing economic crisis, manifested in an inflation rate of about 30 percent a month.

Not surprisingly, Betto had written a short primer on the issue and it was used as the basis for the discussion. Small groups were formed to discuss particular sections of the book. In my group, a great deal of time was spent reading aloud from Betto's booklet, and the discussion had a catechism-like quality. After the groups made their reports, the discussion was lively. A parliamentary system seemed to enjoy sympathy—probably because it was not favored by the Workers Party leadership—but no position was endorsed.

After lunch an automobile worker named Gilberto drove me in his Volkswagen Bug to see various parts of Sao Bernardo. The Workers Party administration in the local city hall had put emphasis on getting urban services to the *favelas* and helping people obtain more permanent building materials. Gilberto also pointed out the drainage problems and consequent flooding being created by both *favelas* and high rise apartments. The Volkswagen complex in the area was the largest automobile manufacturing facility in Brazil and employed thirty-five thousand workers who turned out a thousand cars a day. After years of crisis, the automobile industry was said to be on the rebound, particularly as the result of a government decision to aid Volkswagen in producing a cheaper car. We drove past the modest home of Lula, whom Gilberto had known since the days when they were union colleagues. It was a reminder of how unusual it is that in less than a decade a worker could rise from the shop floor to become (at that moment) the most popular political leader in the country.

When we returned, the afternoon session had moved on to a discussion of various issues facing the *pastoral operaria*. Toward the end Betto rose and posed a question for their reflection: What is it that makes human beings distinctive? His own answer was summed up in the terms "meaning and gratuity" (it did not sound so grandiose in context). This group meets, he was suggesting, not for pragmatic reasons alone, but to reflect on and celebrate their various activities, and to keep alive the dream of a different kind of society. The everyday grassroots work they were doing was important. This group was not like a political party or a union, whose goal is taking power; its driving force was the dream of Jesus Christ for a different kind of society, he said.

His observations prompted further participation. A woman in her twenties, who was obviously one of the leaders, observed that even though raising children involves a great deal of work and occasional annoyance, no one would consider giving them up; the same should be true of one's organizing activity. Dulce said that doing one's utmost so that one's children will be raised even better than oneself is a kind of investment. While organizing for the upcoming International Women's Day, you are tempted to stop and ask, "Why am I doing this?" but the whole effort brings growth.

Betto then asked each person to say what he or she was feeling. He wanted something short and evocative, but he got speeches—about thirty or forty minutes worth around the circle. It seemed to prove that the model of a leader is one ready to speak publicly.

My feelings were mixed. Like Ana Dias, these were people whose experience in the church had awakened their vocation as leaders in union and other struggles. In sessions like this they continued to nourish their faith and ideals, and they cherished Betto both for his long experience and for his role in helping them deepen their faith perspective. At the same time, I felt in them a sense of weariness similar to what I had seen in lay activists elsewhere after many years of effort.

Padre Ticão

What first caught my eye as we entered the vestibule of the church located on a ridge in the district of Ermelino Matarrazo in the eastern part of the city were sheets of newsprint with schedules that bespoke energetic activity. The parish of an estimated 150,000 people was divided into eight local communities, each with its own liturgical and sacramental life, and ten defined ministries cutting across the parish.

Padre Ticão (Luiz Antônio Marchione) is well known, perhaps even notorious. "I was accused of being a communist, a Workers Party (PT) priest, and even today I'm known as a priest who invades land." Because of his involvement in land struggles, neighborhood authorities and police accused him of defending the human rights of bandits. In the late 1980s, local small business owners had brought five legal actions against him; some were still in the courts.

Together with a half-dozen other priests, Ticão said he had been reevaluating their earlier work. "Our discourse was that of liberation theology and we imagined—I imagined—that the people were understanding our discourse, and that even the poor were understanding. But they didn't accept it. Our mistaken methodology created bad feeling." The often cited method of starting "from reality" and then going to the bible had not been accepted. "So today we are in a way going back; we're giving training in the bible, helping people connect the bible to their everyday life. Many people are now beginning to see what we said ten years ago was in the bible."

At a youth mass to launch a program of preparation for confirmation, 150 or 200 people, mainly youths, were seated in a fan shape around the altar. Rather like Protestants, parishioners had their bibles in hand, instead of mimeographed or photocopied sheets typical of Catholic parishes, and Ticão read from the bible rather than the lectionary. After the gospel (on the "salt of the earth"), a group of young people presented a short play in which various items were tasted. The young people were seated in groups according to the section of the parish where they lived, and adult catechists were present alongside them. During hymns people swayed to the music or held their hands or bibles high.

Confirmation preparation was one of the ten parish ministries which included marriage, catechesis, health, social, pastoral, youth, liturgy of the word, and so forth. These were a legacy of the Sao Paulo archdiocese before this diocese of Sao Miguel was cut off. Each month, on a Saturday afternoon, those in charge of ministries met for common reflection. Ministry teams were expected to do some kind of outreach each month (for example, those involved in health ministry would visit the sick).

Other activities took place in the parish besides the ten ministries on the official chart. A literacy training effort that was started in the parish in 1982 had grown to 125 adult literacy groups. Small groups meeting to help the disabled or retarded in the parish had expanded to the point where a full-time staff was working with fifty or sixty children; this ministry was now supported by the municipal government. At a recent mass for recovering alcoholics and their families, three men stood up at Ticão's invitation and described how they had stopped drinking and no longer beat their wives, all to extended applause. With their superficial Marxist analysis and with notions that the family would disappear, said Ticão, the progressive church and liberation theology had "reinforced machismo with leaders who were in the community and are now involved in politics, who are very domineering and unethical." Ticão and the parish had returned to various traditional practices such as recitation of the rosary, which he occasionally led. Although he was not personally sympathetic to charismatics, he allowed them to use the church facilities, and he acknowledged that they had two positive features: use of the bible and of the body.

Such rethinking and shift of emphasis notwithstanding, Ticão was clearly still in the thick of social involvement. At mid-morning, after the youth mass, we went to an open grassy area where several dozen people were meeting under a tin roofed open shed. The previous Workers Party (PT) municipal administration in Sao Paulo had approved a housing project of four-story walkup apartments for twenty-five hundred families. Rather than contracting with a private firm, the government had pledged to allow the people themselves to organize into work crews and do the work, thereby saving money and providing jobs.[7] The project had been halted by the incoming right-wing city administration as part of a larger process of reversing the programs of the previous socialist mayor Luiza Erundina.

Ticão, who participated in city-wide housing movements, said that sixty organized groups were struggling to obtain housing in his diocese of Sao Miguel. He allowed the movements to use church spaces and shared information with them, but the leadership was theirs. In his mind, there was a distinction between the pastoral work embodied in recognized ministries and this work of "accompanying" the popular movements.

At this meeting, a mustached man of forty or fifty was speaking to the people assembled on plank benches and standing under the roof. Because of the buzz of conversation, he could not be heard beyond the first three rows. No one seemed to be disturbed, however, perhaps because they had little idea of what was supposed to be accomplished. Some may have been present primarily to keep their names on the list for housing, should the project go through.

At one point Ticão stepped forward and began to address the people in a voice loud enough to be heard. He had the people repeat after him *A união é nossa força* "Unity is our strength" (like Cardinal Arns in the cathedral on Ash Wednesday). He mentioned that the theme of the National Brotherhood Campaign was housing and urged them to come with banners to a day-long rally that was being organized. If the city government did not comply with this demand by April 1, they would organize a demonstration to apply pressure. As he warmed up, Ticão moved closer to politics. When he suggested that Brazilian behavior at election time was suicidal, the implication seemed to be that people had voted for Collor over Lula against their better judgment, as had been proven by Collor's disgrace and impeachment. A Workers Party activist would probably be pleased. The distance between Ticão's former and present style was perhaps less than he imagined.

Padre Zaga

Ticão gave me the name of his friend, Luiz Gonzaga—"Padre Zaga" as he is known—whose parish was in Vila Cisper, about a half-hour bus ride from one of the eastern metro stations. The church sat on a flat area facing the soccer field.

The district was relatively new and had been named after the container manufacturing plant up the hill that employed many local people. The people were poor, but not the very poorest, and were struggling to complete their houses. One sign of the economic crisis was that many people rarely left the neighborhood. They could not even afford to visit the shopping centers near the metro station.

Zaga had reassessed his earlier position even more emphatically than Ticão. "Starting around 1968 or 1970 our discourse became political. You had to talk to the people about faith and politics—there was no other key for addressing them...We did everything: Elections for Lula in Sao Bernardo? We were there. Strikes? We were there. Campaign to get schools? We were there—Ticão and I and about fifteen or twenty other priests. We were tremendously paternalistic with the people. We were very judgmental—God didn't accept anyone on the right." They had wanted to lead people toward socialism, and had instilled their ideas in the people, but were incapable of grasping the people's own feelings.

After five years in the priesthood, Zaga began to suspect that something was "rotten." Driven by a personal crisis, he went to the Peruvian altiplano (he had previously traveled to Central America and over the years he had been to Cuba eight times). Upon returning, he spent a year being treated for tuberculosis before coming to Vila Cisper.

In Peru he had learned that "people are thirsty for spirituality. They are so thirsty for God that we often don't know how to read it, to interpret it for ourselves and reinterpret it for the people." His parishioners were from the interior, especially Minas Gerais, a traditionally Catholic area. "The religion of the people is their soul, and God is there in their simplicity, in their petitions, in their lives, in everything." He had set out to understand the people's "religious imaginary"—post-structuralism was much in evidence among Brazilian intellectuals—and saw that it was "so beautiful."

"So, when I returned, I was very clear about the fact that my religious practice was not going to be like that of the 'guerrilla' period." Whereas the people's religiosity had once been viewed as something to be harnessed for political purposes, he became convinced that "God is much greater than our own ideas and schemes." He was now willing to serve the people's religious needs and aspirations.

The beginning was not easy. At his first mass in the parish the church was full of his friends from around the city. The following Sunday there were only three pews of people. The building he had inherited was small and its walls were soiled with pigeon dung. Such disrepair was symptomatic of the attitude of social activist priests. On one of my visits Zaga showed me a chapel dating from Operation Periphery, and he said that the people disliked it for the same reason they disliked his church, namely that it did not feel like a church. He accordingly had an ample and solid church built. The Sunday eucharist was the center of his ministry and the life of the parish. Although he described himself as a "coordinator" of a number of activities, Zaga was willing to accept his role as a priest and to be sensitive to the people's expectations.

At the Sunday 10:00 A.M. mass, I found a full church. There were at least four hundred people, and many were standing in the aisles. Addressing God with feeling at various points, Zaga was clearly a leader in prayer. At some moments the congregation paused for silent prayer, and at other moments people waved their hands overhead during a song, or placed one hand on the back of their head while praying. Zaga's liturgies did not have striking innovations, but I sensed an atmosphere of prayer that was considerably more intense than that in the usual Catholic liturgy. The highlight of the Holy Saturday liturgy was a beautiful Exsultet sung to a Brazilian folk melody by one of the parish musicians.

Zaga's parish had a base community, a youth group, a bible group, a liturgy committee, and organized retreats for dozens of couples. It was my sense, however, that organization was not his major focus. In contrast to Ticão, whose parish seemed to have a program for every identified need, Zaga was willing to suffer without answers and to let his own emerging attitude be shaped by the people. For example, he now took seriously people's reluctance to engage in politics; they saw all politicians from any party as people who are "overpaid and get nothing done." Whereas he might once have regarded such an attitude as "false consciousness" or as the effect of centuries of oppression, he now regarded it as "popular wisdom." Not that he automatically went along with all such "wisdom": he was dismayed at a recent poll showing that 67 percent of Brazilians favored the death penalty (in the wake of the notorious murder of a TV soap opera star), but he at least understood the frustrations over crime and violence that had produced such sentiments.

Both Zaga and Ticão had not only been rethinking, but had changed their approach to ministry. They regarded their earlier approach as overly political and as an illusion. Unlike priests who sought to be utterly "like everyone else," they accepted their role as religious leaders. Popular religiosity was no longer an embarrassment or something to be utilized for other ends. It was itself at the heart of the people's spirituality, something from which both priests felt they had much to learn.

This shift was not a simple return to a more conservative position or model of ministry. As noted, Ticão was thoroughly involved in social ministry, and Zaga denounced the injustice of the "capitalist city," but he no longer believed that a viable socialist alternative was on the horizon.

Ana Dias, Frei Betto, Ticão, and Zaga embraced the post-Vatican II church in Brazil and wagered much on it. The first two were persevering largely in the same direction and the second two had changed their minds on some matters and shifted the direction of their work. All four were struggling with questions of how to remain faithful to their commitment in a changing context.

5
Questions about Base Communities

T HE *FAVELA* IN DIADEMA in the southern part of greater Sao Paulo was named "18 de Agosto" after the day in 1989 when the people invaded it (with the tacit agreement of the Workers Party mayor). Around dusk on a Saturday, I went with Father Luiz Carlos Marques to the house where the host couple welcomed us. A dozen people somehow squeezed into the sub-divisions of the cinderblock house. We sang hymns prepared for the "Broth-erhood Campaign." The scripture portion of the mass was somewhat awk-ward since the questions that a young leader asked in order to elicit participation were met with silence. The real highlight was the baptism of two children. By candlelight Luis Carlos explained each gesture, obviously finding his liturgical role fulfilling. A eucharist in the home followed.

Luis Carlos and his fellow Redemptorists were living in one corner of a large parish (probably one hundred thousand people) and by agree-ment with the pastor did some pastoral work. He pointed out that one of the women from the *favela* who worked as a domestic in several houses had gradually taken courses in theology and was now responsible for cate-chetics for the whole parish. He wondered whether those who paid her to clean their houses realized that this poor woman carried such a responsibil-ity. She was really more cultured than they.

That evening celebration was similar to many others taking place in Brazilian base communities the same weekend. It had once seemed that such small communities would gradually become the characteristic Latin American form of the Catholic church. Indeed, around 1970 it seemed only logical that, given the ratio of only one priest for every ten thousand Latin American Catholics, at some point ordinary married men would be the ordinary ministers of the eucharist in settings just like this one in Di-adema (women's ordination was not yet being proposed).

Over the years, what had once seemed inevitable had become in-creasingly unlikely. The base-community model of pastoral work was on the average being implemented in no more than 10 percent of parishes in Latin American countries, and even in those parishes such communities were small islands in a vast sea of Catholics whom the church scarcely touched. Moreover, base communities required considerable input from priests and sisters. A parish team in Guatemala, for example, was proud that approximately four hundred people were participating in weekly meetings of one kind or another, but ten priests, sisters, and seminarians were involved in maintaining the programs. Meanwhile, two hundred Catholic charismatics were functioning with little input from the parish team, and a third of the sixty thousand people in the area were said to be evangelicals.[1] Despite the efforts of a generation of church workers, Christian base communities were quantitatively a minuscule part of the religious scene in Latin America.

One of the first pastoral theologians to raise uncomfortable questions about base communities was Jose Comblin in a 1990 article in the *Revista Eclesiastica Brasileira*.[2] An often unresolved question, he notes, is whether the base community is a "quasi-parish" where the emphasis is on ritual actions, or is rather like a "social movement." At one point Comblin makes a series of observations on what Catholics could learn from pentecostals. One of his harshest observations has to do with the "authoritarianism of love," his description of the real power that priests and/or sisters (and behind them the bishops) have over base communities. As well meaning as priests and sisters might be, they have the power and lay people will never develop on their own, especially when they are poor and devoid of their own resources. Comblin proposed that base communities should be allowed to become institutionalized with their own lay autonomy, alongside other movements (such as the Charismatic Renewal, the *cursillo,* and so forth). Such a development would be tantamount to admitting that base communities are not *the* model of church, but one legitimate current among others.

The article stirred up controversy. The sociologist Pedro Ribeiro de Oliveira replied that Comblin had failed to see that the relationship between pastoral agents and base-community leaders was not one-sided but was dialectical. He also said that Comblin was assuming that base communities should be parish-based, whereas it might be better to coordinate them through a higher-level structure (to some degree bypassing the parish). Acknowledging that the time was not propitious for base communities, he suggested that they could become the normal church structure only in some future truly democratic society—which was nowhere on the horizon. Jorge Atilio Silva Iuliannelli sought to find the strong points of both positions. Another writer argued at length that the base communities were experiencing a crisis of adolescence. In a short note ("Defeat of the CEBs?") (CEBs = *comunidades eclesiais de base, "ecclesial base communities"*) Eduardo Hoornaert noted that thirty years previously Comblin had written an insightful article raising basic questions about European

Catholic Action (*Echec de l'Action Catholique?*). Hoonaert's implication was that although that article had aroused little discussion when it appeared, time had proven Comblin correct and his questions should not be ignored now.[3]

Secular social scientists had originally taken at face value what was said about Christian base communities by theologians, clergy, or some members of base communities, and were slow to raise questions. By the mid-1980s, however, on the basis of fieldwork in Sao Paulo, H. E. Hewitt found that the members of base communities were not the very poorest, but tended to be people who were steadily employed.[4] The fact that leaders had to be literate in order to read the bible and other materials screened out most of the very poorest. Moreover, despite the progressive interpretation put on base communities, participants were often seeking something of the traditional devotion that they remembered from their youth.

Two works that I read on the flight to Sao Paulo intensified my questions. John Burdick, an anthropologist, had first become aware of the role of the progressive church in connection with Central America. However, as he read the literature he came to see two paradoxes: 1) the numerical paradox that while base communities were intended to reach the masses, large numbers of people were gravitating toward pentecostal churches or Afro-Brazilian religion, and 2) the political paradox that most members of base communities are far less socially active than much of the literature had implied.

In a community on the outskirts of Rio de Janeiro, Burdick systematically compared a progressive Catholic parish that was using the base-community model, the Assemblies of God church, and the Afro-Brazilian religion, *umbanda*. His major finding was that people consistently found evangelical and Afro-Brazilian religion more helpful for facing everyday problems. For example, he found that a base community tended to avoid dealing with situations of spousal abuse because addressing the issue might threaten the unity of the group, and because the prevailing ideology was that such matters as machismo were only symptoms of deeper societal injustice. By contrast, the Assemblies of God church would take the problem seriously and would offer consolation—even a solution, if the man was converted. The Afro-Brazilian religion would offer advice and prayer. Poor blacks also found that despite opposition to racism in Catholic teaching, subtle but real racism was at work in base communities. Base-community members and leaders tended to be lighter, while evangelicals, both leaders and lay people, were mulatto or dark.

Looking for God in Brazil was one of the first studies to suggest that base communities and evangelicals are in competition and to examine them from that standpoint.[5]

Questioning the Figures

The other work I read on my flight to Sao Paulo was a draft essay by the Canadian sociologist, Jean Daudelin, who began by asking why the resistance of the progressive church to the attack from the Vatican (disciplining of theologians, choice of bishops) was so weak. If the progressive church had been as strong a movement as often alleged, it should have offered greater resistance, he believed. It was perhaps disingenuous to pose the question in this manner, but some of his observations were nonetheless important. He was perhaps the first scholar to question systematically the often-made claim that 80,000 to 100,000 CEBs existed in Brazil and that participants numbered from 2 to 4 million. He noted that the Sao Paulo archdiocese had a total of 765 base communities in 1983 and 875 in 1987. If base communities were represented throughout Brazil as they were in Sao Paulo, which contained about 10 percent of the country's population, the number for the country would be 9,000 or 10,000. Assuming an average of 25 members per community (based on three research projects in different areas), Daudelin concluded that the total number of participants throughout Brazil was perhaps 250,000. "These results suggest that the number of both communities and their members has been exaggerated by a factor of ten or more in the literature."

The second and longer portion of the article was about the "myth of 'the Church born of the People' or the Church of the Poor as a lay, democratic, and autonomous movement." Like others, Daudelin found that the base-community movement was dependent on the good will of the bishops (he cited the ease with which Archbishop Helder Camara's work had been dismantled by his successor in Recife) and, at the local level, on priests. He also observed that the progressive church is overwhelmingly dependent on money from foreign (usually European) agencies. This is obvious to anyone familiar with the proposals submitted for funding, but is scarcely ever mentioned.[6] Thus, the progressive church has little independence and has been powerless to resist the Vatican's moves.

Daudelin did not intend to detract from the accomplishments of those working with base communities, and the humble people who meet to discuss the bible and deal with community problems or struggle for land, often risking their lives. But he did observe that, "Obviously—one more time—many intellectuals from the north thought they had found in Brazil's Progressive Church the meaning of their life and of history, the promise at last of a true revolution."[7] The rhetorical excess aside, Daudelin's essay exposed the willingness of even social scientists to accept the conventional figures at face value, when a pocket calculator and a modicum of suspicion should have been enough to raise questions.

While interviewing a priest who had served in a parish in the eastern part of the city for over a dozen years, I pointed out that he was referring to the base communities in the past tense. He paused, and when I pressed, he said that "they seem to be non-existent" in the diocese (Sao Miguel). He observed that priests who had once been involved in base communities were now working in *pastorais* (ministries) such as those of the street children. For the liturgical seasons of Lent and Advent his parish might organize *grupos de rua* (street groups) to meet for a few weeks, but they had no ongoing existence. Based on what some others told me, including a bishop, the temporary "street group" seemed to be what was most akin to base communities.

Another priest explained that the heyday of the base communities "was in the late seventies, around 1978. It seemed like there was a new model of church really being born. We were developing a lot of lay leadership and a lot of deep formation. Political courses and those kinds of things were flourishing" [meaning, I think, consciousness-raising courses about people's rights, not a political party]. "It seemed that this was the way: a way of transforming church and—indirectly—society. There was a lot of hope." With the economic crisis and the political opening—which was really managed by the military—people had become confused, dispersed, and frustrated. The church had been on the front lines, especially in the prophetic voice of Cardinal Arns, and it was the focal point for the progressives. With the shift to civilian government, however, the church returned to its "specific function." The church's prophetic voice had been displaced by the rise of Lula and the Workers Party.

Base communities in Sao Paulo, it should be recalled, were part of "Operation Periphery," the thrust to put personnel and resources in the outskirts where people were building houses and new neighborhoods. One priest described arriving in a neighborhood where people were building their homes while the streets were still unpaved. He and the others on the team downplayed their identities as priests and sisters and encouraged the lay people to make decisions, including planning liturgies. Using the exodus story as a background during meetings, they encouraged people to discuss what had prompted migration to Sao Paulo (drought in the Northeast or lack of jobs). "This was the promised land. Some didn't come here right away; they may have stopped in Minas Gerais or Rio before coming here. And when they started reading the story of the Exodus, they got to see their own journey.

"There were a lot of things going on; people were involved in issues like building schools and getting electricity." Sometimes people became excited about a particular project, such as getting a neighborhood health post, and would hold meetings and organize visits to the mayor's office. When they achieved their goal, however, it seemed that they had no further reason to meet. Eventually the whole routine of the city, especially two hours of commuting by bus each way to work, exhausted people and made it difficult to continue with the communities.

A sister put the point more sharply, "When people invade land, they get thrown off and then come back, get thrown off and come back. They get their little patch of land and start building their house. They get electricity and water and then they put up a wall. That's all they wanted. You can't get them out to meetings. They still don't have sewage and don't have paved streets but they close in and say, 'I've just got to take care of my family. We've got this much and now little by little we'll take care of our own house, but we're not going to go out for any more.'" The observation may reflect an organizer's frustration, but such behavior is shrewd. The activism of the early stages of a new self-built community—whether resulting from an invasion or not—is a transitory phase. It is rational for people to struggle as a community for what can be attained through such solidarity. When that limit is reached (when it becomes obvious, for example, that the municipality will not have the resources to install sewers), it makes more sense to use their time and energy at the household level rather than in community activism.

Operation Periphery apparently caught the wave of the rapid expansion of Sao Paulo in early and mid-1970s, but that early phase of community activism would inevitably subside. In Brazil the heyday of the base communities also coincided with the dictatorship when "the space for people to come together was the church, the community," explained the priest. That was the time when the working-class ministry was most active and many leaders were trained. It was diocesan-wide but different parishes had small core groups of working-class pastoral workers. "When the unions became stronger or louder, and especially when the Workers Party emerged, a lot of the leadership from the community or the *pastoral operaria* went into that, and this created a vacuum of leadership in the communities." Likewise, when political parties could function again, "people weren't coming to the community or the parish to have problems resolved. So the church at that time was beginning to ask, 'Well, what is our role as church?'"

The emergence of the base community in the 1960s seemed wonderful in several ways: it had a scriptural precedent in the New Testament house churches; it was a method of evangelization; its pedagogy was one of mutual respect; it formed community; local leaders were lay. Indeed, to see ordinary people with their profound common sense express basic realities of Christianity was inspiring. Furthermore, it seemed to solve the vocational crisis of Catholic priests and sisters in the confusion of the post-Vatican II period. A parish priest or a group of sisters in a village or barrio could focus their pastoral approach on creating and sustaining base communities.

Serving Whose Needs?

Was it possible, I began to wonder, that the rapid formulation of the base community idea and its implementation throughout Latin America was a reflection of the needs of the priests and sisters who were looking for a model of work? If poor Latin Americans themselves had been its primary creators, would it have taken a different form? When I expressed my doubt to one priest he replied, "That's our big question: whether the base communities were more for gratifying the pastoral agents than for answering the needs of the people."

To a similar question, Jose Comblin replied, "Of course. Many became involved with base communities out of a personal calling, not so much out of concern for the church but because it was personally fulfilling.

"Several things came together. Among the people some were searching... They found a priest who was in crisis and also looking for a new way. There was a convergence. But after a while the priests no longer felt fulfilled. The crisis is a crisis of the pastoral agents, not of the base communities. The people are still the same.

"Deep down pastoral agents thought that base communities would be the spearhead of a social revolution, a social transformation, a new society. So, working in base communities was a way of preparing for the new Latin American society. At that time the base communities were seen as at the spearhead of the opposition. They were the alternative. People said that basic change might take time, even into the next century, but base communities were the alternative."

The return to democratic government turned out differently, however, bringing a series of defeats. Brazil has gone back into the hands of the old "captains and landholders, the traditional elites who have no interest in change but simply want to make money." When it became clear that the base communities were not the spearhead of change, "the priests were no longer so interested. They began to say that base communities weren't achieving anything.

"But the lay people who entered the base communities had no intention of engaging in social revolution or changing the church... They didn't have such vast ambitions. What they wanted was greater independence, a community life with more independence from priests. And that's still what they want but the priests aren't very interested." Lay people do not need complicated courses, he insisted. They need a "strong initial spiritual push, a very strong message. The pentecostals do that and so do the charismatics. They get started and go to work. But if you begin with very intellectual meetings, things are going to be slow. What is required is entering into the people's psychology. It has to be a conversion movement, like the early

Baptists and the Methodists." He was speaking on the basis of what he and his colleagues had been doing in Northeast Brazil.

Comblin was incisively articulating something I had suspected but had not heard from others. Some Latin Americans would no doubt resent the tone and disagree with the thrust of his remarks, but I found it salutary to see them stated forcefully.

From another angle, the theologian Ivone Gebara confirmed this assessment. "I think we Catholic pastoral agents and theologians wagered on a new model of society and a new model of church—one in which the base communities were the new model of society. I'm confessing to you that I always felt uncomfortable with this exalting of the base communities, and I had to endure a lot of criticism.

"I also have the impression that a great deal of the enthusiasm over base communities comes from people who don't live in poor barrios, who don't share the daily life of the people as they struggle for survival. So my impression is that it is a kind of investing in a dream, but a dream that isn't dreamt out of the real situation of the people. That is a bit of my impression of liberation theology's understanding of pastoral work.

"I'll admit that I'm somewhat happy to see this idea of base communities come tumbling down, because what there is among the people is so frail and also so different from what the theories say." She did not mean to say that everything had been a mistake, but "when I live in a poor barrio, and when I talk with my neighbors, and see how their situation is—the poverty, the unemployment, the violence—I sometimes think that for years we were using the poor to buoy up our own triumphalism about the church. I'm not denying all our good will," but this church of the poor has been largely the "church of an intellectual elite."[8]

Like Comblin and others, Gebara was questioning not base communities but the exaggerated expectations that had been invested in them. To do so was to question one's own life options, but it was essential for confronting the challenges of being the church in the present.

6
Ministries to the Marginal

IF SAO PAULO HAS A CENTER, it is Praça da Se (praça = "square," like Spanish *plaza* and Italian *piazza*) where the cathedral stands and the two major metro lines cross underground. Paulistas with automobiles have little occasion to go to this center, however, which lies in a busy but decaying part of the metropolitan area. After the evening rush hour passers-by become fewer and fewer.

At 8:30 on a Thursday night, I arrived to observe the ministry to street children. Some of the kids were already there when a tall blond man arrived and began playing with them, holding their arms and swinging them around. He was obviously part of the team. Others soon arrived, including John Drexel, the American Oblate priest who had invited me. Soon six or eight were present: an ex-sister, a sister who was studying theology (in full habit), a sister who was studying law, a woman psychologist, and a young Argentine priest who was going to work in Angola. Over twenty volunteers took turns coming here.

One of them had brought a heavy jump rope and for the first fifteen or twenty minutes he continued to play with the children. A woman team member went looking for first-aid materials to treat one child's open sore. When she treated him, several others produced their sores or other problems and were also treated. Their clothes were obviously seldom washed.

With no systematic plan, the team members sat on benches and the kids approached. Team members put their arms around them, or allowed the kids to lie in their laps. What contact with adults to these kids have? I wondered. During the day, most passers-by tried to avoid them. The police no doubt hassled them. They might be sexually propositioned. These people—sisters, priests, lay—were probably the only adults who showed them any affection without expecting something in return. Physical activity—jumping rope, swinging them around, holding them—were obviously central to their mission.

Most of the kids were between ten and fifteen years old, but some were as old as twenty. One eleven-year-old was nowhere near the height of

71

my twelve-year-old daughter and looked closer to seven. The older ones often bullied the younger ones, but some offered protection.

Early in the evening, two members of the team left with two of the girls, one of them pregnant, to take them out to a *favela* where they would have a place to stay, perhaps deal with a drug or alcohol problem, and where the pregnant girl could have the baby. The team had aided six pregnant young women that way. During the evening some older adolescent girls who were on crack cocaine or had alcohol problems passed through briefly, but the team members were not optimistic that much could be done.

At any moment throughout the evening one or more kids were sniffing nail polish from transparent plastic bags. Drexel told the boy lying on our two laps, "If you're going to lie here I'm not going to let you sniff," but he continued to sneak off to sniff. More than one had AIDS, and John thought several would not live long.

The team's number-one principle was simply to accept the kids: a minimum rule was that they should not be stealing here and now—although they stole John's cigarettes from him. Team members encouraged the kids to get off the street and were able to offer a way out when they were ready. An older youth named Alex, who was now off the street, came by to say hello. Another had lost the job that John had helped him get at a bar, and John now offered to help him get another job.

The square was almost deserted. A woman hurrying through clutching her knapsack to her chest testified to the feeling many people had about the area. I could not avoid the suspicion that a red-faced older man who came through several times and sat on a bench was waiting for a chance to proposition one of the kids. One of the girls went off with a man passing through and soon returned alone.

Three police in the gray uniforms of the Sao Paulo state police periodically passed through the square. Once they forced the small group of kids to turn over their plastic bags but, as soon as they left, the kids drew out more. A single container of nail polish lasted hours. They obtained it through petty theft, just as they obtained food. One of the older youths was strutting around in a windbreaker that he had apparently just stolen.

On their third or fourth swing through, the police, who were plainly annoyed but no doubt had instructions to avoid conflict with church people, struck up a conversation. Why didn't they take the children to a home? they asked. The tone of the question implied: "Why are you hanging out here? You're only encouraging them." When they expressed concern for the fact that the children were hungry and sniffing glue, John replied, "Well, take that to the state government. They're the ones who should be doing something." He mentioned a welfare agency that had a thousand people on the payroll but did nothing for these children. "Give me a thousand people and see what I can do," he said. Politely but firmly, he was pushing the police-men's feigned concern for the kids back at them and putting his finger on the societal source of the problem. Most Sao Paulo residents would nonetheless probably think more like the police than the priest.

Not all of the children were without family. The kid lying in our laps talked about the rosary and the white shirt and white pants he wore at his first communion. John suspected that he came from a slightly better-off family.

At about 10:00 P.M. a larger number of kids came through, including a number of girls; they looked like some sort of gang. By the time I left, twenty-five kids were present in the area. The kid who had been lying in our laps said he was going to go off to sleep on a grate above the metro with a concrete slab overhead for protection and warmth.

Team members took turns doing their *plantão* (= being on duty) every night of the week from 8:30 until midnight or 2:00 A.M. according to the circumstances. The focus was on "presence," being available for these kids. Team members were volunteers in the sense that they were not paid for this activity, but at least half of them were full-time church people doing this in addition to their regular activity. The next day the rector of the cathedral told me that he took his turn on *plantão*. This was clearly a ministry, but it had no immediate payoff in terms of "building up the church" or improving religious practice among Catholics. Church capital was being spent, not accrued, so to speak.

The ministry maintained contact with around three hundred children. Most street children, said Drexel, were not orphans and most were actually *meninos na rua* ("children *in* the street") not *meninos da rua* ("children *of* the street"). "Children in the street" might spend days on the street but they had a place to which they could return; the smaller number of true street children organized themselves in groups or gangs.

Typically, "children in the street" left home because their father had abandoned their mother and the stepfather beat them; in the case of girls, he may have raped them or attempted to do so. Some remained in the street for three or four days and then went home. They might be beaten for not bringing home enough money. "So when they decide to live in the streets, it's because they've been rejected, not because they don't have a mother or father," said Drexel. Recently a mother had arrived at Praça da Se and said to her child, who was huddling by a vent, "Vagner, what are you doing here? I'm not going to hit you." She had brought a clean sweat-shirt and sweatpants (so he wasn't even so poor, said Drexel). He changed his clothes in the plaza and they walked away, the mother with her arm around her son. According to Drexel, it was the mother who should have been questioned: "Why did your son run away?"

Street children came from all over the metropolitan area to gather here downtown, near Avenida Paulista and at the major centers of movement. "That's where the people are: more watches, more attache cases." Food might also be more available, for example, from a McDonald's that might otherwise throw away hamburgers at closing time.

Team members called themselves "street educators." Drexel emphasized that the first contact with the children was simply a matter of being there, sitting in the plaza, and waiting for the children. You had to listen to them, let them build up enough confidence to speak. The first step was to show that you didn't want anything from them; you simply wanted to be with them. It was like going from flirting to being in love to getting married. The concentration on a pastoral work where the emphasis was on direct contact was clearly more satisfying to Drexel than other forms of pastoral work which, despite all their talk of solidarity, seemed to be taken up by planning and coordination meetings.

Drexel, who now headed the ministry to street children for the archdiocese, had been working with children for twenty of his thirty years in Brazil, although it had become his full-time work only recently. His current dream was to have a "House of Welcome" to take kids in. He had visions of them doing art work, perhaps silk screens, and perhaps learning a trade at a Salesian vocational school. Experience had also made him realistic. Street kids accustomed to operating as they please for twenty-four hours a day would need to have a minimum of regimentation. In order to get a job they would have to be able to stop sniffing glue or using crack, and be willing to make themselves presentable.

When Drexel arrived in Brazil in 1962 there were 2.5 million abandoned children. The number was now estimated to be more than 7 million. According to the census agency, 53 percent of Brazilians eighteen and under were in a state of extreme poverty. In 1991, 247,000 children aged one to five had died of diarrhea, dysentery, and respiratory infections. These figures revealed the consequences of the kind of development that had occurred in Brazil during the last thirty years.[1]

Drexel had previously been a pastor and he had worked in television. After years of base-community activity, he had concluded that base communities were not reaching the poorest of the poor, especially the illiterate, who were more likely to gravitate to the Assemblies of God or God is Love where "they don't have to read and write but only pray and sing." He had not moved to his present work out of dissatisfaction with his previous work, however. "I felt that in my life as a missionary—sixty years old, thirty years in Brazil—I had other priorities. I feel now the priority in my life is to work with street kids and I think it's a special charism." Some of his colleagues wondered why he was "wasting his time" with street children. They no doubt also questioned why the Oblates who shared a downtown apartment with him were in prison ministry rather than working for structural change.

In Drexel's mind, however, the Brazilian and global economic and social structures were by no means disconnected from street children. Indeed, the first two chapters of a short book he co-authored on children are about unjust structures, both national—within Brazil—and international. "So when people ask what working with street kids has to do with pastoral work, I say that street kids are prophets. They're crying out, saying 'We're the victims, the consequences.' The church has always worked with poor kids, and street kids, but only recently has it begun to inquire about the causes."

THE SAO PAULO ARCHDIOCESE was heavily committed to *pastorais ambientais*, ministries to and in non-territorial "environments" (labor, youth, street people, housing, etc.) which numbered about fifteen on the organizational chart. Another Oblate, Bill Reinhard, headed the housing ministry, and lived with a small community of priests and sisters in the Moocá neighborhood (a five-minute walk from the God is Love complex).

On one of my last nights in Sao Paulo, I went to Moocá to meet two Brazilian sisters who led me to a meeting where representatives for the housing ministry were to help a group deal with a threat of imminent eviction. The three-story building had once housed public offices but had been abandoned, and had then been occupied by people who needed housing. During the Collor administration, a woman had used her political connections to obtain the building with the intention of turning it into a home for older people, probably more as a business venture than out of humanitarian concern. The occupiers had ceded half the building for that purpose, but the woman was not satisfied and had sought to evict them. Two earlier evictions had been stayed, but the previous day a judge had once more ordered an eviction, and the people were meeting to decide what to do.

We climbed the dark stairs to a meeting site on the third floor. Bare electric wires ran across the ceiling. Perhaps a dozen people were present, as well as the lawyer from the archdiocese and Reinhard. Coffee was served as Reinhard reported steps he had taken to halt the eviction, including contacting influential government officials who would attempt to persuade the judge to change his decision.

The lawyer noted that the judge's arguments were far more political than legal, and that the legal basis for the decision was weak. But, he said, "You are minorities and you really don't have support from your neighbors who would just as soon see you gone." At the moment, I understood the discrimination to be racial, but later I realized that he was referring to the fact that some were gay.

Whether the eviction would actually take place could not be determined at that moment. Much of the discussion centered on tactics of resistance. The lawyer urged them to decide that some would be too sick to be moved and thus, even if eviction took place, they would retain a toehold on the building. He seemed to warm up to the idea that if the police thought that these people had AIDS they would be afraid to touch them. Several did in fact have AIDS, including the dark soft-spoken man who was the president of the association and was chairing the meeting. Another tactic might be to insist that the owner comply with the legal requirement of paying for transportation and storage of their belongings. Plans were made to contact the press and TV and get other allies, including possibly a bishop. It was problematic because they wanted to avoid bringing such resources to bear on a false alarm, and yet if the eviction went through things could happen fast.[2]

Back at the house, Reinhard said that only in the last three or four years had the church been devoting pastoral attention to the *cortiços,* as the downtown tenements were known, even though they had existed for a century. He said seminarians increasingly wanted to work there and sisters were establishing communities in the area.

His colleague Betto recalled a Christmas celebration at which the people who were now facing possible eviction had presented a play ostensibly about rabbits which was a political critique of Brazil (someone had represented Cardinal Arns defending human rights).

When evangelicals arrived offering to help homosexuals be "converted" from their sin, the group leader replied that they knew that God loved them as they were. Betto saw in this response an indication that his own work of solidarity, both in supporting the group's organizing efforts and sometimes celebrating mass, was truly evangelization.

LIKE DREXEL AND REINHARD, Sister Maria Emilia Guerra Ferreira had spent years working in base communities. She had studied with biblical scholars Milton Schwantes and Carlos Mesters and had worked with Jose Comblin training lay leaders in the impoverished Northeast. Like Drexel and Reinhard, she had now turned to people who were more "marginal"—in her case, women at Sao Paulo's largest women's prison where she had been working as a psychologist for eight years. Her congregation, the Canonesses of St. Augustine, was very supportive of its members' activities. Although I had come recommended by a priest who is a good friend of hers, she was wary of me throughout the evening, an attitude probably arising from the common suspicion of any American asking questions.

A phrase that kept recurring in her comments was the need to *sair da casa do pai,* to "leave one's father's house." She understood this phrase in a psychological, largely Freudian, sense, meaning that one must come to terms with the Oedipal conflict. But the phrase also had a trinitarian sense: the Spirit is different from the Father and the Son, and life is not a matter simply of replicating what has been done previously but of promoting difference, variety, and novelty.

She resisted my efforts to elicit from her an analysis of the present and future state of religious life. Of those who had left the convent she said, "If they managed to leave the convent, the father's house, they did so because they were humanly and spiritually mature and have taken another road." Another option is to remain and become more mature in the midst of work. The important thing is not canon law—what is prohibited or allowed—but engaging in tasks and struggles in the world. Women religious were increasingly working independently of priests and bishops, who were "unbearable." They were doing so by undertaking their own projects. "You don't move forward until you leave your father's house."

She was surprisingly sanguine about the tendency of religious life and the church to turn inward that many were deploring. She regarded it as "a natural human process of opening and closing." The traditional idea of religious "consecration" had nothing to do with one's garb but was a "quality of human contact" between a person and those suffering the most. "That is what consecration is, renewing everything as God wants, helping all to attain the dignity that God wants. In that act we are fulfilled as religious." When every human is human, when nature is nature—that will be God's ideal.

In the course of our conversation I mentioned that as a married person I was inclined to regard religious as freer to devote themselves wholeheartedly and to do "crazy" things. She responded vigorously, saying that this was the "old framework. Who says that someone who's married isn't consecrated?"

So why does religious life even exist? I asked. "Ask God; it's his problem. It's a matter of callings," she replied. She likened it to being a musician or an artist, but she had no overarching theory of religious life. "That's one of the various mysteries of the world. Why are you here?" she asked, meaning why was I in her living room at this moment. "There may be a rational explanation, but the explanation may go beyond the rational." Those who sought explanations were insecure. If religious life were to disappear in the next fifty years, it would be because it has been in the image of the father, producing the same thing (like a Coca-Cola factory producing only Coke). "The institution's problem is its inability to live with differences."

So you don't have hope in the Catholic church? I asked. "I have it because the Catholic church is not the father's house. The church is also the Spirit of God which is there, the universal Spirit of God is there. It's also in the evangelicals, in Afro-Brazilian religion, and in esoteric religious groups." What would happen in thirty or fifty years was of no concern. "My concern is this adventure that we are living, faithful to the Holy Spirit. As Abraham and Moses went out, so must we."

Throughout the conversation she had questioned what I was doing. My whole enterprise of spending several months talking to people and eventually writing something struck her as an idle academic pursuit. "The important thing is to live" she said, once again cryptically. "One does what one can," I said, using the common Brazilian way of saying, "I'm doing what I can." It was my most unsettling encounter and what she said gnawed at me throughout the next day. What was I doing, running from interview to interview and from worship to worship?

I was also left wondering whether the kinds of options sketched here are suggestive of something happening in the Catholic church, or at least to a portion of those who had wagered years of their lives on the promise of conciliar renewal. Both Maria Emilia and Drexel had turned away from base-community activity to work with the poorest and most marginal. These activities were officially recognized as ministries, but they were likely to be dropped or downgraded when Cardinal Arns was replaced. More important, I wondered how significant it was that those who had devoted years to Christian base communities and the training of lay leaders were now taking on such ministries. While it might make sense in the life story of particular individuals who grew weary of administrative work or who wanted to work directly with the neediest, might it also signal a retreat from seeking renewal of the church itself? On the other hand, these ministries were bringing the voice of "prophets," such as the street children, into the broader church community.

7

Church within the Church?

The Charismatic Renewal

IN RECENT YEARS THE CATHOLIC CHURCH has frequently been portrayed as a battlefield on which "restorationist" forces led by the Vatican are seeking to undo the achievements of the post-council period, especially through the systematic appointment of loyalist bishops and the exclusion of those who do not meet certain criteria.[1] Certain movements, including Opus Dei, Communion and Liberation, the Neocatechumenate, and the Charismatic Renewal are said to be favored by Rome. Journalists have written about two ambitious plans, Evangelization 2000 and its related media effort, Lumen 2000, describing them as well financed and planned behind closed doors. Along the same lines, two secular researchers on religion in Brazil told me that parishes in the state of Sao Paulo were being taken over by charismatic Catholics who volunteered for tasks such as helping prepare the liturgy.

A number of questions were accordingly on my mind as I approached the Charismatic Renewal: Who are the charismatics? Are they mainly middle class, as their critics say, or are they from all segments of society? How many are there and how fast are they growing? Is the Charismatic Renewal a potential Catholic antidote to pentecostal growth? What does the charismatic movement represent for the future of the Latin American Catholic church?

Although the Charismatic Renewal was no more than tolerated in Sao Paulo under Cardinal Arns, it had a place in the archdiocesan organizational chart, and charismatics met in the cathedral every Monday evening. Arriving at one session, I encountered perhaps two hundred people, a number that grew to three hundred by the time I left. A rosary was in progress, and people in blue smocks were walking up and down the aisles. The participants looked generally middle-aged with a sprinkling of younger people.

After some hymns, a priest in a short-sleeved clerical shirt ascended into the pulpit. I recognized him as Padre Alberto, whom I had seen Sunday morning on TV. Once he grasped the microphone, the evening was his. He prayed, he led singing, he raised his voice, and he lowered it dramatically. At one point he spoke in tongues (staccato nonsense syllables). Leading a large group in worship generally has an element of theater about it, but in Alberto's case, I had a strong sense of calculation, of calibrated actions, rather than seizure by the spirit. The worshippers around me, however, sang, clapped, and swayed contentedly.

Shortly afterward, I attended a weekly service at Patio de Colegio (a small church that is one of the few remnants of colonial architecture in the city). Again the proceedings began at about 6:30 with a rosary led by an older Brazilian priest. The number of people grew from one hundred to perhaps two hundred. "*You* have a friend in Jesus," they sang, pointing to one another. The central figure was not a priest but Carlos, an Argentine layman. At one point newcomers were invited to withdraw to a room in back and a rather large number did so. Although similar to an evangelical acceptance of Christ as personal savior, this moment seemed to lack drama. When the newcomers returned, the priest gave benediction of the Blessed Sacrament. (Afterward he mentioned a group of seminarians on retreat, and asked everyone to pray for them, specifically that the retreat might help them avoid the secularization that has entered the church during the last twenty years. His resentment of post-conciliar developments was unmistakable.) Matters dragged somewhat as Carlos led more meditational prayer and three women gave rather long testimonies.

In the sacristy after the service, Carlos and another man took a rather hard-sell approach with me. In their description of ordinary Catholics as passive and not really evangelized, they seemed to be saying that only charismatics are true Catholics. You can know all the theology in the world, they said, but if you don't have the Holy Spirit you don't know what it means to be a Catholic. Pope John Paul II, they claimed, was *renovado* ("renewed"—not exactly a public charismatic but obviously within the pale). Carlos, who owned or worked for an automobile agency, failed to keep an appointment I had made with him for an interview, and my further attempts to reach him were unsuccessful. It was difficult to avoid the conclusion that he was not really interested in talking with a non-charismatic who was unlikely to join the Renewal.

Padre Alberto had announced that the charismatics would be holding a three-day vigil during Carnival, no doubt to counter its paganism. Actually, there was rather little paganism evident on the streets of Sao Paulo. The Carnival weekend extended from Friday night to Wednesday noon. Most places of business were closed, traffic was light, and people seemed to stay home. Carnival was largely a television spectacle: the parade in Rio was being broadcast each night starting at 11 P.M. and continuing through the night.

The vigil was held in the auditorium or gym of a Catholic school just off Avenida Paulista (the major artery of the banking and business district). Those present, who looked like traditional churchgoers, sat on folding chairs spread in a fan shape around the stage which held a small rock band. A number of young people—from Catholic high schools, I surmised—were present. The words "Jesus Christ is the Lord" were the backdrop (as they are at the Universal Church).

While the group was still returning from lunch, "Padre Eduardo"—a Jesuit named Edward Dougherty and a major figure in the movement—spoke about media plans. Emphasizing the need for evangelization, he repeatedly said, "We are the majority," implying that the minority (Protestants) were monopolizing religious broadcasting and that it was time for Catholics to produce their share. His organization had produced some religious spots and had more ambitious plans that included a religious soap opera.[2]

After worship had resumed, a sister began to encourage the people to be ready to speak in tongues: When you pray to God using conventional language, you soon run out of titles like "Almighty Father," "Lord," and so forth, but when you speak in tongues you don't have that problem; speaking in tongues is simply praising God. What had seemed bizarre to me suddenly sounded more reasonable. Would those who have not yet spoken in tongues but would like to please stand? she asked. Perhaps a third or a half did so and others approached them and laid hands on their heads or shoulders. The sister said "Do this," and began to speak in tongues, offering a lesson and a model. This did not strike me as manipulative, since she was not concealing anything, but simply setting up a situation in which praying by uttering random syllables felt easy.

Dougherty, a central figure in the Catholic Charismatic Renewal, is an American Jesuit who came to Brazil in 1966. After studying theology in Sao Paulo, he went to Canada, where he heard about the Charismatic Renewal. On a weekend in March 1969, "I was baptized in the Holy Spirit," he told me. "I had a pentecostal experience. The grace of Pentecost happened in my life. Whereas before I had been timid in public, after the pentecostal experience of March 15, my faith grew, my love for the word of God grew, my prayer life improved very much. Something deep happened in my life through the imposition of hands." On a visit to Brazil later that year, he told his Jesuit confreres of his insight that besides the grace of the cross and resurrection there is the "founding grace of the Catholic church called the grace of Pentecost. Pentecost is possible."

A fellow American Jesuit, Harold Rahm, who had likewise had such an experience, was the first to spread the Charismatic Renewal in Brazil. He organized a course called "Experience of the Heart." Dougherty had worked full time with the movement since the early seventies, specializing in giving priest retreats. His travel was facilitated by a free pass from Varig airlines (whose prices on flights within Brazil are quite expensive).

I mentioned my uneasiness over the impression I was getting that some charismatics felt that they alone were true Catholics; I could not accept the implication that the Holy Spirit was scarce until the late 1960s. Dougherty agreed that the Holy Spirit has been in the church. "But have we really wanted the spiritual gifts? Have we really been trained to expect gifts? Prophecy? Or does that mean just 'denouncing'? What about discernment of spirits?" The Catholic church needed discernment of spirits, and had said little about the "outright spiritual warfare" now taking place with the spread of the occult, belief in reincarnation, and New Age movements. If we can have a biblical renewal and a liturgical renewal, why not a charismatic renewal?

He described an experience at Carnival time. "We had benediction and I went among the people. There was a lady who had been hit by a bus seven years ago and her right arm was run over. She had had sixteen operations...I saw this lady and approached her. I put the monstrance in my left hand and put my hand on her head and then on her arm. Right after that she raised her arm. She hadn't been able to do that for the last seven years. She went up and gave witness, saying that she was healed, physically healed...Was that healing? Suggestion? Psychosomatic? Or are we really open to the power of the Spirit in the way we should be open to everything God has done? People come because of the healing even if they don't know the doctor. The same thing happened in the time of Jesus."

After describing this apparently miraculous experience, Dougherty shifted easily to saying that pentecostalism and the charismatic movement have both learned how to market the faith. The pentecostals do not offer theological arguments; rather, people who stand up and tell their stories: I was a Catholic and was drinking, beating my wife, committing adultery— and now I have found God. The Catholic church must look much more at marketing, detecting people's deepest needs and showing how they can be satisfied.

In more than 180 of Brazil's 230 dioceses the Charismatic Renewal had "service teams," people who were in contact with the bishop and with the national office of the Renewal. The moment of takeoff for the movement was a 1986 retreat given by the American preacher, Fr. Robert De-Grandis. Based on the number of prayer groups in Brazil, Dougherty and the movement's leaders were confident that charismatics numbered between 3.5 and 5 million. That figure would be impressive, since it represents about 2-3 percent of the Brazilian population. Some confirmation for that estimate comes from the Datafolha survey, which found that 3.8 percent of electors were connected to the Catholic Charismatic Revival.[3] The fact that most of those involved in the Renewal (70 percent) are women was a matter of concern, so much so that the movement was making an effort to draw in married couples.

The Renewal was not intended to be independent of parishes, but rather a leavening influence, since deep evangelization was needed. Prayer groups were being encouraged to become basic Christian communities. (Most promoters of base communities would not be happy to hear such a statement, since they believe that taking a critical stance toward injustice and working for social change are essential to base communities. It is conceivable, however, that over time the term "base community" may come to be applied broadly to small lay groups meeting outside regular church services.)

Although Dougherty described the relationship with the hierarchy as close, it was clear that he lamented the fact that church authorities did not always esteem charismatics. "Now what happens if the sheep are abandoned by the pastors: Who is to be blamed?" Most renewal in the history of the church has started from the bottom, he noted. People are surprised when the Charismatic Renewal "can fill a soccer stadium with over 100,000 to 140,000 charismatics, and for the Corpus Christi procession they have trouble getting together 10,000" (he was referring to Cardinal Arns and his associates). "Why? What is the charismatic movement doing that is right and what is the Catholic church doing that is not right? Have we really done the marketing well? Do we really know what the people want? Or do we ask our friends who are ex-theology students...what should be done?" He thought that the church should carry out surveys to determine people's needs and be concerned about "packaging," finding the kind of expression that would bring lapsed Catholics back.[4]

Perhaps sensing that he had gone too far with his criticism, he acknowledged that there were "so many graces going so many different ways. It's a grace to have a cardinal with the vision [Arns] has. The Charismatic Renewal is also a grace." Grace is happening "all over the place." The great obstacle was to be closed—the implication was apparently that the pastoral consultation and planning so emphasized in Sao Paulo was closed. "And what is God doing?...It is part of the pastor's main role to discern what God is doing, what God wants, the signs of the times. It really does no good to say, 'Well, I'm the Charismatic Renewal or I'm liberation theology.' You know—'I'm of Paul, I'm of Apollo.'" As long as the bishops did not close the door, the Renewal would continue. Although charismatics carried out some social work, particularly with abandoned children and drug addicts, they did not need to engage in such programs because the church itself was already doing so. Its specific ministry of evangelization was to bring people to a conversion experience.

When I inquired about Evangelization 2000 (which progressive Catholics were convinced was a multimillion dollar "restorationist" takeover that would neutralize movements for justice), Dougherty said that the basic idea was "Let's give a present to Jesus Christ on his 2000th birthday: a world much more evangelized. Let's get Catholics out evangelizing."

"We are training evangelizers...setting up a national offensive to evangelize Brazil, to Christianize Brazil. There are twelve different front lines: a national school, the media, youth, married couples, priests, religious, seminaries, communities..." Charismatics were apparently very much involved in this effort. The appeal would be to get people back to the church, "get their lives in order, get their marriage situation in order, get to know the good news, become Christian, work for a better world." The mechanisms would be to train leaders who in turn would train others who would evangelize. This model borrowed from the work of the Mexican priests, Alfonso Navarro and Jose Prado Flores.

Dougherty believed that Catholics were "timid" and divided (e.g., into dioceses and religious orders). "Who is working on a national level?" The bishops were apparently unprepared or unwilling to undertake the massive kind of media work he regarded as necessary. Hence, the media work that he had described at the Carnival time gathering was independent. Its relatively low budget ($100,000 a month) operation was being financed through many small contributions from an active membership list of 80,000 people, primarily in the state of Sao Paulo (the "buck-a-month club").[5]

To my eyes, Catholic charismatics looked distinctly middle class, especially when compared to most pentecostals. The movement had begun among the middle class, providentially, said Dougherty, "because it is the middle class who have studied more and have gone to the university and can more easily serve as teachers and leaders of a solid Catholic Charismatic Renewal and not fall into fundamentalism...or other things...But certainly I'm convinced that the most open people are poor people." It was they who filled the stadium at the annual Pentecost gathering.

The movement's dream for the year 2000 would be "to see a strong, vibrant, young Catholic charismatic church, which is very much a missionary church with many vocations to the priesthood but also with many lay people clearly living Christianity." In a Brazil that is "materialistic, devoted to sex and consumerism, often easily falling into the occult," the movement would like to see a "committed, alive, and happy Catholic church having a big impact on Brazil."

In interviews with major leaders of the Charismatic Renewal, all of whom were laymen, I sought to pursue my questions further. Adilson Carvalho, the head of the movement in Sao Paulo, invited me to his crowded second-floor office on a commercial street near the Dom Pedro II metro station. He was a wholesaler of imported foods (canned goods, oils, and the like) and the smell of dried fish was in the air.

There were three hundred prayer groups in Sao Paulo, he told me. This was somewhat more than a third of the number of base communities. By the kind of reasoning applied by Jean Daudelin (Chapter 5), if the groups averaged 25 participants, the number of participants in Sao Paulo would be around seventy-five hundred. Since Sao Paulo constitutes about 10 percent of the Brazilian population, national participation in prayer groups would approximate seventy-five thousand. Even if national rates were double or triple those of Sao Paulo, the total would be far below Dougherty's 3.5 to 5 million.[6]

Carvalho, who had attended training sessions for evangelizers, said that in some places in Brazil evangelizers were preaching the "kerygma" (first announcing of the gospel) in public squares. This struck me as a naive transfer of a New Testament concept to the contemporary scene. How can you make a "first proclamation" in a country where images of Christ have been part of the landscape for five hundred years? How can you have a pure kerygma? I asked. The questions seemed to put him at a loss, but he then continued to speak of power in the Holy Spirit, being liberated from death and sickness, and having one's life changed; it struck me that he was repeating the terminology he had learned at evangelization courses. That the coordinator was in fact a lay volunteer was impressive, but I doubted that he would lead an effective evangelization campaign.

A similar contact was Joel dos Santos Ribeiro, who had recently been appointed coordinator for the entire state of Sao Paulo. He operated his business, some kind of trade, from a modest office downtown. He had been a traditional Catholic, but the crisis of his son's drug problem had led him to change his own life. For example, he now refused to falsify receipts for customers so that they could avoid taxes. He was thinking of starting a prayer group exclusively for men and planned to hold gatherings at 6 A.M. on Saturdays.

Unlike the Argentine Carlos, Ribeiro did not seem to judge other Catholics on the basis of whether they were or were not charismatics. In his area of the city, the charismatics were active in social ministry and had recently participated in a demonstration in front of a *favela* in connection with the Brotherhood Campaign. He spoke approvingly of his parish priest—not a charismatic—who housed homeless people and recently had used parish funds to buy a house for a woman who had lost hers.

They had held one workshop to train trainers for the evangelization schools. These trainers were to train one hundred others, each of whom was to reach out to at least seven others, thus ultimately reaching seven hundred people. Such a multiplication scheme left me skeptical.

I met the national head of the Charismatic Renewal in a modest office in an already decaying concrete building in Brasilia. Evaldo Pina Silho, also a layman, was from Rio. He looked to be in his thirties, was physically fit, and had an affable manner. As we talked, we drank several cups of coffee and he smoked—an obvious feature distinguishing Catholic charismatics from pentecostal Protestants.

He divided the bishops into three groups: those who were charismatic, those who were not but accepted the movement (the largest group), and those who opposed it. The Charismatic Renewal is not a movement, he assured me, but "the church in movement." Liberation theologians had made the very same distinction about base communities a few years previously. This (non-)movement was structured in a pyramid form, going down to states, dioceses, and local groups. He could not provide figures but said that they were being prepared at the lower levels of the organization.

So as not to suffer the fate of all waves which break and foam away, the Charismatic Renewal was now organized to work on various fronts (mentioned by Dougherty above), each with its secretariat and so forth. The national office intended to make mobile teams available for helping local groups.

The first loyalty of the Charismatic Renewal was to the Catholic church. "We do not own the truth." Evaldo agreed that, because of the influence of pentecostalism, there was a danger of fundamentalism in the Renewal. On the other hand, ecumenism was taking place in practice: evangelicals were often found in Catholic charismatic prayer groups. The opposite danger was that in poor areas evangelicals could make inroads into charismatic groups.

Liberation theology was indeed beautiful, but charismatics were concerned that some people put material things first. When I pointed out that the Catholic church had overcome such a dichotomy in Paul VI's *Populorum Progressio* (1967) and at Medellin (1968),[7] he seemed unfamiliar with what I was saying. God, he said, proceeds the other way around, putting the spiritual first.

Some assessments of the charismatic movement may be made on the basis of these admittedly limited observations and contacts. The Charismatic Renewal obviously has appeal and satisfies a religious need in some people, as evidenced in the numbers of prayer groups and in events such as filling the Morumbí soccer stadium at Pentecost. Such success is especially interesting in Sao Paulo where the movement has had only grudging acceptance at the archdiocesan level.

Determining the number of participants proved elusive. Dougherty's estimate of 3.5 million adherents, however, was implausible. Those who entered the Charismatic Renewal tended to be already church-going

Catholics. Although conversions and change of life (from drug use) do occur, they do not seem to be the norm. The association with the rosary suggested that some participants find in the movement a connection to pre-Vatican II Catholicism. It might indeed be that a relatively high proportion of parish activists (helping prepare and lead the liturgy and serving on parish councils, for example) were charismatics.

The Charismatic Renewal is both lay and clerical. The fact that three major leaders were lay (two of them volunteer) was impressive, but I had a strong sense that their strength lay in administration, not spiritual leadership, a role filled by priests like Dougherty and Padre Alberto. In fairness, it should be noted that the leaders and spokespersons of the progressive church are most often clerical. (This is one of Comblin's central criticisms.) Like the Catholic church itself, the Charismatic Renewal is multiclass, but its center of gravity is middle class.

There was no evidence that the ambitious aims of Evangelization 2000 and Lumen 2000 would be realized. It seemed likely that the scheme to train evangelizers with a multiplier effect all over Brazil would remain on paper. The charismatics might establish a greater Catholic presence in television, alongside the existing evangelical programming, but that presence would remain modest.

8

"No, We Don't Accept..."

Challenging Machismo in the Church

IT WOULD HAVE BEEN ENTIRELY POSSIBLE to research this book by moving about in an almost all-male world, that of Catholic clergy, Protestant pastors, and some academics. Even if two-thirds of those active in pentecostal congregations, base communities, and the Charismatic Renewal were women, the spokespersons would be overwhelmingly male. In addition to the women whose voices have appeared thus far, it seemed important to seek out those who could specifically address the situation of women in the churches.

The crucial role of Catholic sisters in the post-conciliar renewal has been insufficiently acknowledged. Base communities and other kinds of community development and leadership training programs owe much to the steady work of sisters visiting homes, counseling, giving lifts in their jeeps, and so forth. Such work may have remained somewhat invisible because of the concern to ensure that lay people would be credited with the results of their struggle.

One looks in vain for any sustained reflection on women in liberation theology—except that done by women. Women are of course mentioned in passing among the groups of the exploited, but there is little sense that the major male theologians have really been challenged by the feminist critique of patriarchy. The male God continues to reign in language and theology.[1]

The fact that they cannot be ordained plainly keeps women outside the inner circles of the Catholic church. Male liberation theologians, with the notable exception of Leonardo Boff, have not raised the issue of women's ordination, both because it has not been widely proposed in Latin America as a pastoral need and because they do not want to aggravate tensions with the Vatican.

Pentecostal ministry is likewise largely male, symbolized by the lone woman standing in the doorway while twelve hundred or so Assemblies of

God ministers carried on their business (Chapter 2). The Foursquare Gospel church is a notable exception. Although women do not head congregations in other churches and are generally not allowed to preach, they can give testimony. The position of women in evangelical churches is not unlike what it is in the Catholic church: they are a majority of active members, do most of the everyday work, are excluded from major leadership positions, and are defined by their maternal and housekeeping role, seemingly with biblical sanction.[2]

This chapter gathers the voices of several women who were devoting their lives to service within the church in Sao Paulo and Brazil, all of whom raised serious criticisms.

THE LUTHERAN CHURCH, said Heidi Jarschel, who normally served in the south of the country but was then living in Santo Amaro, an industrial suburb of Sao Paulo, did not invoke Paul to tell women they must be silent in church and indeed had no theological objections to women's ordination. The fact that women served as pastors in Germany was a helpful precedent. Nevertheless, patriarchy continued to shape the mindset of church leadership and the expectations of congregations. Even after women had been formally admitted to ministry in Brazil, progress had been slow: at first only one woman per year was allowed to study for the ministry.

As women moved into the ministry, communities and women pastors themselves were insecure. The community was accustomed to the pastor having the last word. "The pastor is a man and he decides. He speaks at the end to sum things up. The community says, 'Okay, the pastor has spoken and this must be the way to go.' After all, our church is a church of the word." Women pastors did not have the imposing self-confident voice that male pastors had, and that made them insecure. One woman pastor had been sent to a rural parish where the previous pastor was in the habit of referring to women as "stupid."

Attitudes and practice, however, were changing, particularly under the influence of a younger generation whose thinking and behavior were more democratic. Women were feeling freer to speak up in meetings. Jarschel believed that women's non-authoritarian style was more attractive than the common practice of pastors who would arrive at women's bible study groups and offer a half-hour exposition of a text. Some congregations were now requesting women pastors.

Jarschel and her colleagues had recently published the findings of a survey of women Lutheran pastors in Brazil. They found that these pastors were suffering from great stress and exhaustion. One of the reasons she gave for this was the fact that women experience everyday life differently from men. A woman away from home continues to worry about her family and her duties there. By contrast, men away from home, including pastors, do not think about whether their children are safe, and do not experience guilt feelings when absent. Women pastors were carrying a double burden—or a triple burden, if one included the political commitments that most had.

Women theologians were likewise constrained. "We write very little about our pastoral experience. It doesn't get systematized either individually or in groups. I'm not sure of all the reasons, but one of them is that it is hard to get together. We don't have money for air fare and it would take three or four days by bus." As a result of the heavy workload in the parish and the demands of political commitments, "there's little writing, little theorizing, little theologizing." Moreover, few women theologians held university appointments.

When I urged her to present a view of how things might be, she insisted that for the present it was important to keep the constraints in mind. "I think there is a great pastoral wealth among Lutherans based on 'the everyday' and on women's experience, but very little is written. We ourselves do not make it a priority to write about this. I think that in order to motivate ourselves we would need to sit down for at least four days to reflect on the issue and from there to put something in writing. We don't do that." She contrasted their situation with the ease which feminist theologians elsewhere seemed to have in writing and publishing, especially collaborative works in theology and biblical reflection.

She and others were preparing for the second seminar on reproductive rights (the first had been held the year before) in which women theologians would meet with women social scientists. She had not suffered repercussions within the Lutheran church for publicly advocating the legalization of abortion. Most Brazilian feminist theologians, however, were working in "institutional spaces" (which I understood to mean primarily theology departments at Catholic universities and Catholic religious orders) in which they were not free to address the issue.

Women theologians of her generation had embraced liberation theology. "It was very progressive because it stood in contrast to classical theology. My concern for another kind of theology arose from the 'everyday,' when I began to work out my own position on abortion. It arose out of my dealings with women, from many cases on the outskirts of the city where I was working, and from women who came to go to confession to me, because they were afraid to go to confession to a priest. I got a sense of their guilt and I began to deal with this underground reality. That led to another type of theological reflection—one on the foundations."

Initially, Latin American women theologians devoted considerable attention to "archetypes." Catholic theological writing took up the figure of Mary. Given their own background, Protestants had not written much on Mary, although Jarschel felt that they should do more. Since most of the well-known biblical heroes and figures are male, theologians had sought to redress the problem by seeking women heroes and leaders. "You open your bible and there you find Mary, and then Deborah and Sarah. But that doesn't question the structural roots of theology." Jarschel was concerned that the net effect of such an approach might be to leave patriarchal theology even looking a little better and easier to digest.

Heidi Jarschel had taught at two Catholic theological institutes in Sao Paulo, including the one attended by most archdiocesan students. One semester was devoted to doing a deconstruction of "the feminine" using Rosemary Ruether, Elisabeth Schussler Fiorenza, and others. North Atlantic feminist theology was fifteen years ahead of Latin American feminist theology. For example, a translation of Ruether's *Sexism and God-Talk* was about to be published, ten years after the original had appeared in English; most important works were still unavailable in Portuguese. *Teologia sob a otica da mulher*—theology from women's standpoint—as practiced by many women theologians was ultimately reformist in nature because it failed to deal with underlying patriarchal structures. Ivone Gebara was an exception insofar as she was striving to reach down to the roots.

When I noted that the male theologians are aware of sexism but not really of patriarchy, she said, "But women [themselves] often don't recognize patriarchy." They talk of discrimination but fail to recognize "that there is a patriarchal system, that it is a complex thing, and that it must be broken. They don't recognize that there is a man-woman conflict." Biblical studies and theology had focused on class conflict, but had ignored gender conflict.[3]

MANY OF THE ISSUES NOTED by Heidi Jarschel were articulated even more pointedly by Barbara de Souza, an ordained United Church of Christ minister. She had been in Brazil since 1966, working in the church and in health and development programs, and most recently organizing women's programs in a Catholic parish. With little prompting from me, she spoke from sometimes bitter experience.

"This is a thoroughly male dominated society. But women historically have always been stronger. They are the childbearers, caretakers, and homemakers, and in this society they also work outside the home, and so they have the larger role. As they get more power, they threaten the male's single role, that is, to bring in the money and have sexual privileges inside and outside marriage." As an example, she mentioned a town in northeast Brazil where, when a boy reached puberty, the women were sent out of the house; then the mayor, the boy's godfather, and other male relatives would bring a prostitute "and this young boy would have to prove he was a male."

Lula was a "typical macho," she said, pointing to the ongoing controversy within the Workers Party (PT). Recently Luiza Erundina, having completed her term as mayor of Sao Paulo, had accepted a position in the administration that had replaced President Collor. Most PT activists—at least males—were angry that she had done so on her own, thus violating party discipline; most of a two-day meeting with representatives from around the country had been devoted to this issue.[4] Barbara de Souza interpreted it as Lula's problem. "Suddenly this single woman from the Northeast appears. She is a social worker who is educated; and not only does she have a reputation in the party, but she is drawn above him into the government and is a threat to him not only as a male but as a figure in the party. There are sexual issues and power issues here." Such an idea—whatever its analytical merits—simply would not occur to the many PT sympathizers I was encountering.

The groups de Souza organized provided a context in which women could talk about their lives, including their bodies. They discussed the right to make decisions about their bodies, and to take pleasure in them, whether sexually or otherwise. They discussed how women were controlled, even with justification from the bible, and they sought to demystify the bible. "One day a woman who took this course said, 'You know, before I took this course, I was happier. Then my eyes were opened and I realized how oppressed I was, how I was used in the church, and in my family. I'm sad, but I could never go back.'"

This work led to clashes even with those who fancied themselves progressives. In a recent article de Souza had referred to the "myth around Mary's virginity." The article was "cleaned up" by removing the myth observation and references to Mary's body and sexuality. On another occasion, she was elected to be a coordinator of working class pastoral activity in their pastoral district, but the priests did not allow her to assume the post; they were supported in this by Cardinal Arns.

The issue, she said, is power. De Souza believed that the sense of superiority that comes with ordination affects even progressive priests and bishops: "All of a sudden that male is God-like. He has a power in his hands that has to do something to him psychologically. This is dangerous for women." By the same token, priests are afraid of women having power. Barbara de Souza believed that even when progressive priests praised what the women's groups were doing, they were being condescending and did not truly regard the work as important.

FOUR SISTERS OF A SMALL CONGREGATION in the eastern part of Sao Paulo described how the general conservative shift was affecting sisters like them. During "Operation Periphery," Cardinal Arns and the other bishops had been desperate for pastoral agents and had asked the provincials for sisters. Hundreds of small religious houses were opened in poor outlying neighborhoods. Now, however, conservative bishops were replacing Arns's team, and priests were tending to go along with the change. Even women's religious orders were becoming conservative. Of the two thousand women religious in the archdiocese, only about three hundred met to discuss issues of this kind of work.

The sisters who had contributed to the prophetic stance of the archdiocese had become disillusioned with Cardinal Arns, because in any conflict between a priest and sisters, the bishops—including Arns—sided with the priest. The bishops had little understanding of women's religious life, which is different from that of men whose situation is closer to that of diocesan clergy. Some sisters had moved away to the Northeast or to the dioceses of the remaining progressive bishops. Even within their congregations, they felt questioned because they were working with women or with street people and could not follow a regular convent routine.

Sister Ruth Mauch said that the recent observances of the 500 year anniversary of the conquest (and evangelization) had helped to put the most recent twenty years into perspective. One of their mistakes, she thought, may have been to "put themselves underneath a big father, the bishop."

SISTER MARIA ISABEL SALES, the coordinator of the Association of Religious for Sao Paulo, confirmed some of these impressions. She regarded herself as on the side of the *inseridas* (those "inserted" into ordinary neighborhoods), but she was also skeptical of religious who became too radical. Not long ago, teaching in schools had been regarded as "bourgeois," but today it was being re-emphasized and many of the students were from *favelas* and *cortiços*.

She warmed up, however, on the question of how women religious are treated. "Priests generally don't value women's work and specifically the work of sisters. Our church is still very macho. You know, if there is clash between a priest and a sister, the priest is listened to, not the sister." Once, when she had been working in catechetics at the diocesan level, the director was changed and the new director informed her in a letter that she was dismissed. "What do you mean dismissed?" she had responded. "I work for free; at least I should get a conversation." She went to the bishop who listened and agreed that she had worked well, but said that the letter was still in effect. "So if they could do that to me, imagine what they do to other women."

SUCH HIGHHANDED TREATMENT OF WOMEN was typical of the behavior of priests in the diocese of Sao Miguel in eastern Sao Paulo, said Sister Judy McDonnell. She cited the case of a woman who one day went to her church (probably a neighborhood chapel without a resident priest) to meet with the other people, mainly women, who prepared the Sunday liturgy. They found the door locked. Taped on the door was a sign from the new priest listing a schedule of masses—that is, indicating that there would be no more lay-led services. There had been no consultation with the community or with this woman who had led the community for sixteen years. Something similar had happened to many of the other women; after years of lay leadership, the priests and the bishop were reasserting their authority and in effect largely bypassing lay leaders and ignoring existing structures. She and Sister Lyn Kirkconnell had "entered at an opportune time, because the women were feeling rejected and abandoned by the official church."

A sympathetic priest had helped a group of church and community activists to organize and to establish an organization named AMZOL (Association of Women of the Eastern Zone) legally independent from the church. McDonnell and Kirkconnell had worked together in Bolivia for a number of years and there they had begun to explore the roots of patriarchy and violence against women.

"When we came here, we went to some of the small group meetings and said we would like to accompany them in their consciousness-raising among women. We tagged along with them and their groups for a while. There came a point when they said, 'Okay, now what are you going to do?' And we said, 'Well, in Bolivia we were doing this kind of work; we've been analyzing violence against women, we've been looking at patriarchy and the church, and we're starting to develop a feminist spirituality.' This seemed to be something they had not heard about, and they asked for it."

With the women they developed a course called "Woman, Faith, and Spirituality," then composed of four segments. Weekly meetings typically began with singing, followed by relaxation exercises led by one of the sisters. The sessions were made up of participatory exercises involving drawing, brainstorming, group discussion, and plenary discussion and concluded with a ritual. Although the bible was prominent in the sessions, the course was centered not on the bible but on women's spirituality; the biblical portion entailed as much unlearning as learning.

McDonnell explained, "We are trying to reclaim women's heritage, reclaim our history that has been written out of the bible and has been written out of history books...Everybody quotes the bible; we demystify that, we demythologize the fact that the bible is God's word. It's not God's word; it's men's word: men's word to men in a patriarchal society." Thus, one of the early sessions devoted considerable attention to the Genesis accounts as creation myths, and to setting the bible within the time frame of human history and human history itself within evolutionary and cosmic history. Patriarchy was said to have arisen in approximately 4000 BCE, following several thousand years when goddesses reigned.

During the following session, the figure of Eve was examined, with ample time to explore how Eve has been used, and to expose the patriarchal elements in the Genesis account. The exegesis in the course connected the biblical myth to earlier myths. At one point, in a kind of review, the course considered scientific creation, the (patriarchal) culture of Jewish society, the subsequent uses of the creation myths, and the consequences of the patriarchal myths. The ritual was both a celebration of Eve, "our mother," and a rejection of the uses of the Eve myth through a litany:

"That we are weak,"
    "No, no we don't accept."

"That we are evil,"
    "No, no we don't accept."

"That we are tempters,"

"That we are seducers,"

        "cursed..."

        "quiet..."

        "submissive..."

        "dependent..."

    "No, no we don't accept."

Biblical texts celebrating human equality and the goodness of the human being and especially of women were highlighted. At one point, a drawing of a woman elicited aspects of a new Eve—themselves: "our freedom, our courage, our love, our sensitivity and natural beauty, our intelligence, our self-confidence, our curiosity, our perseverance...mother of all the living." "Let us do this in memory of her," they proclaimed—as all ate apples.

"One of the things that has made the course grow is the intuition that women have of the feminine image of God. We can point out times when goddesses were worshiped or when there were both gods and goddesses." The idea was not to claim that God was either male or female, but rather to make it clear that other images have existed. "That has taken a huge burden off the women because it's very hard to relate to Jesus, this man, as the answer to our salvation. So they begin to question the whole Christian basis of what we're about. It's interesting, because we struggle with how can we help women to take a look at this church."

Among the most powerful group exercises was simply to have the women draw their image of God: what they thought of when praying. They were then asked to list the terms for God found in church prayers or hymnals. Those words were then compared to their drawings. "They never connect: the names for God are the almighty, the powerful, the king, lord, the judge, the whole list. And their pictures are pictures of nature—of animals, of what they say is 'my spirit.'" When their attention was drawn to the disparity between the words and the images they would respond, "There's no problem—these pictures are our image of God, and those words, that's what the church tells us." McDonnell concluded that the rituals of the church and certain traditional Christian symbols did not speak to women, and they were therefore devising new rituals.

"Women are generators of life, and the whole thing of suffering and death and sin and destruction, and that God is other, that God is transcendent, that God is not here present" was alien. "To them God is very much here in their life constantly." The divinity they sensed was more immanent than transcendent. They were not attuned to the "ritual sacrifice" of the mass with its overtones of death and destruction. When women celebrate, "they want to bring flowers and...their own bread, and they want to celebrate with dance and music...We try to use our senses." The woman whom the priest had summarily dismissed from preparing the liturgy said that she been more enriched by this experience of women's spirituality than by anything she had heard in sixteen years of base-community work.[5]

McDonnell painted a rapid but incisive picture of the routine humiliations of women in Sao Paulo: "Even in house building you see women and children carrying the cement blocks, water, and sand and doing the digging. They have to pay men to do the building and bricklaying. Who takes the child to the clinic? The woman. Where are the men? They're not even working—count the bars on the street. The women are sewing something, cooking something to sell, so they can have something to eat.

"To get a job women have to dress in miniskirts, have the right kind of looks, and put up with the foreman molesting them. Women get paid less. They are searched, even strip searched. Women have had to have forced sterilizations to get a job (to guarantee that they won't get pregnant). Brazil is the country with the highest rate of Caesarian sections in the world. Why? Money for doctors.

"Those are the kinds of women's issues that aren't brought into the open. The church doesn't ever speak out against those things. The only thing it takes a public stand on is abortion—something a woman decides about her own body. That's when they take a stand."[6]

The annual Brotherhood Campaign, for example, never dealt with rape. "Rape is a women's issue. Men don't get raped." The theme for the 1990 campaign was to have been "Woman"—for the first time—but in the end it became "Woman and Man." The biblical reflections were on "Miriam and Ruth and Deborah as women who struggled for the people. It was not aimed at exploring women's dignity and their daily struggle."

The impact of AMZOL could not be measured in numbers. Although many women had taken at least segments of the course, what gratified Mc-Donnell most was the quality of about fifteen women who had participated in all levels. "This is our dream, that we are creating women-church. They get together to nourish their faith in the divine; they encourage one another and try to chip away at the patriarchal structures." Their vision was a kind of ecofeminism. "We're hoping to develop a kind of spirituality that will keep women in the struggle to change things."

Although their primary group was AMZOL, McConnell and Kirkconnell were networked into other women's groups and had distributed five hundred copies of the first booklet growing out of the course. They also met periodically with other feminist theologians and pastoral workers and sometimes held joint rituals and retreats.

NANCY CARDOSO PEREIRA, a Methodist pastor and professor at IMET (Methodist Institute for Theological Studies), described a simple research project on the clothing of evangelical women. Even one as insensitive to clothes as I could easily spot evangelical women on the street with their plain colored, long sleeved, loose fitting long dresses and lack of makeup. To Catholics and liberal Protestants they are the embodiment of the rigidity and fixation on rules of conservative evangelical churches.

Pereira simply approached women, usually members of the Assemblies of God, and asked them to explain their clothes. To her surprise, she found that they were not uncomfortable but happy to be recognized as evangelicals and as women standing apart from "the world." The stated reason for such modesty is that a woman's body should not lead another to sin. Although this was undoubtedly a sincere belief, most of them were older and were unlikely to be "temptresses."

Pereira interpreted this behavior as a kind of protest, a way of saying "no." In a society shaped by advertising, where women's images were used to sell consumer items that were out of their reach, the clothing these women wore was a way of negating a world that in any case did not accept them. Most of them had been born in the city but were children of immigrants. They had not been accepted by the city and were living on the outskirts, in the *favela*. Pentecostal churches were sites of resistance to this culture—a counterculture. Whereas fashion gives consumers identity in style, pentecostalism gives identity in negation, in creating a countermodel. It is a way of saying, "I'm different from the women of the world who live in their passions; they want to be more, to compete, to be more beautiful. Not me, I belong to my family, to the spirit. No man is ever going to say anything to me in the street. He is going to say I belong to God." Pereira interpreted this refusal and dissidence as a stance of self-esteem and a basis for how these women viewed their husbands, families, and children. The seemingly negative dress code could be interpreted as an affirmation.

Working with similar women in the Methodist church, she had become aware of how overwhelming their problems are. Many poor women, she said, "have lousy marriages. Most women are not loved or respected, and almost all are single women with children. Their husbands are dead or have left. This [pentecostal] moral discourse shields these women. It gives them a dignity that the overall situation does not give them. They aren't pretty, they can't compete, they don't have money. The television image of women is unattainable."

While working in a Rio *favela,* Pereira once proposed to a group of women that they all go downtown to see a movie. The idea was initially shocking: normally it would never have occurred to them that they could do so. With some encouragement, they warmed up to the idea, chose the film, and decided on the time. That day, they dressed in their best clothes. Whether or not they were pretty, married, single, or abandoned did not matter: their strength as a group gave them the confidence to confront the city. The outing later served as the basis for further discussion. That something as simple as going to a movie theater could be a powerful pedagogical and pastoral action was an indication of the class and gender divisions in the society, divisions that affect churches and pastoral work. Although Pereira was more at home with the relative latitude of her own Methodist tradition, she admired the spirit of resistance in pentecostal women.

She thought that dress served a similar purpose for Catholic sisters as it did for pentecostal women. Even when not in habit, nuns were easily recognizable in the street. The principle was the same: dress provides identity and is a "militant discourse of rebellion... You are refusing to accept the model that patriarchal society gives the woman. In this sense it is rebellious, but there is something ambiguous about it because it's a movement of refusal; it doesn't create a countermodel by standing up to the hegemonic model, but remains in rejection." Both the nun and the pentecostal woman were alike in their purity or chastity. Pentecostal women are organized to serve their family, their church, and God and not to be involved in the things of the "world."

Pereira did not hold out much hope for the Methodist church (which she said was undergoing pentecostalization), and like other women she looked toward ecumenical spaces where women were coming together over their concerns, even starting with their concerns in the local community. Women were active in many areas, with street children, health, and school issues. Out of such activity, they might reflect on the bible and even celebrate liturgies "despite the priest or the pastor."

She insisted on the reality of female-headed households. If women could discover that the *favela* is already organized around them, they might affirm their own value and not depend on men, society, or fashion. Thus, it was fundamental that women discuss their bodies. When they did so, they were also discussing economic issues. To the extent that the Catholic church pays any attention to the woman's body at all, it is as a victimized body. Churches may allow a woman to discuss herself as victim, but not to discuss abortion. "Ah no, because there she's no longer a victim. She wants to be a protagonist." It was very hard to find room to broach such matters in the Catholic church, and only somewhat easier in the Protestant churches.

Work with women was very ecumenical, said Pereira; indeed, many women pastors were also involved with the Catholic ministries, such as those to street children, the homeless, and the *cortiços*. In this effort to find common space for women of faith, the major issue was how to engage our "pentecostal sisters" (*companheiras pentecostais*) who had sometimes participated in land struggles and might participate in matters affecting the family or children (which for them is an absolute value) but avoid anything related to reproductive matters.

VIRTUALLY EVERY WOMAN WITH WHOM I SPOKE singled out Ivone Gebara as the most important Catholic woman theologian; she was the most courageous, the boldest, the one least fettered by the institution. I certainly found that to be true in a number of ways as already noted in her willingness to question the exaggerated view of base communities (Chapter 5).

Gebara said that it was not only in "ecumenical spaces" that women had freedom to speak about their own bodies and other issues, but also in other spaces organized by women. These, she said, were a kind of *ekklesia* (assembly or church). Because such matters could not be discussed in Catholic parishes, she believed that "the hierarchical church and its parish organization is increasingly ceasing to be a space of revelation for women's truth. It may continue to be a space where they go seeking consolation or where they continue to recreate the domesticity that they experience at home, but the churches, with some exceptions, have not been where women of the popular classes—and intellectuals—are growing."

Nevertheless, her own option was not to seek spaces outside the Catholic church, because she was concerned that such groups could be quite marginal and have little effect on decision making. Acknowledging the problems she had experienced within the Catholic church, she said that she wanted to continue to struggle within its "institutional space." She was also wary of certain approaches that might be inappropriate. She was especially suspicious of the tendency of some feminists to romanticize women's "leadership." The fact that women were more active economically, working outside the home, especially in the informal sector (washing clothes, selling sweets) might reflect worsening economic conditions, not any kind of liberation. She questioned songs being composed about a "superwoman" who could earn a living, raise her children, and be a community activist, and asked whether such a woman was not actually a "superslave."

Although liberation theology had been Gebara's "daily bread" for many years after she had returned from her studies in Belgium in 1973, she had begun to see its limitations. The male liberation theologians were mistrustful of women theologians, especially those who said something different. A Chilean theologian had recently told her that Latin American theologians were not interested in examining patriarchy. "I tried to explain to him that patriarchy is not simply an issue between men and women, but that it is a structure affecting how society is organized. It's an ideological structure, an anthropology, a way of taking a stance toward different human groups. He gave me a very distrustful look and said, 'That's an issue for feminists; it's not an issue in Latin America.'" The male liberation theologians were willing to consider race alongside class, but not gender.

Gebara spoke slowly, haltingly, both because she was struggling with the ideas, and because she was expressing deeply felt pain and frustration. Her major concerns were not about church governance but about how God is conceived and understood. She repeatedly said that she no longer thought the "humanist God" was adequate. I understood her to mean that even the most well-intended and up-to-date theologies were hopelessly anthropomorphic.

How do we speak of God in a time of so much violence, and in a world in which the media, and particularly television, are so all-pervasive? On many questions and issues, theologians had to be willing to wait and "to admit that we don't know." It was important to reexamine Christian faith in the light of what is happening to the planet, to seek another cosmology and another anthropology (she admired the ecological theologian, Thomas Berry). She regarded her own mission as "not writing for scholars. I have to write very simple things that the people can understand because things have to change."

Gebara was hoping to explore images of God that no longer took the human male as the model; she was looking to find images of a God who is the energy in all humans, all life, all reality. She now questioned the traditional idea of "the will of God" and its liberationist variant, "God's project." Gebara did not aspire to write a major treatise, however, since most of her writing was in response to specific requests (even a recent book on the Trinity had arisen out of a request to speak on the Trinity and religious life).[7] "I'm not a pure intellectual," she noted, smiling, but "an impure intellectual."

Her painstaking honesty was at the root of her disciplining by the Vatican. When asked by a magazine interviewer whether abortion was a sin, Gebara had answered that the question could not be answered abstractly, and had sought to take into account the real conditions of many poor women. She was speaking from her years of working with poor women, and had been told by the interviewer that her remarks were off the record. Nevertheless, the interview was published with the headlines, "Nun Says Abortion Not a Sin." After some dialogue, representatives of the Brazilian bishops conference were satisfied, but not the archbishop of Recife and Vatican officials. Hence in mid-1995 her community, the Canonesses of St. Augustine, was ordered to have her sent to France where she was to observe two years of silence and study.[8]

The action was a clear demonstration of Barbara de Souza's observation on power: what Gebara had said would pass unnoticed in a Catholic university in the United States (which must observe academic freedom) and indeed in practically any Catholic context in the United States. As a sister in a country where there was no room for any discussion of reproductive issues whatsoever, Ivone Gebara was vulnerable, and church authorities chose to make an example of her. In a deftly written letter accepting the action, Gebara compared herself to a honeybee who had angered the drones by tasting certain flowers too freely.

As the viewpoints presented here indicate, women, including sisters and pastors, were questioning the blind spots of and abuses by male authority figures in the churches, and their roots in patriarchal ideology. The kinds of questions raised here are almost certain to be expressed and examined in society and in the churches in the years to come, despite all efforts to suppress them.

CARACAS

9
Crisis and Polarization

A S I APPROACHED MY FIRST CARACAS INTERVIEW at the Bible Society, Avenida Paez had been blocked off and traffic was being diverted. Crowds were gathered on the sidewalk looking into the closed-off area toward the Pedagógico (teacher training school) as plainclothes police rode by on motorcycles shooting into the building where snipers were firing back. Having telephoned and found that Bible Institute staff people were at their desks, I waited about an hour and then took advantage of a relative lull to make my way down a block.

The standoff continued through most of the afternoon. As far as I could ascertain, no one was killed or seriously wounded. These clashes usually did not merit mention in the press, since they occurred regularly (as I soon observed since I was living a few blocks away). Such an exchange of gunfire in the capital city in a country that had been an orderly democracy since 1958 was an indication that things might not always be as they seem in Caracas.

Like Sao Paulo, the city is elevated (about three thousand feet) and the climate is pleasant. A wall of mountains rising to six or seven thousand feet runs along the north side of the city, thereby blocking any hint of the sea which lies just beyond them. Greater Caracas has almost 4 million people[1] and hence is about a quarter the size of Sao Paulo.

Certain features set Venezuela apart from other Latin American countries. Most obviously, oil wealth has given Venezuela the highest per capita income in Latin America. That very wealth retarded agricultural and industrial development, since Venezuelans could import what they needed. For much of the twentieth century, Venezuelan social critics and politicians have argued that Venezuela should use its oil wealth to build the basis for its own development (with the slogan, "*Sembrar el petroleo*"—"sow the oil") but to relatively little effect. Falling oil prices in the early 1980s plunged the country into a crisis. The most dramatic manifestation of that crisis occurred in February 1989 when spontaneous looting broke out.

As it happened, my time in Caracas coincided with a political show-down. President Carlos Andres Perez had been caught in a financial scandal involving $17.5 million.[2] There was nothing new about politicians enriching themselves—the novelty was that the press, public opinion, the congress, and the judicial system were deposing a sitting president for corruption. Whether his unseating was a step toward dealing with the larger crisis in Venezuelan society or merely a transient spectacle was by no means clear.

When an evangelical preacher made a passing reference to "the crisis," his poor, and perhaps illiterate, audience knew what he meant. During my stay, the Catholic hierarchy and Catholic university held a week-long "Encounter with Civil Society" in which leading intellectuals offered proposals for what should be done in the areas of the economy, education, law enforcement, and the like. These ideas were then discussed and eventually codified into a series of proposals intended to represent the areas of consensus (and disagreement) as a kind of agenda that could help move the country forward. Whatever its effectiveness, the fact that the bishops felt impelled to make the effort attested to the widespread malaise.

That malaise could be revealed at unexpected moments. One evening, shortly before sundown, I happened upon a commotion on a residential side street of the district of El Paraiso, the older middle-class area where I was staying. Dozens of people were standing on the sidewalks near a house where a young man was lying on the grass in a small front yard; his sister or girlfriend was screaming. He had been pulling into the driveway when two youths accosted him, shot him in the leg, and stole his Toyota pickup. I watched as he was carried to a Volkswagen Bug and driven off, presumably to the emergency room of a nearby hospital. Neighbors commented that parked cars had occasionally been stolen, but nothing like this had happened in this relatively safe neighborhood.

A woman approached and introduced herself as a neighbor from one of the nearby high-rises. "I saw them come speeding around the corner and I knew it was stolen." She was also certain of where they were going—into the hills of the nearby neighborhood of La Vega. "It's either them or us that are going to be left" she said.

She did not have to specify whom she meant by "them"—the poor who constituted half of Caracas and lived in makeshift houses on the hillside neighborhoods. This polarization could be sensed in conversations, and was visible in the architecture of the city. As in Sao Paulo, most of the middle class lived in apartment buildings of twenty stories or more, with gates and security guards at the entrances.

Such matters as the immediate political crisis, the longer-term economic decline and political gridlock, and the social polarization and anxiety over security were a backdrop to my own questions on the state of the churches in Caracas. The Catholic church had not produced any figure like Cardinal Arns nor had it experienced any period of resistance to widespread political repression. Most Protestant churches had been in the city for only a generation or so.

Chronic weakness has beset Catholicism in Venezuela. Noting that clergy and religious are 80 percent non-Venezuelan, Wagner Suarez, who directed the theological training center for religious orders, said that the challenge was to establish the indigenous church—it did not yet exist in Venezuela. His fellow Jesuit, the theologian Pedro Trigo, pointed to the historic roots of the institutional weakness of Venezuelan Catholicism. The church was well established in a number of cities in the west and into the Andes as early as the sixteenth century, but three-quarters of what is now Venezuela was neither colonized nor evangelized. Although the Spanish king declared the new world conquered in 1664, those territories remained beyond the control of Spain for another century, although some missionaries carried on work there. The upshot, said Trigo, was that Venezuelan Catholicism has been transmitted largely by the laity.[3]

Simon Bolivar, the "liberator" and most well known leader of Latin American independence, was Venezuelan. The house in which he was born and raised stands on a square in what is now a pedestrian mall in Caracas. Although five priests signed the declaration of independence in 1811, the independence leaders were fiercely anticlerical. Two bishops had to leave the country within the first two months, and in the years from 1810 to 1819 the number of priests, diocesan and religious, in the diocese of Caracas plummeted from 547 to 110.[4]

The hostility of the elite continued throughout the nineteenth century. In other Latin American countries the political tug of war between pro-church conservatives and anti-clerical liberals offered the church some protection, but such was not the case in Venezuela. Thus the Catholic church entered the twentieth century poor and weak, without lands or rental properties, for example. Trigo recalled that the effects were still visible in the 1960s when he and his fellow seminarians had few clothes and little disposable money.

Early in the twentieth century religious congregations began to send personnel from Europe, particularly to open and staff schools. Elite anti-clericalism gradually subsided, partly because of the influence of these religious. A major influx occurred at mid-century. In the 1950s, for example, 262 religious houses were founded, 156 of them for teaching purposes.[5]

The political context of the Catholic church in Venezuela differs notably from that of Brazil and elsewhere.[6] The guerrilla movement that arose in the early 1960s and was suppressed by the middle of the decade had had no contact with the church. Two political parties, Accion Democratica (social democratic) and COPEI (Christian Democrat) have alternated in power since 1958, with AD being the dominant party. These parties are not just political entities; they have extensive influence throughout society, in labor unions and neighborhood organizations, for example. During the past three decades, virtually all political actors have assumed that, whatever the limitations of Venezuelan democracy, revolution is not on the horizon. Moreover, the country is one of the few in Latin America that for close to forty years has not experienced a phase of direct military rule or widespread violation of human rights.

With the exception of the early 1970s, the Venezuelan Catholic church has known little of the turmoil found in other countries. In 1970 Francois Wuytack, a Belgian priest who had been involved in demonstrations in front of the Venezuelan congress building with people from his barrio, was expelled from the country with the public approval of Cardinal Quintero. Shortly afterwards, four Spanish priests who had been working in the country were not allowed to return.

Commentators on the Catholic church looked back to that period as a turning point. A number of priests and sisters from religious congregations chose to move into poor areas of the city and work there, largely ignoring the Venezuelan hierarchy. In some instances, sisters were assigned to "vicariates," areas in which they were officially recognized as doing pastoral work. Their ideal was to share the lot of the poor. Although the bishops initially mistrusted these initiatives, perhaps fearing further conflict, they eventually came to respect the value of such work.

Thus, in the early 1990s, those Venezuelan Catholics whose ideals might be similar to those of progressive Catholics in Brazil had not experienced a heroic phase similar to that of the church under the Brazilian dictatorship; by the same token, they were not as perplexed or disillusioned as those who had entertained high hopes of a different kind of society. Familiarity with events in Cuba, Chile, Colombia, Brazil, and Central America and with the ideas of Latin American social scientists and theologians no doubt had an impact, but any temptations to radical positions were tempered by the obvious reality of an orderly political process and the relative prosperity trickling down from oil revenues.

The history of Protestantism in Venezuela is relatively brief. Although itinerant bible salesmen had passed through in the early nineteenth century, the first Protestant congregations in Caracas were established in the 1870s. For decades missionaries were attracted more to the rural areas, and hence there were practically no Protestant congregations in Caracas until the 1940s and 1950s. Many of the first-generation church leaders were still active in the 1990s.

The sharp and unexpected decline in oil prices in 1982 triggered a crisis in Venezuela that lasted through the 1980s. Shortly after his inauguration as president in February 1989, Carlos Andres Perez turned his back on his party's social democratic tradition and announced a series of austerity measures at the behest of the IMF (International Monetary Fund). Early on the morning of February 27, when passengers found bus drivers charging far more than the officially approved price rise, spontaneous demonstrations began to break out. Buses were stopped, traffic jams formed, and at 2 P.M. a group of people occupied a freeway. As the protest spread spontaneously, shops and businesses closed their doors. By mid-afternoon some trucks had been looted, tires were burning, and crowds had begun to break into stores in a number of neighborhoods. The fancier shopping centers in the eastern part of the city were spared, since most of the looting took place in the market areas closer to the poor neighborhoods.

The first fatality was a student shot by a motorcycle policeman. By evening, morgues were receiving bodies from various parts of the city, and flames and smoke were visible in a number of sites. Looting continued into the following day. The army and the police engaged in gun battles with snipers in public housing buildings. Residents later said that government troops came through their neighborhoods with heavy weapons shooting both to exact revenge and to intimidate the people. A list of 310 victims was compiled from the morgues. Some later estimated that as many as 2,000 had been killed, but no proof was offered.

A newspaper article written shortly afterward was titled "The Day the Hills Came Down." Whether intentionally or not, the author was giving voice to the middle- and upper-class fear that at some apocalyptic moment, hordes of poor people living in their ever unfinished houses within constant sight of the Caracas of freeways, shopping centers, and art galleries might come pouring down to vent their rage.

The 1989 disturbances (which occurred not only in Caracas but on a lesser scale in several other cities) were a watershed. Like the 1992 disturbances in Los Angeles, they initially prompted widespread soul searching but were soon forgotten by many. In the poor neighborhoods at either end of the city, where four-inch bullet holes could be seen on the walls of public housing units, those events were still a living memory in 1993. For other people, the events fueled the "It's-either-them-or-us" sentiments that I observed in reaction to the carjacking.

If more than three hundred people had been shot by police in London or Tokyo, it would have been deemed a shocking tragedy and would have received extensive media coverage. Why were the events of February 27, 1989 virtually ignored in the international press? The victims were poor Venezuelans—many of them looters—and hence "unworthy." Indeed, I saw only one modest monument to them in Caracas. Moreover, in announcing austerity measures President Perez was doing the bidding of the Bush administration and the international financial institutions and hence there was little inclination to undermine him. (By contrast, Washington had already made General Manuel Noriega of Panama into an international villain and thug, even though he had far less blood on his hands than did the Perez government.)

By 1993, economic decline and pervasive corruption indicated that no end to the crisis was in sight.

10
Hope and Reality

Catholic Pastoral Portraits

THE JESUITS CAME TO THE WORKING CLASS NEIGHBORHOOD OF CATIA, which is separated by hills from the historic center of Caracas, in the 1940s. After operating a vocational school for decades they had accepted parochial responsibility for the surrounding area, and their chapel had become a parish church. In the colonial manner, houses formed a solid wall along the sidewalk and the main street bustled with shops.

Father Javier Asate took me toward the part of the parish where the poorer people live in what are appropriately called *bloques* ("blocks"), bare rectangular public housing of about ten stories, often dating from the Perez Jimenez dictatorship of the late 1950s. Architecturally, these buildings looked like poor cousins to high-rise public housing in U.S. cities. One of the young people hanging out in front of a building motioned to Asate, apparently offering to sell drugs, but halted upon seeing the cross around his neck.

Asate was quite convinced that from the standpoint of the people the number-one problem was that of youth violence and criminality. The local high school had frequently been forced to close because of violence. He pointed out bullet holes from the 1989 disturbances. Although snipers may have been firing from the buildings at some point, much of the shooting was sheer vengeance and intimidation by the police and army against the people. More recently, rival gangs shooting at each other from different buildings had also left bullet holes. On the top floor of one of the buildings we said hello to a bathrobed young man who was recovering from a gunshot wound. Asate saw no possibility of ending the violence, but only of "winning back space from the *malandros*." (The word, which is apparently borrowed from Portuguese, has no exact English equivalent and refers to a male criminal who lives with bravado, not necessarily a gang member.)[1]

Plastic bags of garbage thrown out the windows were piled several feet high. Garbage chutes in the buildings had fallen into disrepair. Asate was encouraged by the pledge of the new leftist city administration to re-construct the chutes using local labor.

The Jesuit team used various approaches in the parish. In the area near the church they had had some success organizing traditional religious observances, particularly a nine-day pre-Christmas celebration. That led to biblical groups, one of which had recently formed a consumer cooperative. In this kind of work the Jesuits were drawing on people's ties to the reli-giosity of their rural past and on what was perhaps a more solid working-class and lower-middle-class family stability.

It was clearly more difficult in the high-rises. Asate believed that many of the people's problems (with garbage, water service, lack of recre-ation facilities) stemmed from lack of organization, and he summed up the parish's pastoral approach as "helping people live with more dignity." The Jesuits had organized a youth group in the high-rises and had set up two local communities. They celebrated Sunday mass at an open space near one of them. Even though the Jesuit church was only a ten-minute down-hill walk away, they had held separate Holy Week processions and Easter Vigils, perhaps because of the social gap between the two groups.

THE FOLLOWING SUNDAY I VISITED a nearby parish where the people had prepared a "Mass for life." Father "Diego" (the adopted name of the Bel-gian pastor) began his sermon by speaking of life in scriptural terms: we desire life, and life in abundance, and that freedom which is ultimately identical with life. Unfortunately, many people think that living means having a fancy car and a gun, and some believe that in order to live they must take the lives of others. Citing the day's epistle, the priest noted that the weapons of believers are not of flesh and blood.

In a short address after communion, a representative of an organiza-tion called Women for Life referred in passing to young people being killed for a pair of sneakers. Most of the 250 to 300 people present were women, along with a large youth contingent (including the boy and girl scouts who marched up the aisle at the head of the initial procession). In most of Latin America in recent decades, a "Mass for Life" would have been a response to human rights violations by government forces, not youth gangs. In this case, the violence sounded disturbingly like that in U.S. inner cities.

Later that same day, I left a Franciscan residence and had to walk down a series of cement stairs on a steep hillside in order to reach the bus stop along the road below. When I arrived at the bottom several minutes later, I glanced back up the hill and saw the student with whom I had been talking; he waved. Without saying anything, he had chosen to remain watching while I traversed a potentially dangerous area. This was yet another confirmation that people in barrios are frightened by the breakdown in behavior codes taking place around them.

This social breakdown is relatively new in Latin America. In eight years (1965–73) in the barrios of Panama City that some outsiders regarded as havens for thieves and criminals, I was never mugged or threatened (except for a minor pickpocketing attempt that I warded off). In Guatemala (1976–80), while surrounded by political violence, I never worried about criminal violence even while walking alone in any part of Guatemala City at any time of day or night. In the last fifteen or twenty years, however, common crime and gang activity have become endemic in many Latin American cities and are now increasingly part of the pastoral context.[2]

MATIAS CAMUÑAS HAD COME FROM SPAIN sixteen years earlier and had served in a parish in Petare, the poor area of a half million people at the eastern end of the city, for thirteen years. Camuñas was well known for his human rights work[3] and for occasional writings of a theological nature growing out of his pastoral experience. He was a member of the "Petare Group" which had been formed around 1971-72, when the wounds from the expulsion of Father Wuytack and the four Spanish priests (Chapter 9) were still fresh. Among the original ten priests and sisters were some who had been dismissed from the seminary faculty.

In its early years, the Petare Group reflected the "contestatory" or anti-institutional mood of the times. By the 1990s the "Petare Group" was an informal structure with about eighteen to twenty members, priests, sisters, and lay, living and working in an area that included six parishes and several hundred thousand people. The group continued to meet on the last Wednesday of each month to share, "our utopia, objectives, and demands," said Camuñas. They had recently held a week-long evaluation. For their retreats they invited outstanding figures in the Latin American church, such as Bishop Pedro Casaldáliga from Sao Felix de Araguaia in central Brazil. Maximo Cerezo, the Claretian artist whose prints are on the cover of books from Central America and Brazil, had spent a period in Camuñas's parish house. Cerezo's drawings, combining a formal iconic look with touches of the barrio, now hung on the walls.

In the early years, the emphasis had been on living in the same kind of housing as the people, sharing their conditions and way of life. Group members felt that they were not in the barrio to baptize, organize first communion, or officiate at wakes—and for some years they shunned such ritual activity. The reason, Camuñas explained, was that at that time (before he had arrived) those doing this kind of pastoral work understood the "option for the poor" to mean struggling for justice against an unjust system. They were not very concerned about popular religion in those early days.

Camuñas himself reflected the partial shift that had taken place. Although his church, parish office, and residence were modest—they were tucked behind some apartments and were not visible from the street—it was a parish complex, and Camuñas's daily duties were those of a parish priest.

Camuñas stressed that he and the Petare Group had evolved and learned much over the years. "I tell you that during the thirteen years I've been here these people have helped me to live the gospel and to deepen in a spirit of prayer and contemplation. I find that in all these struggles and fights" (which were incorporated into his contemplation), "these people have helped me to have greater faith in providence." "Have faith, Father, trust," they would tell him when he should be consoling and supporting them (for example, when he accompanied youths and their family members to court cases at the other end of Caracas). The experience of the Petare group has been to return to the Jesus of the gospel from within the people, he said.

On the basis of his experience, Camuñas had come to question even well-intentioned reforms such as regulations requiring people to attend preparation classes before receiving the sacraments. "Who am I to tell someone 'You're not ready for baptism?' Who am I to impose on the people more demands than those that they already bear? Who am I to give an interpretation to the word and to say 'This is what has to be taken to the people'—even turning it into specific kinds of moral behavior?" The gospel is understood much better from within the people, "who have values that you yourself have not experienced, such as sharing, love for life, brotherhood, simplicity of life. These are gospel values and the people have them. It's we who have to be learning from them, little by little."

Like Asate at the opposite end of the city, Camuñas seemed at his wits' end over the violence. Recently he had attended a ceremony at a Fe y Alegria (Catholic) school in the neighborhood. Sixteen or seventeen former students had died during the previous five years; one of a stroke and another of an accident—but all the rest had been murdered. All were under twenty-five, and all were "dead before their time" said Camuñas. Two days previously, four funerals had been held in the parish for young people who had been killed. One of them had gone out to buy snack food for his daughter; one was a thirteen-year-old girl. A layman on the parish staff later told me that four local high schools had been closed by the Ministry of Education for the past month due to parents' concern over violence.

Camuñas spent much of his time with young people who were in trouble. He mentioned a boy named Tato whose mother had just come by. The stepfather beats the mother and the boy had said that when he got older "I'm going to grab a machete and kill my stepfather." The same thing happened over and over: fathers absent, children in the street, involvement with drugs, getting weapons, gangs, death. One of the Fe y Alegría graduates killed had been involved with a horse race gambling operation. The police and military themselves were selling weapons. The plainclothes detectives who were supposed to be combating the *malandros* were themselves *malandros*. For young people with no prospects, drugs were a way out. Others came to the barrio to use drugs or to act as couriers.

Camuñas believed that social breakdown accelerated after the disturbances of February 1989 when heavy weapons and tanks were used against the people, and so "violence was legitimized." Later we stopped at a shrine to those killed. Crosses and a painting of a rural scene with flowing waters expressed a yearning for another life. (It reminded me of the murals depicting "rivers of living waters" as the backdrop in some pentecostal churches.)

"I never imagined any situation in the world where life could be so degraded as what I am experiencing and feeling now," he said. "It's affecting me psychologically down in my soul. I can't stay out of it. I can't just look at it objectively, or make it an 'object' of my pastoral work." It was a kind of "flaw" in his character that he could not hold back, that he had to become involved, and, he said, " it pains me so."

The previous day a tall youth had come by to ask Camuñas to bless a cross for his grandmother. Hearing where the boy lived, Camuñas said he remembered meeting a boy named René there. "I'm René," the youth had replied. Camuñas had not recognized him because the René he had met had been in bed with five bullet wounds. The priest now told him, "I've already prepared the prayer I'm going to say when they kill you," and joked about how big the casket would have to be. He wanted to impress on the young man that if he tried to return to his barrio after healing from his wounds, three or four of his enemies would be after him. "It was just luck that you weren't killed."

Once while he was blessing a shrine in a neighborhood, Camuñas had spotted one young man and told him that he should go away to the city of Maracay to avoid being killed. "No, it's not my time yet," the boy had answered. Ten days later they were praying at his wake.

At this point in our conversation a dark and obviously needy woman from a poor section high up in the hills entered the room. Her partner, a Colombian, mistreated and beat her. He sent her fifteen-year-old daughter and eleven-year-old son out to the streets to earn some money, and cursed them if they did not bring home any. The children had no identification papers and had never been to school. She wanted her oldest son to leave for his own good. When Camuñas asked the woman whether she could work, she responded that she suffered "attacks of nerves." He urged her to consider participating in women's groups that met in her area, and mentioned the names of several women leaders who might be able to help. Camuñas also promised to follow up with her personally.

Theologically Camuñas agreed with the idea that "you can hear cries only where they are uttered"; that is, it is important for the church's representatives to be close to those who are suffering. Even so, he said, it sometimes becomes too overwhelming, and he wondered whether it might not be better to allow someone else to take over his position.

IN PETARE AND SIMILAR AREAS IN CARACAS, people get around not on buses, but on jeeps that ply regular routes from the busy market areas below to various hillside communities. On a Saturday afternoon I caught one of these passenger jeeps and rode for about fifteen minutes with a dozen other people. I got off perhaps a thousand feet higher at a basketball court where scheduled games were being played all day long. There I met up with a tall, curly-haired, handsome young man named Yulman, who was part of the Petare team and who was refereeing. After the game ended, we headed down a trail and up to another hilltop, where I met his mother. Their house was near the area chapel for which they were responsible. (In the rear of the chapel I noticed the statue of a somewhat distinguished man in archaic clothes, but not the typical garb of canonized saints. It was, Yulman explained, Dr. Jose Hernandez, a physician who died in 1905 and is widely revered as a miracle worker in Venezuelan popular culture.)

We then trekked up and down paths to six or eight local areas, each with its own chapel or community center, and met the lay people in charge. Most of the buildings were substantial cement structures, often on two or three levels set with firm foundations into steep hillsides. They were multi-use buildings and were usually called "community houses" (as in Sao Paulo's "Operation Periphery"). One of these centers, for example, had a clinic and a main meeting room used not only for mass but also for classes. The couple in charge of the site lived about two minutes down a steep trail. This particular community met regularly to pray the rosary. One of their activities had been an excursion to Mérida (a colonial and university city nestled in the Andes ten hours away by bus). Without such an initiative, most people in Petare would never see Mérida. These communities were good examples of the kind of "presence" of the church I frequently heard about. Although it was only twenty minutes away by car or jeep, the parish complex on the flat land below seemed distant from these communities.

A Spanish lay volunteer said that she had spent her first two years living "like anyone else," as priests and sisters often say when they undertake this kind of work. She meant that she had not arrived with any particular pastoral duties or assigned role. She spoke of her own work as "family catechesis," although in fact it was almost entirely with women. Most men in Petare were irredeemable in her eyes.

Taken altogether, the Catholic church had a considerable presence in Petare: the small community houses, Fe y Alegria schools, a day care center, and a number of religious living in the area (not all members of the Petare Group). Some activities were linked to the formal structures of the six parishes while others grew directly out of contact between groups of sisters or priests and brothers and their neighborhoods. At the "community houses," sacramental and children's catechesis took place, the dead were waked, the rosary was prayed, and processions and other devotions were organized. Indeed, the emphasis on popular devotions and the fact that they were organized by lay people bore out Camuñas's observations of how the Petare team had changed: initially they had seen popular devotions as an obstacle to their aim of standing alongside the poor in solidarity and struggle, but now such activities were central to the parish.

On a Sunday afternoon, I returned to one of these community centers for the monthly meeting between a group of local leaders and Pedro Trigo, Venezuela's best known theologian. Also along was a sister visiting from Bolivia. Trigo pointed out that the people in the group were not a local community but were leaders, most of them engaged in community projects independent of the church, and that they met once a month as committed Christians to nourish their faith (and his own). In that sense, the meeting was akin to the gathering of Frei Betto in Sao Bernardo (Chapter 4), although the latter gathering had a stronger working-class thrust.

At a recent meeting in Europe, Trigo had found theologians dismissing this kind of work. (One well-known German theologian had said that it was "small scale communitarianism" which had already been attempted and had failed.) Outsiders, and particularly these theologians, were judging matters in Latin America on narrow political criteria: they assumed that work was of value insofar as it contributed to taking power, and hence they could not see the importance of steady, unspectacular work. Latin America was considerably less interesting to these theologians after the Sandinista electoral defeat. Trigo's own reaction was rather the opposite: the Nicaraguan experience had demonstrated that the kind of change required involves far more than taking power. He evidently thought that I needed to have the point emphasized as well.

About twenty people, almost all women, sat in a circle of folding chairs on the concrete slab floor in the middle level of the community center in Barrio Bolivar. The sound of accordion-led Colombian music blared from a stereo in a house across the street. These neighbors deliberately turned it up when they observed a meeting, said Juana, our host.

Trigo had been proceeding through the gospel of Mark for more than a year. Today the text was from Mark 14, where Jesus goes to the garden and prays to his Father. Under Trigo's leadership, the group considered other occasions when Peter, James, and John are with Jesus, and then the occasions when Jesus prays in the gospels. As a good teacher, Trigo led with questions. He was also good at improvising comparisons, and even at dramatizing the voices of different types of characters. The participants read some of the scripture passages. When the Spanish lay volunteer arrived, she tended to dominate the discussion (despite her claim that she was a participant like everyone else).

Whereas Trigo was clearly most fascinated with the mystery of Jesus—his sadness unto death, what it means that he prays to the Father—the participants tended to draw rather conventional moral lessons. After Trigo asked for observations on what the passage meant for one's life, a woman said, "I see that when we are unwilling to do something, it's often due to pride," and then continued to speak about pride with little connection to the text. Others spoke of the need to love one another, to work together, and so forth.

That this was spiritually nourishing to Trigo and meaningful for the participants, I had no doubt. It was also salutary to be reminded that the expectations of outsiders might prevent them from appreciating the importance of such apparently humble activities.

This type of dialogue was central to Trigo's understanding of liberation theology. For him, liberation theology was just beginning—what had gone before was pre-history. True liberation theology must arise out of the "everyday," not out of the Enlightenment framework that characterized much of written theology, including the early work of Gustavo Gutierrez. Trigo viewed *We Drink from Our Own Wells*[4] as the "first stammerings" of what he understood to be an emerging theology. The difference lay not in the content but in the process or method. He was rather unfazed by the demise of existing socialism. The collapse of the Berlin Wall meant "nothing, absolutely nothing" for his theology and pastoral work. The liberation of the people is essential to being Christian, but it must be patiently built up "from the everyday." He reminded me of what he had said before: to focus on political change is like starting to build a house with the roof. We still need at least eighty years, he said.

He was implicitly replying to those who said or assumed that the moment of liberation theology and its associated pastoral work had come and gone. From within Venezuela it had always been clear that no "complete overthrow" of the political and economic system was going to take place, despite the dreams of some on the left. In international meetings he had expressed his reservations about what he regarded as the illusions of some well-known theologians about the possibilities for change. Similarly, a Jesuit who had arrived in Venezuela eager to apply what he had learned in Central America and in Central Brazil with Bishop Pedro Casaldaliga had to unlearn some things in order to work in Venezuela. For years Trigo and others had resolutely sought to avoid being infected with insufficiently grounded enthusiasm from elsewhere in Latin America. Recent developments had only confirmed his position.

Camuñas was somewhat less sanguine than Trigo about the future. Our "hope is stronger than the reality," he said, and "our utopia is stronger than our accomplishments . . . Some of us are thinking it's time to pause and think things through." Nonetheless, he said that their response must be to stick it out.

JOEL CASTRO, A FRANCISCAN IN HIS THIRTIES, was pastor of a parish, headed the archdiocesan human rights commission, and worked in the formation of aspirant Franciscans. The parish was located in the "23 de Enero" district, which was made up largely of public housing units to the west of downtown Caracas, not far from the parish of the Jesuits in Catia and the parish where I had attended the "Mass for Life."

The area had a reputation for left-wing activism dating back to the Perez Jimenez dictatorship (1948–58), and the 1960s. Some veterans of earlier struggles still maintained their loyalty to leftist ideals and informally encouraged and helped the people to organize and defend their rights. Drugs and criminal violence were also a reality. The daily papers frequently reported killings and other violence in 23 de Enero. Castro said that after returning from their jobs, people were loath to venture out, and hence it was difficult to schedule evening activities. Partly as a result of the area's history of militancy and violence, the police regarded it with suspicion. On one occasion, the police had entered the building in an adjacent apartment building and thrown every family's TV out the window in vengeance or frustration over the killing of a policeman that day.

The three Franciscans who first arrived in the parish were attracted by the idea of working in a compact area where they could make a difference. Indeed, the whole parish was contained in a half dozen twelve- or fourteen-story public housing *bloques,* and was only a few minutes' walk from one end to the other. Castro said that they had started with catechesis for the sacraments, base communities, and various organizations, including cooperatives, but all such activities had fallen apart. Rather than maintaining permanent ongoing communities in each apartment building, the team had opted to work with what he called "living presences," two or three people in each building acting as contact points for the parish.

When I asked how he would summarize their current pastoral approach, he said, "The basic thing is to approach the family. That's the foundation, and that's what's most missing in this world of violence." He mentioned children who spent hours in the street and observed violence between their parents. Change would come through the family, not through individuals, he insisted. Part of the pastoral approach was family catechesis, led by adults. Meetings were held in the apartment buildings, with parents who in turn were expected to discuss the themes with their children, who also attended catechism on Saturdays. (In fact, we were meeting on a Saturday morning in a small room off to the side of a larger hall that echoed with children's voices.) They were using materials adapted primarily from Peru, as well as from Chile and Honduras. Castro admitted that, in practice, "family" often meant the women of the family.

Community problems also included a general decline in services, such as the water supply. Castro did not see a need for the parish as such to be directly involved in organizing, particularly given the area's long history of activism. If the parish team were to become too involved, people would let them take the initiatives. Hence, he and other members of the parish were taking part in community activities, "like anyone else." The aim was to "reach the community through the family." Speaking more theologically, he said, "Out of our faith what we are seeking is to feel a presence of the living God in the midst of the people. I wouldn't say that we are liberating or anything of that sort." The parish facilities were one site where people could come together. Several times he emphasized the parish team's desire to be "like everybody else"; they were seeking to be "incarnated."

The language is similar to that of "insertion" heard among religious communities, and indeed Castro easily elided from a pastoral vision for the people in the area to a vision of the four or five Franciscans on the parish team, including the provincial. They met once a week as Franciscans to examine their "community project of life," and in order to "decipher the signs of the times." That morning, as they reflected on the gospel text for the day (Jesus' words that his disciples are not "of this world"), they considered the seemingly imminent resignation of President Carlos Andres Perez and determined that their response should be to give people encouragement and stand in solidarity with them in such a moment of national crisis.

SISTER LEONOR WAS A FIXTURE IN ANTÍMANO, where she had been living and working for twenty years (after first spending almost a decade teaching middle-class students in a Catholic school). The years had taken their toll, and she could not move about easily. When I asked her to summarize her group's pastoral approach, she replied, "The idea is to be a presence of the church, but to do it in a very simple way, with no structure and nothing complicated." Their work was one of the dozen vicariates established in poor barrios in the archdiocese. The vicariates had pastoral responsibility in an area but were not formally parishes. The sisters had little relationship with the parish to which they formally belonged; for example, Sunday mass was said by Jesuits from the nearby Catholic university. Much of her work could be described as *promoción* (lit. "promotion"), that is, helping people acquire skills and confidence through participation in local development projects.

The accent had been on local-level specific projects. Initially, the sisters had responded to many requests for literacy training. More recently they had organized training classes in sewing, dressmaking, handicrafts, and so forth. Later I visited the ceramics studio where women made household items and handcrafted goods, some of which were sold in Europe. For most of the women these activities supplemented family income, and did not constitute full-time work.

Two young men working on the vicariate team described some of their projects as "popular economics" aimed at helping people set up enterprises, most concretely in four bakeries. What made them different from small businesses started by individuals was that they were in partnerships and provided services to the community (in this case locally prepared fresh bread). The program also provided technical and business training. The same principle could be applied to other types of endeavors. For example, someone who knew how to fix household appliances could share that knowledge to set up a repair shop, thus relieving neighbors of the necessity and expense of traveling to the business district in Antímano to have things repaired. The idea was not that one person should make money off the labor of others—as a shopkeeper would from low-paid employees—but for people to be partners with others. Twenty-five percent of the profits from such enterprises were to be used in the community. For example, one of the bakeries was using some of its profits to provide day care for the children of the workers.

In practice most of the team's work was with women. One difficulty was that women who became involved in community activities were sometimes beaten by their partners. Team members said that the process of winning over the men was slow, but that some progress had been made. Just by coming together, many women had realized that their individual problems were much the same as those of other women. They were beginning to understand that they were active and responsible agents. "Many women have changed and many spouses have changed." When I noted that only two women panelists had been scheduled for the week-long conference on national issues to be held at the Catholic university, Sister Leonor gently observed, "Our holy, Roman, Catholic church is not immune to machismo. Priests are as inclined to machismo as any man out there."

Like other poor areas of Caracas, Antímano was experiencing an economic crisis and rising violence. One sign of declining living standards was the fact that two of the three butcher shops along the main street had closed. It used to be feasible for people with even poor paying jobs to acquire land, save money (perhaps with their Christmas bonus), and start building a house. That was now impossible: statistical data showed that pay in real terms had fallen to what it had been almost thirty years earlier. Based on their house visits, the young men on the team confirmed that living standards were indeed declining.

Gang violence was a reality; Antímano had the second highest murder rate in the city. Gangs were involved in drug dealing and auto theft and had automatic weapons. As a by-product of coup attempts in 1992, even more weapons had reached the barrio through members of the military who stole the weapons for resale. The various names of the gangs were well known. In fact, some gang members lived across the street, although Leonor said that she and they greeted one another as neighbors and made small talk. Violence "is a problem for the people...and it leads us to despair; we have no idea what to do."

THE CATHOLIC CHARISMATIC RENEWAL came to Venezuela—as it did to other Latin American countries—from the United States in the early 1970s. Although one of the downtown parishes was said to be its focal point, I had been told that there was a Claretian parish organized around the charismatic movement. So, I took buses to the parish of San Miguel Arcangel located in a part of town named El Cementerio after the cemetery nearby. Eighty percent of the people lived in self-built homes in the hills, said Father Angel, and the area was regarded as "dangerous, violent, and impoverished." Many of the people worked in the informal sector, and the street outside was lined with vendors.

Sixty percent of those active in the parish were involved in the Charismatic Renewal. Other parish groups included the Cursillo, the Legion of Mary, Alcoholics Anonymous, and Friends of Christ, a youth group. Parishioners who not only participated in prayer sessions but were also committed to some further action in the community were called "servants." After taking part in two or three basic retreats, people were invited to participate in one of four ministries: that of the word (teaching), healing (visiting and praying for the sick), order (maintaining the physical plant, preparing meals, cleaning), and music (for liturgy). Each ministry met once a week to share not only their activities but also their lives. Six of the seven base communities in the parish were made up of charismatics; they read the bible, discussed it, prayed, and dealt with problems, both their own and those of their communities. It was in this sense that the parish was built around the Charismatic Renewal.

"The family isn't evangelized in Venezuela," said Father Angel. Eighty-five percent of the people were living in free unions. Over the years he had sought to work with couples, sometimes sanctifying longstanding common-law unions by marriage in the church. He had organized fifteen matrimonial retreats in a retreat house run by his congregation.

Unlike many Catholic charismatics, Father Angel did not absolutize the movement to the point of regarding non-charismatics as second-class Catholics or worse. Far from being triumphalistic about the movement, he believed that people were becoming disenchanted, and that numbers were declining—by at least 20 percent in the last two years, he thought. The movement had grown enormously for five or six years, but perseverance was very difficult.

Without any prompting, he spoke respectfully of those in Petare and other poor neighborhoods because their liberation theology was action rather than talk. He echoed the idea that I had encountered elsewhere that it had been the religious communities living prophetically in poor neighborhoods who had persuaded the hierarchy to move away from its pro-government stance; it was they who had prompted the bishops to issue some forthright pastoral letters, which then found support among the people who recognized that the bishops were speaking the truth. The religious "have incarnated liberation theology for the people and in the people... for years. And now the bishops are admitting that the religious were right. I also think liberation theology has gradually calmed down." He thus saw a gradual convergence between what had once been polarized sides.

I returned to observe the weekly evening Assembly as an example of a central activity of a charismatic parish. Although Father Angel had said that normal attendance was 140-160 people, I counted 55 or 60, no more than 10 of them men. Some were young, particularly the musicians. The leader was a young man, possibly a seminarian. The style was relatively low-key with periods of silence and meditational prayer. A woman prayed, "Thank you Holy Spirit for dwelling within us." She sang and spoke in tongues. Then she moved into something like a chant tonality. Another voice joined hers and they raised the tone by thirds, with half-tone embellishments. The dimly lit parish church contributed to a spirit of contemplation. This group, however, represented one-tenth of 1 percent of the 60,000 people said to make up the parish.

On the Saturday before Pentecost, the Charismatic Renewal was holding its annual prayer meeting at the Velodromo Teo Capriles, a racetrack. Having frequently heard of the ability of charismatics to fill large soccer stadiums in Brazil, I went to the racetrack hoping to be able to observe something of the mass appeal of the Charismatic Renewal and its spiritual intensity. Arriving at about 3 P.M. I was told that the event had been canceled in the morning for lack of sufficient attendance.

11
Preaching to the Tribe of Caracas

IN CHOOSING CARACAS I hoped to be able to observe a city at the "take-off" stage of evangelical growth. I knew that the numbers of evangelicals were low; only 1 percent of the city was evangelical (the figure for all of Venezuela was 4 percent). More than one article in the church-growth literature, however, suggested that church leaders had large ambitions. The organizers of "Plan 15,000," launched in the late 1980s, had hoped to bring "15,000 new Christians" into the churches by April 1990. The planning group had aspired to make the city 10 percent evangelical by the year 2000.[1]

It was therefore a surprise to find that, despite repeated organized attempts to stimulate church growth (some described in this chapter), evangelical leaders and church growth specialists were not claiming that a take-off phase had begun. "In my missiology classes," said Brad Smith, an American seminary professor, "I joke that the Caracas tribe is the tribe least reached by the gospel in all Venezuela. The percentage of Christians among the Yanomami and other groups in the Amazon region is often higher than it is in Caracas" ("Christian" evidently being synonymous with evangelical).

It was also somewhat harder to get an overview of the evangelical churches than it had been in Sao Paulo, where the landscape was dominated by a half dozen large pentecostal churches as well as several of the historic churches. In Caracas, the most well known evangelical phenomenon was the independent Las Acacias pentecostal church, which was widely known in Latin American evangelical circles. Otherwise, the evangelical presence seemed somewhat more dispersed and more difficult to characterize.

Taking Venezuela as a whole, about half of the estimated 325,000 Protestants could be found in six churches: Assemblies of God, Light of the World, OVICE (Venezuelan Organization of Evangelical Christian Churches), Peniel, the National Baptist Convention, and the Presbyterian church.[2] The first two churches are pentecostal, and the second two are of the free church tradition. Aside from the Baptists and Presbyterians, the historic churches have had relatively little presence.

Within Caracas itself, however, the impression was one of greater dispersal. Aside from the two main branches of the Assemblies of God (possibly 40 churches), the Baptists (9 churches), and the Light of the World (8 churches), most of the 231 churches in the city were independent, or were linked to two or three other independent churches.[3]

Evangelical churches had been slow to reach Caracas. Early missionaries went primarily to rural areas and small towns farther west, where several denominations had arrived in the early decades of the century. One writer notes that the only Protestant church established in Caracas before 1940 was the First Presbyterian church. In the 1940s, three churches were founded, one of them Baptist. Samuel Olson, the pastor of the Las Acacias church, noted that as a child he played marbles with virtually all of those who would later become evangelical leaders. Church expansion in Caracas began in the 1960s (23 churches) and continued through the 1970s (52 churches). A survey made in 1992 found that the 231 churches in Caracas had thirty-one thousand members, estimated to be a little more than 1 percent of the three million people in the area surveyed.[4]

As low as the 1 percent figure is, it should be kept in mind that Catholic practice is low. In his dissertation Brian Froehle estimated that 6 percent of people in Caracas attend mass on any given Sunday and that the percentage is 2 or 3 percent in poorer areas. Since a high percentage of evangelicals attend worship—often more than once a week—the numbers of active evangelicals may be at least comparable to that of active Catholics. Indeed, the assumption of Froehle's work is that a situation of competition exists.[5]

This chapter will provide windows into a few examples of evangelical churches (most notably the Las Acacias church) as well as organized efforts to promote church growth.

WHEN SOME OF THE PROTESTANT LEADERS I interviewed used the term "radical pentecostals," they were reflecting their own distaste for religious expression that they regarded as extreme or fanatic (they were either non-pentecostal or relatively open pentecostals) but at the same time they recognized that these were fellow members of the Protestant fold. The Emmanuel church near the central bus area was an example of what they had in mind. Like the "God is Love" churches I had seen in Brazil, men and women occupied separate sides of the church and all were obviously poor. As I entered, an older woman with a strong metallic voice was leading hymns with a guitar and percussion background. A man gave a testimony about his visits to hospitals. Another man warned that the Legion of Mary was brainwashing people in an area near Caracas.

A thin, energetic man whose lightweight orange suit made him look like a salsa musician gave the sermon. He began by referring to "the crisis" which perhaps meant the slow-motion downfall of President Carlos Andres Perez, or corruption scandals, or economic stagnation, or rampant crime— or all of them. The "crisis" was due not to politicians but to religion: the activities of Mormons, Jehovah's Witnesses, and other unnamed groups and the practice of idolatry (presumably meaning various Catholic practices or Afro-Caribbean *santeria,* also widely practiced).

Shifting topics, he said that science and religion are not opposed, as some people think, since science shows how wonderful God is. Scientists have been discovering that earthquakes are occurring more and more frequently (he gave figures from the twelfth, eighteenth, and twentieth centuries) and are now predicting a major earthquake. From the scriptures, however, we already know that creation is in birth pangs (Romans) and that the earth will tremble, the nations will tremble, and the people will tremble, when God sends his Anointed.

Such conviction about the travails of the last day are part of the stereotype of Protestants held by Catholics and secularists in Latin America. What I heard in the Emmanuel church made me realize that I had encountered relatively little such vivid apocalyptic preaching in Sao Paulo and Caracas. About two weeks later, however, I went to the Petare metro station for the last night of an evangelistic campaign. As the connection point for the bus and jeep routes that take people to their communities in the hills, the area around this station was a strategic site. About three hundred people, largely evangelicals, had gathered around a platform illuminated with floodlights. A few passers-by stopped to observe, but most were not intrigued by what was no doubt a familiar sight. The backdrop to the platform that held the preacher and a small band was a picture of Calvary and three crosses with the words, "The Miracle You Are Seeking."

"How many believe Christ is coming?" asked the preacher. Hands went up with cries of "Alleluia!" Jesus, he said, was "the most controversial figure in history, one who divided human history in half." Jesus' power is evident not only in the gospel accounts, of which the preacher gave several examples, but continues to this day. To illustrate, he told the story of a pastor who, as a hurricane moved toward Puerto Rico, had a vision. He and his congregation, rather than going to shelters as they had been warned to do, went toward the seashore to confront the storm head-on with prayer. Just before hitting the island, the storm split and the people were spared. "That was because our God is not dead but living."

That Christ is coming, he said, can be proven from both the Old Testament prophecies fulfilled in Christ and the New Testament prophecies about the last day which are now being fulfilled (in the return of the Jews to Israel, for example). He then pointed to the signs of moral degradation prophesied in the New Testament, especially homosexual marriages in various countries and the general turmoil in the world. In a vision, a pastor had seen a beautiful and well-dressed woman, whose name turned out to be Venezuela; in a later vision he saw the same woman beaten and disfigured.

When the stage went dark for several minutes due to an electrical equipment problem, the preacher continued unfazed. He said that we know what will happen when Jesus comes: one day your evangelical colleagues at work will not show up; one day a mother who has evangelical children will find them not there. The harvest of those who stepped forward to accept Christ as their savior looked modest to me, a dozen people perhaps.

The event left me troubled. How typical was this preacher's understanding of Christian faith? To what extent was such literalism a part of the everyday world view of his hearers? At the same time, I could not but reflect on pre-Vatican II Roman Catholicism. The notion that only those who die "in the state of grace" go to heaven might be less picturesque than "the rapture," but it still divided humankind into sinners and saved (primarily well-behaved churchgoers). Even though Tridentine theology allowed for a "baptism of desire" on the part of sincere unbaptized people and insisted that individuals would be judged in accordance with their (rightly formed) conscience, the Roman Catholicism I knew as a child was a type of fundamentalism (more papal than scriptural). The great strength of such literal belief is that its adherents are not hindered by doubts or qualifications, and the obvious urgency of the times impels them to share their faith. The theological liberals with whom I feel more spiritual and theological kinship are not preaching in metro stations.

AS IS THE CASE IN VIRTUALLY EVERY LATIN AMERICAN COUNTRY, the Assemblies of God is the largest single evangelical church in Venezuela. Arriving in the country in 1947, the denomination had grown to about 60,000 members and 400 churches. However, its presence in Caracas was modest. A smaller group calling itself the National Assemblies of God exists (discussed toward the end of this chapter), and many of the independent churches can be traced directly to the Assemblies.

At the Assemblies of God headquarters in an older part of downtown Caracas, I interviewed Heliodoro Mora, the newly named superintendent, who had pastored one of the main churches in the city for many years. In his office, surrounded by ministers coming and going and by a continual flow of members on benches waiting to see him, Mora looked like a scaled down version of Jose Wellington whom I had seen in Sao Paulo; both seemed "episcopal," although the Assemblies do not use that terminology.

That sense of an established church was confirmed at a service I attended at a church in Gato Negro on a Sunday which happened to be Mother's Day. A flowered plaque stood behind the pulpit and the church was quite full of people dressed up for the occasion. The woman giving testimony, perhaps the pastor's wife, said that many of the mothers present would not have the satisfaction of seeing their children in church that day, and she made an emotional appeal for prayers on their behalf. In our conversation, Mora had stressed that the doctrine of the Assemblies is common to that of evangelicals, and that the church does not give detailed regulations on dress and customs. He said, for example, that television is permitted but that members are discouraged from attending movies.

ALTHOUGH PENTECOSTAL CHURCHES were generally growing faster, some non-pentecostal churches were also experiencing success. A well-known example was the Dios Admirable (Wonderful or Marvelous God) church, which for eighteen years had been meeting in a theater in a shopping center in Chacaito, whose metro stop made it accessible and relatively central to all portions of the city. The church traced its origins to worship services held in the apartments of American missionaries in the 1960s. When I entered on one Sunday morning, most of the seats were filled. The site felt more like an auditorium than a church. The minister, Francisco Liévano, was sitting on a light blue and gold sofa positioned against a red background. One of the hymns was a translation of "When the roll is passed up yonder" (*Cuando allá se pase lista*), and the general style was that of a non-liberal church in the U.S. heartland.

To my eyes, the congregation looked quite middle class, although perhaps some poorer people had dressed up to attend. On this particular morning the church was taking steps to build its own church after years of meeting in the theater. Five architects from the congregation (two of them women) as well as a woman lawyer were presented to the congregation as those who would be working on the matter. The elders shook their hands in what I took to be a formal launching of the project. (Many evangelical leaders regarded land scarcity and prohibitively high prices in Caracas as a major obstacle to church expansion.)

The prayer of intercession might have been heard at a moderately progressive Catholic church: the petitions mentioned the corruption resulting from free-flowing money and the poverty of many Venezuelans despite the country's wealth. At this political moment (as congress and public opinion were pressuring Perez to resign) invocations implored God to control the situation so that there would be no looting or violence.

The church offices were located about a half mile away in what was once a private house, and included a sizable chapel. Francisco Liévano embodied in his person much of the history of Venezuelan Protestantism. He had been baptized during adolescence after his parents were converted. He studied for four years at a bible institute in San Cristobal, near the Colombian border, and first served in that same area. Then he worked in evangelical publishing and in seminaries, much of the time as a rector. He had spent his life working in the conservative, but non-pentecostal, free church tradition. His congregation was not exceptionally large. At its peak it had reached 285 full members, but then it had declined to 85 before Liévano became pastor. After two years under his leadership, the church had rebounded to about 235 members.

Liévano was most proud of a program that he had devised called Basic Discipleship Groups, which he presented as a response to the challenge of cities. Rather than expecting people to come to church, the church must go to where the people are: small communities should be formed where people live and work. Members of such a group should have an affinity with one another based on residence, occupation, age, or profession. The core should be made up of those "born again," but the aim was to draw others also. Such cell groups are relatively common among various church traditions. Liévano had packaged the idea rather tightly and insisted on certain rules: punctuality, limiting the meeting to an hour, and following a set schedule. He had prepared detailed questionnaires to be used as the basis for discussion on scriptural themes. Each group had an elder prepared to lead who was generally more highly educated than the other members. Twenty-seven such groups were functioning, primarily in Caracas but also in some other areas. They met not only in homes but in the teacher training school, the university, and in private companies. The groups were normally supposed to be made up of from seven to twelve persons, but in some instances the numbers were much larger.[6]

Although as described these discipleship groups might resemble Catholic base communities, the discussion outlines were entirely devoted to the scriptural texts rather than to the interplay between faith and lived experience that was crucial to the base-community methodology.

THE EBENEZER BAPTIST CHURCH is located in a busy market area near the Plaza Sucre, four metro stops west from the center of the city. Two young women began the 10:00 A.M. Sunday service with a hymn about Jehovah sinking chariots and other symbols of Old Testament victories; the singing continued for about a half hour. People swayed to and fro and waved their arms to a slower hymn that spoke of a "fountain within me like a river of living water." Pastor Hector Navarro eventually appeared and led spontaneous prayers. At one point he appealed to people to peer into their consciences and discern what God wanted them to do. At another point, those bearing heavy spiritual burdens were urged to come forward and were prayed over.

What was "Baptist" about the worship service? I asked Navarro a day or so later, since to me it looked indistinguishable from that of any pentecostal church. He responded that Baptist worship had no fixed pattern and that it could vary from charismatic to non-charismatic. A spiritual awakening was taking place in the church, he said.

The Ebenezer church's approach to evangelism was person-to-person. One of the congregation's tools was a series of cassette books on family issues. The congregation sold these cassette books both because of their content and because selling them was a way of establishing contact and paving the way for future contacts. Navarro said that the church sought to integrate family, health, and community service. He believed that it should serve people's needs, even when doing so did not bring in more members directly, in contrast with some churches that are more narrowly focused on proselytizing. Jesus cured the ten lepers, he noted, although only one returned to give thanks. Violence and murder were a real concern, but the only answer was conversion: people did not fear God and families were inadequate.

Ebenezer was clearly an example of what observers have called the "pentecostalization" extending into the historic churches in Latin America, that is, the adaptation of at least some of the practices of pentecostal churches. These practices include moving from reformation hymnals and classical instruments (organ, piano) to a much wider ranger of musical styles and instruments (guitars, drums, and percussion); sessions centered on prayer, praise, and testimony, as opposed to the pulpit-and-pastor-based focus on preaching the word; and practices like healing and speaking in tongues.

One indication of the extent of the movement is the fact that in the early 1980s the First Presbyterian Church in Caracas, which had been the first Protestant church founded in Caracas (1900), broke away from the main body and became pentecostal. (One of the reasons for the break was a belief that the Presbyterian church had accepted liberation theology.) A small presbytery of like-minded churches had been formed.

ALONG THE LOW EVANGELICAL SKYLINE OF CARACAS, one tower is visible from afar—the Las Acacias Evangelical church. In Brazil I had encountered a Baptist pastor eager to visit Las Acacias, and it is mentioned frequently in writings about Venezuelan Protestantism.

Shortly after arriving in Caracas, I jostled with evening bus commuters as I headed toward a part of the city that was still unfamiliar to me. A nearby public housing complex and the dim street lamps suggested that the location was lower middle class.

The church building itself was a former movie theater. The pews were comfortable but firm and upholstered with a blue carpet-like material. A man opened the service ("Glory to God!") by establishing an atmosphere of calm: "Here we are in God's presence. Let's relax and thank God for whatever good has happened today, and thank him for getting us through whatever has happened."

Contrary to almost all the pentecostal worship that I had witnessed where the intensity of prayer seemed to be measured by decibel level, at Las Acacias there were periods of silence, and the climate was one of recollection, with some gentle hymns and prayers during the first twenty or thirty minutes: "Our God is not an angry or harsh God, but a loving God," was the continual message. The leader was darker than most Venezuelans, and that fact was especially noticeable in a church regarded as middle-class in its style and perhaps in its demographics. At a particular point he invited the congregation to read scripture. He read most of the text (1 Cor. 15), pausing to make only a few remarks—the accent was on thanking God for victory: resurrection.

At one point the leader found himself forced to lead singing unaccompanied. He moved from a fast-tempo tropical rhythm to some slow songs ("I'm not going to give myself to anyone but Jesus" and, with similar lyrics, "...not going to adore..." etc.). A pianist arrived, found the key, and began to accompany and embellish. A younger man then arrived and preached on a text from John: "If you love me, keep my commandments." These commandments he found in other scriptural texts: "pray always," "read the scriptures," "be perfect as your heavenly Father is perfect."

Eventually the congregation grew to about 150 people, most of whom to my eyes seemed to fit some sort of broad middle-class category. Samuel Olson, the Venezuelan-American pastor associated with the church's distinctive style and success, had been unable to attend. What struck me were the signs of difference between this congregation and much of what I had observed in pentecostal churches: no discernible dress code, no accent on exorcism or healing. I was tempted to call this "lite" pentecostalism, but the stress was plainly on a positive sense of God's presence.

Olson later insisted to me that the pentecostal world was originally not as rigid as many of the churches in Venezuela and elsewhere in Latin America had turned out to be. (I was again reminded of Aimee Semple McPherson, the founder of the Foursquare Gospel Church.) Much depends on the background of a particular missionary or set of missionaries. The Plymouth Brethren, a church strong in some parts of the country, had been influential in setting a tone of legalism and separatism in Venezuela.

On a trip to the United States, Olson's parents, who were Assemblies of God missionaries, observed that other pentecostals were leaving rigid customs behind. "So when we came back in 1954, my parents decided to establish this congregation without any type of code. The basic idea or sense was that we needed to obey the Holy Spirit and the word, and that we would have to learn how to lead our own lives in terms of a sanctified life. That varied from person to person, but it no longer meant that the church had a code, and so this church has never taught that type of mind set." He admitted, however, that something like "unverbalized rules" might exist.

"Here everyone does what they want," explained Ursula Hahn, the general church administrator. The church "is for sinners, not for saints. We have to provide an opening for people to come. They have to know the gospel. Once they know it, we help them escape from their problems and live as well as possible." She distinguished between matters of custom and serious matters, "like adultery or embezzlement," in response to which the church might send an elder to talk to the person. If such people refused to accept their fault and change their behavior, they would eventually be informed that they could no longer be in communion with the church. This attitude toward discipline sets Las Acacias apart from other churches. "Oh yes, they call us heretics," she said. Recently, Olson had officiated at a mixed marriage with a Catholic priest. That would be a "scandal" to other churches.

At the 11 A.M. service on a Sunday morning the auditorium was nearly full. The initial portion of the worship occupied the first hour. Hahn had explained that this period, led by an "adoration team," is very important. About eight ministers, including Olson, stood together in a row. Music was provided by piano, keyboard, guitars, and a mandolin. I estimated those attending at over a thousand, 60-65 percent of whom were women, and many of whom were younger people. One song had an Exodus motif, "The Lord did not bring us here only to turn back." The leaders segued from readings to songs (for example, from Psalm 22 to a hymn about green pastures). During a song with the words "Dance, Dance," some young people danced in a circle, while others swayed in their places. Some songs were the kinds of Israeli melodies I had heard in Guatemalan churches, while others had a bit of tropical syncopation—but nothing resembling rock.

After an hour of standing in such worship, we were told to sit down —easily, said Olson, so as not to break the spirit. At one point we sat in silence for about three minutes. After some announcements, "Brother" Pablo Rosales came forward to offer a testimony: he had persuaded the army high command to allow an evangelical Puerto Rican salsa band to play for a large group of troops and give their testimony for Christ. Rosales, it turned out, was a general, and belonged to the Evangelical Military Confederation. Having learned that Bobby Cruz and his group were coming to Venezuela, he had requested and received permission to have them play for the troops. Permission was granted on the condition that there be "no political or social proselytizing."

That restriction was clearly an obstacle to what Rosales and Cruz intended, but they decided to go ahead with the concert and leave the result in God's hands. Rosales said that five thousand attended. Some of the evangelical troops left as soon as they heard "worldly" music. Rosales wanted to tell them that something worthwhile was coming, but could not because of his orders. Eventually Bobby Cruz gave testimony to his own conversion and called on those who wanted to be prayed over to step forward. According to Rosales, all had done so.

This story prompted applause and Olson thanked God and spoke of the armed forces as defending the country. There was no hint of anything problematic about the army—which, it should be recalled, along with the police killed hundreds of people in Caracas in 1989.[7]

After the collection, a couple from the Iglesia las Catacumbas (Catacombs Church) in Puerto Rico, now making their third visit to Las Acacias, related how a group of evangelicals had become concerned about immorality on a radio station; the man mentioned "pornography," referring, I presumed, to graphic song lyrics. A group of about five or six evangelicals began to hold a vigil outside the station located in what sounded like a seedy part of town. They prayed and called down God's judgment. Within a month the station was out of business; it was then bought by a multimillionaire group of evangelicals in the United States. Now, he said, when evangelicals undertake action, other stations pay attention and correct their ways.

At this point in the service another minister called for God's blessing, but his prayer evolved into a kind of "exorcism" as he prayed that God rid Caracas and Venezuela of corruption, abortion, pornography, and other evils, and the congregation said "Out, out!" Olson himself set the mood for the final part of the service, the invitation to come forward. About a dozen people or more did so, and he and the other ministers prayed over them.

Attendance at the three Sunday church services was around twenty-five hundred people. Only about six or seven hundred people were formal members of Las Acacias, however. Olson insisted that the church was not trying to draw members away from other churches, and hence many attended Las Acacias while remaining members of their own churches, including Catholics who "love our worship and our teaching and feel they are learning," and yet they continue to attend mass.

Las Acacias used an evangelization method called "Explosive Evangelism" devised in the United States by James Kennedy. Ursula Hahn said that the church had one hundred or more teams of three people who go out to evangelize each week. They did not do much door-to-door visiting, because people were reluctant to accept such visits. Forms of evangelism included calling on those who had filled out the blue cards in the pews and visiting the sick.

The Las Acacias approach had led to numerous social ministries. The church complex now occupied the entire block around the theater and the church staff numbered thirty-five people. Hahn referred to their conviction that human beings are "body, soul, and spirit," and that they should be attended to in an "integral" or "holistic" way. Olson added that the church engages in "a lot of pastoral work and counseling...and so we move from a pulpit-based and church-based discipline to a counseling attitude and mode, which helps people work through their struggles." One example of such ministry is a twelve-week pre-marriage course, half of whose participants are from other churches. "Marriage enrichment" courses were provided for couples already married, with topics such as conflict management, crisis states, self-esteem, roles, and money management. The course was arranged on four levels, with one weekend for each.

Olson said that the approach of Las Acacias was different from both the "Catholic mindset" which "wants the leaders to tell them what to do" and the "Protestant mindset" which says "you are absolutely responsible for your conduct." At Las Acacias the individual was "ultimately" responsible but was aided by the church's ministries. Olson and Las Acacias thus rejected the legalistic framework of many other pentecostals on theological grounds. Their refusal to oblige people to adhere to a rigid and detailed behavior code was rooted in the "basic Protestant tenet that salvation is ours by faith, the expiatory redemptive work of Jesus Christ. That work is not lost unless I negate it totally by my word or absolutely deny Christ. So there's much more grace than legalism."

Many pentecostals held to their rigid rules-centered morality and their worship in which intensity is measured by loudness because they had encountered no other tradition. Olson's own background had exposed him to diverse approaches, "and so I try to transmit slowly the understanding that the work of the Holy Spirit is going on in so many different ways whether in the individual or in the corporate life of the church." He had deliberately sought to provide a variety of forms of preaching, teaching, and music so that people would understand that the important issue is not belonging to a particular form of church. "The driving matter is to follow the Lord, to follow Jesus, whatever one's denomination or religious style may be." Contrary to the practice of other churches, Las Acacias consciously distinguished water baptism from membership in a particular local church.

Many of those attending Las Acacias "have come from other churches, and have been wounded or hurt for one or another reason. They take refuge here," said Ursula Hahn. A number of observers made this point. It seemed plausible to me that individuals and families who at one point in their spiritual journey became evangelicals and then grew estranged from their particular church might find a home at Las Acacias.

Although most pentecostal churches in Caracas firmly opposed Olson's approach to "customs" and relative openness, both he and Las Acacias were plainly influential. Olson estimated that perhaps 20 percent of pentecostals in Caracas would be sympathetic to his approach: three thousand in Las Acacias itself, and another two thousand in other churches. Other ministers frequently sought Olson's counsel and the church had sponsored pastoral clinics and symposia on worship. Olson said that he had always rejected the idea of setting up any kind of association of churches. However, the church had created an association for church-related social ministries of various kinds, and another association for individuals involved in particular ministries. In each case the motivation was both to offer a measure of institutional support and to provide an opportunity for like-minded believers to come together. One spin-off from the church was the Evangelical Seminary of Caracas, which was temporarily being housed at Las Acacias. Olson saw this activity as networking; he also admitted that Las Acacias was in some ways a "mother church." Las Acacias is widely discussed among evangelicals because of its positive growth and because its approach represents an alternative to the customary rigidity. [8]

AS I APPROACHED A "MINI-CONGRESS" ON CHURCH GROWTH jointly sponsored by a network of churches called the Coalition of Evangelical Churches of Caracas and the Venezuelan office of the U.S.-based organization DAWN Ministries, which assists in church growth efforts worldwide, I anticipated a meeting of one or two hundred people. It was thus a surprise to find only about forty people, at least five of them the organizers of the event.

The unease of some with the opening music led by a young woman playing a four-stringed guitar hinted at the fault lines running across what was by no means a homogeneous "Protestant community." During the opening prayer the group was encouraged to envision the city and to pray for it. The first major speaker, Brad Smith, drew attention to the church growth pattern. The big spurt of church growth in Caracas was from 1971 to 1984 when the number of evangelicals grew from five thousand to twenty-five thousand. From then until 1992 the number had grown another 34 percent and the number of churches had grown 22 percent.

According to church-planting theory, a church should be established for every group of one thousand people, so that individuals can be confronted with the gospel. In that sense, all of Caracas was a mission field. For example, the area of La Candelaria near the historic center of the city should have had sixty-six churches, but had only four. Smith stated that if the churches followed such a strategy and even if only 10 percent of the population became evangelical, their goal would be accomplished; this is because everyone would have an (evangelical) church nearby, would encounter believers, and would have to make a decision about Christ. The best way to spur church growth was to multiply sites of church-planting activity. The high-rise apartments of the middle class were especially difficult to penetrate. Smith mentioned his own efforts in the apartment where he lived and how they were frustrated when another church undertook activity in the same area. The implication was that evangelicals should coordinate their efforts and strive to have a church for every one or two high-rises.

In addition to geographical areas, specific human groups should be targeted. For example, Smith pointed to the large number of immigrants (from Spain, Portugal, Italy, Colombia, and elsewhere) in Caracas. Another example was the large number of unmarried people over fifteen: it would be a mistake to limit ministry to the family as traditionally understood. The church should be alert to people's specific needs. For example, noting the large number of women who worked outside the home, one church had formed a child care cooperative; a church in the interior had organized to help people deal with problems associated with having a family member in the hospital (relatives have to provide meals, change sheets, and so forth). By taking advantage of what is known about Caracas and by working together, the churches could grow. Late in the morning participants formed sub-groups along geographical lines to meet one another and to pray for their particular areas while visualizing them.

The major afternoon speaker was Hipólito Avila, a Baptist minister who was on the staff of the Coalition and who was trained in demography. To do evangelism in a neighborhood means approaching in a spirit of service and being involved in the problems of that neighborhood, he said. Questions to be asking when entering a place included: What is the history of this area? What is its music? How do the people think? What are their needs? He cited a complaint he had heard: The evangelicals are preaching in the park but are never around to clean up. The church must go to the community, not expect the community to come to the church. In fact, he himself had been unable to attend the morning session because he had been at a civic event.

Avila observed that in many areas there is little Catholic presence. When doing outreach in a new area Protestants should identify themselves as such but they need not ask permission from the local priests. That observation came from his own experience of encountering resistance from priests. In one district of Caracas, for example, the Baptists had begun an athletic program, and soon the local parish initiated a similar competing program. Avila told how the Baptists had organized cultural activities, including sports during the recent Holy Week. Although to Catholics this might sound offensive, my observation was that most people in Caracas would not participate in the Catholic liturgy or processions; many people went to the beach, but even for those without cars, Holy Week was primarily a vacation. The Baptists were only seizing a potential opportunity.

Avila and Smith both advocated "holistic mission," a notion that is conceptually close to what Catholics call "integral evangelization." Despite all the talk of service to the community, however, in the end the aim was to bring people to personal decisions for Christ and membership in a church. Further, all those present did not necessarily hold holistic views. At lunchtime a young pastor enthusiastically told me of a course in which he was learning that, according to the scriptures, churches should be governed in a theocratic rather than a democratic manner. Members of a group called Faith Crusade did street preaching outside the McDonald's in a pedestrian mall near a metro station. They had gathered ten thousand cards from people who had stepped forward and accepted Christ.

The problems entailed in direct efforts to "grow the church" and to "think in the reproductive mode," as I heard American missionaries put it, were made even clearer at a week-long evangelistic campaign by the well-known Argentine preacher, Alberto Motessi. The location could hardly have been more dramatic, I thought. Nuevo Circo was an old bull ring purchased by the Renacer church (apparently no relation to the one in Sao Paulo). The circular area below was still yellow with sand; had the platform been removed, the site would have been ready for matadors.

On the ground near the speaker's podium sat about two dozen church leaders. Most of the audience was concentrated in the area facing the speakers' podium; there were no more than a thousand people in the entire ring. Motessi spoke enthusiastically of the recent successes in spreading the gospel, with examples from Nepal, Nigeria, and the former Soviet Union. He read a scripture passage—from Habakkuk, I believe—about the kings paying homage to Jehovah, and claimed that Islamic Arab nations would soon do so. To have said the same of the USSR a few years ago would have sounded absurd, but recently the vice-minister of education in Russia had been converted, and he had immediately allowed the film *Jesus* to be shown. Motessi recounted his own trip the previous year to meet with Latin American presidents and other leaders. The climax had occurred in Mexico, where he and a large group of church representatives had met with President Salinas. For the first time the gospel had been preached inside the presidential palace of what had long been the most anti-religious government in the hemisphere.

By comparison with the "Christ is Coming" campaign that I had observed at the Petare metro stop, Motessi seemed moderate. The general tenor was that the evangelical cause is marching forward. His book, *500 Años Despues* (Five Hundred Years Later), on sale that night, was a general statement on what evangelicals had to offer Latin American society—yet another sign that evangelicals were feeling that their moment had arrived.

At the closing session on Saturday evening, I estimated attendance to be no more than fifteen hundred people, mostly evangelicals who had presumably attended one or more of the earlier evenings. Motessi seemed to tailor his preaching to this fact. He had the people read John 3:16 ("For God so loved the world...") after him. Toward the end of the evening, he first asked people to pray to Jesus in their hearts, and then—if they had so prayed—to raise their hands and come down into the ring. Fully 40 percent or perhaps even half of those in the stands went down, the vast majority not to accept Christ for the first time, but to "confirm" their acceptance in some fashion.

Measured by the number of people who accepted Christ as their savior, the crusade could hardly be regarded as a success. The very act of putting on such an event was a kind of statement from evangelicals to the city, but at some level the organizers must have recognized that vast amounts of money, time, and energy had been expended not to convert non-believers, but to bring churchgoers together to hear a famous evangelist deliver well-worn sermons.

"MY IDEA IS THAT if you're going to have an evangelical crusade it should be designed for non-Christians," said Chet Seapy, an American who had come from Orange County, California, to Caracas to help churches grow. To him, the Motessi campaign "was like a church service—with pentecostal leanings." If you really intend to draw in non-Christians you would not call on those present to "raise your hands, we're going to praise God," since that simply puts people on the spot.

The campaign must have been targeting lower-middle-class people, he said, since the "middle and upper class won't go to the Nuevo Circo."

That was an eye-opener to me, since I thought the metro stop location and bull ring ambience were quite effective. According to Seapy, the style of the campaign would not "minister to an upper-middle-class person." A stadium might be apt "as long as it wasn't at night in a bad section of town. If you have a nice car, where are you going to park it and not have it stolen?" Continual newspaper accounts of murder in the area reinforced such feelings.

Seapy had been seated among the church leaders near the platform, and so it was helpful to hear his frank assessment. As numerous studies had shown, he said, the most effective evangelism was "personal evangelism, sharing one-on-one, cell groups, small bible groups." Inviting people to one's home is far more effective than crusades. When asked in a survey what kind of evangelism they do most, pastors put crusades at the top, largely, he believed, because it was a tradition. When they were asked about effectiveness, however, crusades were toward the bottom in rating. The examples of Wesley and of historical revival periods indicate that "crusades may be better when you're dealing with a churched population that may have strayed away from God," but it is not an effective tool for first-time evangelization. "How many non-Christians go to a crusade? Why should a non-Christian walk through the door of your church?" It would be as unlikely as having a Christian go through the door of the imposing mosque recently built in Caracas (with money from Saudi Arabia). "The most effective way of reaching people is through a network of relationships: your neighbor, the person you work with."

Seapy's convictions were based on his own experience of being "discipled" by a farmer. While out harvesting corn, he would show the farmer verses he had memorized and the farmer would discuss how he applied his belief to dealings with his neighbors. The point is to "be not just hearers but doers." Discipling was 2 Timothy 2:2: "What you learned from me, confirmed by many witnesses, entrust it to trustworthy men who can then instruct others." It involved conversion, taking a person from non-Christian to Christian, helping him or her to become mature in the faith. "You can't disciple from the pulpits; it has to be done in small groups and one-on-one." Jorge Rodriguez of the Bible Society had told me that there was an "emerging consensus" that large campaigns do not produce results, and that the most effective evangelism was through person-to-person contact.

Seapy was also unapologetically interested in working with the well-off in Caracas. We were on one of the upper floors of his family's apartment tower toward the east end of the city, far removed from the makeshift houses on the hillside. Since most churches had "targeted the lower middle class," the upper middle class was largely unreached. Protestant missionaries, many of whom were themselves of rural background, had gone primarily to the rural areas. "Nowadays a lot of the missionaries coming in are targeting the upper middle class because they feel that it's an unreached section—and it is—and also because they can probably reach that class a little easier than some of the pastors could." Seapy spoke approvingly of a church that was being pastored by a missionary and a Venezuelan sociologist. Upper-class people were unlikely to seriously listen to someone less educated than they. At the same time, he acknowledged that there was a growing group of pastors who had full-time jobs or professions (as doctors, lawyers, or economists, for example) and who were capable of reaching the upper classes.

SUCH ISSUES—concern over what would make the churches grow; the need for approaches tailored to particular segments of the population; ways of taking into account educational level and class—arose repeatedly in discussions with observers of the larger evangelical scene.

Over the years repeated efforts had been made to jump-start evangelical growth. The Baptist church had announced ambitious plans for rapid growth that seemed to have produced few results. When considering why evangelical growth in the city was scarcely faster than the rate of population growth, most observers mentioned the stress of coping with life in Caracas, hectic work schedules, and commuting. Brad Smith told of a man who left for work before his children rose and arrived home shortly before they went to bed; this man did not want the good news of Jesus Christ to mean three more meetings a week. People also felt it was "increasingly dangerous to be out—everybody has either been attacked or had their car ripped off or something of the sort." Like other church growth specialists, Smith was enthusiastic about cell groups meeting in homes and apartments, but at some point people want a church building and then they run into the problem of prohibitively high real estate prices. A warehouse that would cost 300,000 bolivars in Maracay could cost 10 to 15 million in Caracas.

Another recurring theme was the contrast between "radical pentecostalism" and a more open view. One of his seminary students told Smith, "You need to know that nearly all of us Venezuelans have either a Catholic God who is sitting far away and from whose table we can only snatch crumbs, or we have a radical pentecostal God who will never ever be satisfied with us." For radical pentecostals, the heart of Christian faith seems to be in the behavior codes. Those codes may have played an important part in the conversion of some people, and for them may have been liberating. Others, however, including their children, may not experience the codes in the same way. Many pentecostal preachers apparently sought to instill fear and guilt, and in doing so they took advantage of the poor self-image of many Venezuelans.

Although "radical pentecostals" might still be the majority, a significant number of believers were "recovering" from a fear-oriented type of faith in which every detail of life was to be regulated by rules provided by a church. Samuel Olson pointed to churches that had broken away from the Assemblies of God because they no longer wanted to impose such constraints. Second-generation evangelicals in particular were unwilling to be subject to such control over the details of their lives. Many had dropped out of conservative churches, but some had moved on to other churches.

THE TEMPLO EVANGELISTICO DEL ESTE (Evangelistic Church of the East), located amid the bustle of Petare's markets, small businesses, and street vendors, indicated that the kind of searching that Olson was talking about was taking place within poor churches. A group of pentecostals had started an Assemblies of God congregation at the site of what had once been a Baptist church. The congregation grew and the church building itself expanded. The church now had 250 active members, over 1,000 people attending worship, and 550 enrolled in Sunday school.

When the church began to do missionary work elsewhere in Venezuela, it ran into territorial disputes with the national leadership of the Assemblies. "We understand that God's call has no limits or borders. We don't have to ask permission," said Inesio Murillo, the pastor. At that point the group decided to break away from the Assemblies of God. Together with other churches they formed the National Assemblies of God, which now had 130 churches in the country. Although throughout Venezuela this denomination had only a tenth as many members as the Assemblies, in Caracas it had twenty churches, rivaling the twenty-seven that belonged to the main body of the Assemblies.[9]

When asked to describe what was distinctive about his church, Murillo said that it was pentecostal but that it was neither conservative nor liberal. The word "maturation" frequently came up as he described the process that they had been through. To take an example, for a long time pastors had said that it was sinful for a woman to wear slacks, use makeup, or dress up. "But it's not a sin; it's just part of the culture." The "maturing" process he described was largely a matter of learning "that there are things in our doctrine that have been patterns set up by human beings—dogmas of men."

Another example was the requirement that a person receive a year or two of instruction before baptism. "I personally think this is an extreme, because in the time of the apostles the only requirement was to believe in Jesus Christ, and that was it. In biblical terms, instruction came afterwards." In simplifying the process, Murillo believed the church was simply following Jesus' instructions (Mt. 28:28).

About ten years previously, he had begun to feel uneasy and asked himself why the church was not growing. Years of prayer and study had led him to conclude that the obstacles lay in "certain denominational, doctrinal, social, and spiritual barriers." He likened the situation to that of the church in Corinth where people said, I follow Paul, Apollo, Peter, or Christ. All agreed that the doctrine was the same: one Lord, one Christ, one faith, one church. Deep down there is agreement, but in matters of "form" the conservatives say that women should not wear slacks and so forth. He made certain distinctions among the various customs. Although it might be normal to have a TV in the home, the "distorted" nature of most programs left believers with little to view. The same was true of movies. Smoking and moderate drinking were normal for Christians in some countries, although he hastened to add that he did neither. Another area "where God has renewed us" was that of social ministry, which was now basic to the church, although for many years the church had "spiritualized" its work and forgotten social ministry. The church ran a rehabilitation center, a children's home, a home for older people, and a school.

Although he admitted that Las Acacias had gone through a maturation process much earlier than his own church, Murillo insisted that he had not come to his own position through Las Acacias, but by observing missionary work and other churches in Venezuela and Colombia, and by making his own trips to Miami and the Houston area.

The church had been involved in both the Motessi campaign and the one I had observed near the metro station (about a three minute walk through teeming streets from the office where we were talking). The objectives of such campaigns were to bring people to Christ but also to bring evangelicals together to *confraternizar*—to share as brethren. The local campaign had been more successful because it had greater support from the churches. The Motessi campaign had been hindered by lack of support, apparently because it had been seen as too liberal by the pentecostal majority. Chet Seapy's idea that people might have been afraid to come to the neighborhood around the Motessi campaign had not occurred to him, since his own church was located in a similar kind of area.

Although Murillo had distanced himself from what others would call radical pentecostals, he was still far from being a theological liberal, as I discovered when I mentioned my own discomfort with the "Christ is Coming" theme of the Petare crusade. He first pressed me to answer directly whether I believed that Christ is coming. Hesitatingly, I answered that it is our faith that Christ is coming, and that God will bring everything to a conclusion, but that we could not know the time. I added—perhaps with gratuitous frankness—that the idea that Jesus would descend literally to a particular location was mythical.

"The second coming of Christ is part of our fundamental doctrine. Of course he himself said that no one knows the day or the hour," Murillo said. He cited approvingly Billy Graham's statement that the church must work as though Christ were coming in a thousand years and be prepared as though he were coming today. He believed that Jesus would literally come and stand on the Mount of Olives, according to the scriptures. We will not all be able to see it directly, just as we cannot see a plane after it goes over the horizon, "but with the media we will be able to see this great event." This was a reminder that even those who "mature" and move away from what they regard as excessively conservative positions may be far from sharing the religious vision of the mainstream churches and (most of) the post-Vatican II Catholic church.

At a Sunday morning church service Murillo had an easygoing manner and addressed his congregation in a conversational style. He moved easily around the wooden platform, amid the exposed concrete of a church perpetually under construction. As he discussed the various leadership roles in the congregation, I guessed that he was answering some kind of challenge to his own role. He insisted that in his absence his wife, who had proven her leadership over twenty-two years, was in charge.

The church was active in twenty sites which might eventually become churches. In recent years Murillo had been moving away from the notion that these should inevitably be independent churches with their own pastors, since individually they would all be weak. His vision was now to build up his congregation as a "mother church," and he had set the goal of having a congregation of "about five thousand at this site by the year 2000. It is easier to do missionary work with a strong church, one strong in people, in finances, and in using radio and TV." You first have to "strengthen Jerusalem," he said. He was already intending to acquire the adjoining area in order to build a church able to hold the numbers of people they planned to attract. His model may have been the "mega-churches" that have appeared in a number of countries.

ACROSS THE DIVIDE

12
End of a Cycle or Crisis of Growth?

Issues and Prospects for Catholics

M Y AIM IN APPROACHING the churches in Sao Paulo and Caracas has been to explore current developments not only in Brazil and Venezuela, but more broadly in Latin America. In the final three chapters, I will offer observations on a sampling of such issues, first on the Catholic church, then on Protestant and evangelical churches, and finally on relations between the two traditions.

Catholic Response to Evangelical Growth

Shortly before I met with the auxiliary bishop of Rio de Janeiro, Josef Romer, the newspapers had reported on the ISER study of evangelical growth. In metropolitan Rio during the 1990-1992 period, 750 new evangelical churches had been founded (about five per week). One new Catholic parish had been founded during same period.[1] What was the significance for the Catholic church, I asked, that in any given week the number of Protestants at worship was on a par with that of Catholics?

"Look," Romer replied, "I'm going to proceed as objectively as possible. First, this is a question of facts, not of interpretation." He went on to say that he doubted very much that all Protestant churches together had as many worshippers as the 230 or 240 parishes in Rio, some of which had thousands attending, although admittedly some congregations could be counted in the dozens. (The growth had brought the number of Protestant churches to almost 3,800.) He did not think that the number of active Protestants was higher than that of Catholics.

In qualitative terms, which he regarded as more important, the Catholic church still had enormous influence, far more than Protestants (he went out of his way to assure me that this influence did not derive from the government, from which he insisted that the Catholic church received nothing). The Catholic church enjoyed "great unity" while "Protestant churches have nothing of the sort." Fundamentalists might offer immediate results, but they would not have impact on universities or the press.

Later that same afternoon, I posed a similar question to Clodovis Boff, a Servite priest, the brother of Leonardo Boff and himself an important Catholic theologian.[2] He likewise resisted the idea that evangelicals might in some sense be on a par with Catholics, and he doubted whether such churches created a profound gospel culture. Their political involvement was weak and they were easily manipulated. They did not see the need for "mediations." Boff and other theologians frequently use this as a technical term to refer to what is required both for comprehending reality (the "mediation" of the social sciences) and for changing it ("mediations" such as movements and parties). The observe-judge-act methodology of the progressive church is an embodiment of what Boff and others mean by "mediations." The implication was that evangelicals proceeded naively as though reading the scripture by itself would tell a Christian what to do.

Boff also suspected that evangelical growth was a passing phenomenon. He had recently read about research indicating that conservative evangelical churches were beginning to decline in the United States and perhaps elsewhere. In any case, the Catholic church could draw on great strengths such as popular religiosity, the form of Catholicism practiced by 80 or 90 percent of those identifying themselves as Catholics (the large numbers who make pilgrimages to the shrine of Our Lady of Aparecida, for example).

A conservative bishop and a major liberation theologian had both questioned the reality of evangelical advance and emphasized the strengths of the Catholic church in very similar terms.

Virtually none of my Catholic interviewees had devoted any attention to examining evangelical churches firsthand. A bishop whose office was located near the large Assemblies of God complex where I had observed over a thousand pastors, and a metro stop away from the headquarters church of the Christian Congregation, admitted that he had never been inside either. A well-known liberation theologian told me that she had never attended a pentecostal worship service. Priests and sisters in barrios were aware of numerous small churches in their neighborhoods, but were little aware of their specific features.

"No one feels challenged by this" said Jose Comblin, referring to evangelical growth, "neither theologians, nor pastors, nor pastoral experts, even though in the large cities of the Northeast, from Salvador to Fortaleza, there are many more [evangelicals] than there are Catholics," that is, there were more Protestants participating in their churches in any given week than Catholics.[3]

The Brazilian bishops were said to be concerned about evangelical growth and indeed in the mid-1980s they commissioned studies on the topic. During his 1991 visit, Pope John Paul II seemed to be urging the bishops to respond to the evangelicals, whom he at one point referred to as "ravenous wolves" devouring Catholics and "causing division and discord in our communities."[4]

Nevertheless, the Catholic church seemed little intrigued by evangelical growth and the reasons for it. A document by Jesus Hortal, S.J., that grew out of a seminar organized by the Brazilian bishops is quite typical of Catholic reactions. Among the "possible reasons for the spread of non-Catholic groups," he cites first the weaknesses of the Catholic church under several headings: the weight of the institution, the clergy shortage, the rural mentality of the clergy, the sociological nature of Brazilian Catholicism, insufficient evangelization, the quasi-federative nature of the Catholic church. The study then discusses what such groups offer Brazilians: association with modernity, a "pure" form of Christianity, moral integrity, and a deeper religious experience.

In one of the most interesting points of his study, Hortal combats some frequently heard arguments against evangelicals. To claim that evangelical success is due to money from the United States (as I continued to hear) ignores the fact that "the Catholic church currently receives far more money (mainly from Germany, but also from many other countries) from outside than the evangelical churches. Even the CNBB [Brazilian bishops conference] would be very seriously affected without that money. Furthermore, the pentecostal churches that I call third generation (such as the 'Universal Church of the Kingdom of God') and which are more aggressive and proselytizing, since they are indigenous and do not have a North American headquarters, do their own fundraising inside the country through massive tithing among their followers, something that the Catholic church neither desires nor would be able to do with the same degree of efficiency."[5]

Hortal's whole essay leads up to his recommendations for a Catholic response: become more participatory, develop ministries, provide a more personal option among Catholics, work together more effectively, (e.g., develop Catholic media), strengthen urban pastoral work, encourage pluralism within Catholicism, develop the contemplative dimension, and so forth. The specific recommendations are less important than the general pattern of thought: the subject of evangelical growth tends to provoke Catholics to consider the weaknesses of their own church and to think about possible responses, without devoting much attention to the specific nature of evangelical churches.

A pastoral specialist at the Brazilian bishops conference headquarters in Brasilia said that the response of the Catholic church was not to engage in polemics with evangelicals but to renew itself "...so that the church may be able to respond to the religious demand, to the Brazilian people's religious searching in this situation of modernity, of changes in the country." The whole church was examining its liturgy, sacraments, preaching, and use of the media. "In fact, we are convinced that in the short run there is no way that we can return to being an overwhelmingly Catholic country. We must live alongside a number of religious groups...The pentecostals are expected to continue to grow until the end of the century."[6]

In neither Caracas nor Sao Paulo did I find any systematic effort at a direct response to evangelical growth by Catholics. I likewise found Catholics little intrigued. Clergy and theologians had had personal contact with colleagues in the historic denominations but their knowledge of pentecostal churches was clearly secondhand (perhaps from lectures by scholars at workshops). They evidently felt no need to expose themselves directly to these religious movements.

Aparecida and Popular Religiosity

It is a two-hour bus ride from Sao Paulo to the national shrine of Our Lady of Aparecida. Made more imposing by its location on a small hill, the shrine, which reminded me of the National Shrine of the Immaculate Conception in Washington, DC, was begun in the late 1940s and only finished in 1990. According to legend, the image of Our Lady of Aparecida was found miraculously in the eighteenth century by fishermen who were casting their nets in the nearby river. (Other shrines throughout Latin America trace their origins to similar miracles.) The fact that the image is black suggests that the poor were appropriating in their own manner the devotion to the Immaculate Conception then being promoted in the Iberian peninsula.

Six million Brazilians a year come to the shrine—more than to any other shrine in the Americas (including Guadalupe, if those from Mexico City are discounted), said the Redemptorist priest who graciously showed me around. The shrine was staffed by twenty priests and ten lay brothers. They maintained contact with eight thousand local pilgrimage coordinators. Every Sunday at 11 A.M. they offered a training session for such leaders.

Attendance varied widely by season. The parish team had a multifaceted pastoral program to serve the many pilgrims, and team members were in contact with an international network of pastoral teams and theologians at other shrines in the hemisphere. The shrine had dining, toilet, and other facilities to accommodate up to ten thousand people at any one time. Social services, such as medical treatment, were offered, and clothes—including wedding and first communion outfits—were made available for the poor. Sometimes groups who were involved in land struggles and had church backing came to the shrine for encouragement. Some pilgrims sought confession and counseling, which the priest called a "beautiful pastoral ministry." From what I observed, lay people on the staff shared the same vision.

These priests and brothers were sincerely seeking to serve people whose religious vision—indeed whose whole outlook on life—was different from their own. The motivation for a pilgrimage, for example, might well be to "pay off" a promise made to God in a moment of need. A scholar familiar with Aparecida told me that in fact the priests really do not believe in miracles. One old priest said that he had been at the shrine for decades and had never seen a miracle. Another commented that he felt "ashamed" at the altar as he looked over the mass of pilgrims; he felt that "no matter what I say it doesn't make any difference." The scholar observed, "The priests don't believe it any more. They are all secularized."

Whether his impression of the priests at Aparecida is fully accurate, I believe the observation states neatly a persistent problem of the Catholic church: how can it engage the popular Catholicism of the majority if its own ministers do not share the religious world view of the people?

Repeatedly, I found priests stating that over time they had been forced to pay more attention to popular religion. Some, such as Padre Ticão and Padre Zaga (Chapter 4) had clearly altered their approach, while others, such as Matias Camuñas (Chapter 10), had willingly accepted their assigned role (Camuñas was often called to bless small shrines that the people had built in the neighborhood). What to do with this new respect for popular religion was far from clear. One priest described working with base communities for a time and being fulfilled with the results, but then gradually realizing that he was not touching a large "mass" of people. How was it possible to "respect what the people feel they need" (for example, holy water and novenas) "when we've discovered that that's not going to bring about [needed social] change?"

Before Vatican II, the gap between the religious sensitivity of the priests and the people may have been less. Tridentine Catholicism, which was focused on the church as the repository of the "means of grace," was not the same as the popular devotions of the people, but priests accepted their role as ritual leaders. The biblical and liturgical renewal enshrined in the Council documents entailed a reorientation of Catholic practice away from practices that had become traditional, such as devotion to the saints (as actually practiced, not as explained and justified by theologians). Involvement in the defense of human rights and the discovery of politics led even further away from traditional practices. In the immediate post-Council years, many priests ignored traditional popular religiosity or merely endured it and sought to minimize the occasions when they had to deal with it. By the mid-1970s, Latin American pastoral theologians were warning against making assumptions that secularization would occur in Latin America as in Europe. They argued that the values of popular religion should be appreciated even while some of its practices were being purified.

While such an approach might be clear in principle, in practice it was less so. In Brazil and Venezuela some priests now recognized that in the past they had sought to harness popular religiosity to political causes (Stations of the Cross that were a critique of political repression). It was possible that progressive pastoral work had attracted relatively secularized people or those open to a more secularized interpretation of Christian faith (such as those in the *pastoral operaria* meeting with Frei Betto), and had alienated those who retained more traditional outlooks. To what extent could representatives of the church enter into the religious world of the poor? To identify the problem was by no means the same as addressing it.

Margarida Oliva, who had been a Catholic activist for decades and who was now pursuing a degree in religious studies, said she believed the Universal Church was tapping into some features of traditional Catholicism. The Universal Church's use of physical things—she cited a ceremony whereby people walked through an arch symbolizing renewal of marriage vows—were like what Catholics used to call "sacramentals," such as holy water and candles.[7] Was it possible that some pentecostal pastors might be more adept at tapping into popular religiosity than the largely secularized Catholic clergy?

A Crisis in the Progressive Church?

"The progressive church is finished," said Rubem Alves,[8] the Presbyterian who was once regarded as a liberation theologian, but who has gone in his own idiosyncratic directions since 1970. Most of the major liberation theologians, however, did not believe that the collapse of communism and the electoral defeat of the Sandinistas along with the winding down of the Central American crisis were a major challenge to their theology. Never had they taken existing socialism as a model for Latin America nor had Marxism been their major inspiration. Their theology was rooted in the poor, not in any ideology. The new world (dis-)order in which the wealthy capitalist nations and their institutions ruled unchecked was even harsher on the poor as policies imposed in the name of debt repayment and opening to free trade aggravated disparities of wealth and power. Although the theologians admitted the need for rethinking, their writing in the early to mid-1990s was largely a defense of their basic commitments.

The secular left was more ready to assess the depth of the changes taking place and how their own view of the world was affected. "The United States and capitalism have won," said Jorge Castañeda in the opening paragraph of *Utopia Unarmed: The Latin American Left after the Cold War,* "and in few areas of the globe is that victory so clear-cut, sweet, and spectacular as in Latin America." Despite the importance of its struggles during the 1960–1990 period, the left was now "on the run or on the ropes." Castañeda presented the hopes—and illusions—that had nourished the left. He believed that the left had a future, but only if it came to terms with its past and reformulated its aims in the direction of social democracy, along the lines of European left parties. Christians who were struggling to come to terms with recent political and economic developments seemed less ready to bite the bullet than Castañeda.[9]

Chapters 4, 5, 6, 8, and 10 have presented perceptions of Catholic pastoral workers. The differences between the experiences of Sao Paulo and Caracas are significant. Under the leadership of Cardinal Arns, the archdiocese of Sao Paulo itself was a center for progressive church forces: the impetus for Operation Periphery came from the cardinal himself. The pastoral plans begun in the mid-1970s were each the distillation of a consultation process that had taken up to two years. Arns had personally confronted the military over human rights violations, and social ministries dealing with housing, street people, and so forth were formally recognized. Some of the pastoral coherence was destroyed in 1989 when the Vatican carved away four separate dioceses and installed bishops who dismantled and discouraged earlier pastoral work. As mentioned in Chapter 1, whoever succeeded Arns at his retirement in 1996 was expected to almost certainly dismantle, by fiat or by attrition, much of what had been done.

The people whom I met were not discouraged about their immediate pastoral work. However, I did not sense great hopes for the church itself. That is why the options of John Drexel and Sr. Maria Emilia Guerra Ferreira (Chapter 6) seemed symptomatic to me; they were following out what they regarded as their own spiritual vocation and were serving people in need, but they were no longer investing their lives in directly building up the church community.

In Caracas, the story line seemed almost the opposite. After conflicts and tension with the bishops in the 1970-72 period, groups of pastoral agents had gone to live in the poor areas, particularly the poor neighborhoods in the hills. From an original suspicion or mistrust, the bishops had gradually come to respect and defend such work, and it was even said that recent social pronouncements by the bishops owed their vigor to contact with church work among the poor. Since Venezuela had enjoyed elected civilian government since 1958 and there had been no serious possibility that a left-wing movement could take power, church forces had not experienced a heroic phase of resistance to dictatorship nor the hopes for change that many Brazilians, Chileans, Central Americans, and others had cherished during years of struggle. I did not encounter any notable sense of letdown because there had never been a period of exaggerated hopes. Pedro Trigo emphasized that while he and others were certainly aware of political developments and pastoral and theological writing in other countries, they had emphasized the importance of not viewing Venezuela through lenses formed elsewhere.

Bryan Froehle comments that with the return to elected civilian regimes throughout Latin America, the once atypical Venezuelan experience has become the norm.[10] Neither Caracas nor Sao Paulo alone reflects the situation of Catholicism, but both offer insights.

Religious Life

About ninety or a hundred men and women, superiors of religious congregations in Venezuela, were gathered at a hilltop retreat house about an hour from Caracas. Pedro Trigo was offering his observations on a Vatican working document intended for a synod on religious life to be held later in Rome. One of Rome's concerns was that religious should fit into the local church, that is, be subject to the bishops. Rome's concern was understandable, said Trigo, but if this idea were to be pushed too far, members of religious orders would be viewed simply as personnel to be used for filling positions in dioceses. Religious life serves the church best by being what it is, not by supplying church personnel. Trigo also insisted that as useful as Vatican documents might be, they should not define what religious life should be, since that was to be found in the documents of St. Benedict, St. Augustine, the founders of religious orders, and the Confederation of Latin American Religious (CLAR). He did not need to remind his audience that the Vatican had cracked down hard on CLAR initiatives.

Observing the leadership of religious orders gathered in one room was a helpful reminder of the dual structure within the Catholic church: clergy (organized into dioceses) and religious orders and congregations. Catholicism arrived in Latin America with the Franciscans, Dominicans, Benedictines, Mercedarians, Carmelites, Jesuits and others, and colonial churches still standing in major cities had been typically built by religious orders. Parishes with neatly defined boundaries came only later. The institutional growth of the Catholic church in Latin America during the twentieth century was also largely the work of religious who had come from Europe. Today the largest numbers of church personnel belong to religious orders, as this table makes clear.[11]

	Diocesan priests	Male religious	Female religious
Sao Paulo	306	655	2,136
Caracas	119	818	1,583

Thus, although the everyday workings (mass schedules, organizations) of a parish run by Franciscans, Claretians, or Carmelites are quite similar to those run by diocesan priests, and religious priests follow diocesan policies, the loyalties of the two groups are somewhat different. To enter an order is to join a family. Each order has its own mystique. A diocesan priest will probably live out his priestly career serving one bishop and his successors, whereas a member of a religious order will move within the boundaries of his province (which might extend, for example, to all Venezuela) and perhaps further. It is also true that the member of a religious order has something of a social security system in his or her religious "family," whereas a diocesan priest is largely on his own. Although it is not widely noted, most of the outstanding figures of the progressive church (theologians, pastoral innovators) in Latin America have been religious.

Certain features of contemporary Latin American Catholicism are better understood by taking into account the role of religious. Consider for example, the concern among religious for "insertion," as it is called, referring to members of religious orders living among the poor. The term is used most commonly by sisters. The overriding concern is primarily to be an authentic "presence" of the church in the community (as in, for example, the case of Sister Leonor in Antímano).

Evangelicals obviously have a rather different goal, to bring people to make a personal decision for Christ and to join their particular church. When I posed the matter to an experienced sister, she said that evangelicals did not suffer the "tensions of the [Catholic] evangelizer who . . . accompanies people in their problems, joys, and sufferings as they live their faith." She observed that some of her neighbors leave the community to become preachers and "two months later you see them in their suits and ties and they no longer even say 'Good morning' to their neighbors. They're off to preach in the plaza in Petare or in their churches." Catholics sought to share their faith, not to impose it. "We have to share the person's whole life, and this creates a demand for service, detachment, anxiety, and joy." That was quite different from Protestants who may "see a large mass of people out there feeling happy and singing 'Alleluia,' but it all has nothing to do with the life of the people." Conscious Catholics were "more concerned for quality than for quantity, while the ordinary evangelical is concerned about masses—the more people there are, the better the worship service."

Whether or not that is a fair characterization of evangelicals, it suggests that the motivation of many, indeed most, Catholic pastoral workers, particularly members of religious orders, is one of "quality rather than quantity," and that such church workers would resist being judged by any criteria that sought to measure the effectiveness of their outreach. The proof lies first in the spiritual experience of living and working with the poor, and second, on whether such a life is considered a sign of the presence of the church. Even if only a small portion of the people participate actively (those active in the community houses in Petare, or those in discussion with Pedro Trigo), it is assumed that a much larger portion of the population is aware of that presence, thereby giving the church "credibility." A further indication of how religious view their pastoral work came from a sister who said that she and her colleagues had originally envisioned themselves spending a period in one community and then moving on to another, but that "now we find we've been in a community for twenty years and still haven't finished there."

The extent to which such work will continue is open to question. In both Sao Paulo and Caracas I was told that the congregations of sisters that are receiving the largest numbers of new vocations are those closer to traditional religious life with its characteristic practices, including the wearing of the habit. Wagner Suarez, head of the theological training center for religious orders, said that living in small religious houses had to some extent become normal for the Jesuits in Caracas, but these houses are likely to be found not among the poorest hillside shacks but in older working-class neighborhoods of the city.

Suarez said that his own generation (he entered in 1969) had sought to "get beyond institutional barriers" and become part of the people. "Our ideal was to get rid of the cassock and look more and more like the people. If there was a strike, we were there; if something else was going on, there we were." His generation wanted to break with everything. One effect was that, of the eighteen Venezuelans in his group, he is the only one still in the Jesuits.

"That's all over," he said of the period in which the only thing that counted was to be involved with workers, peasants, or in the Amazon region. "Institutionally, it is impossible." Today the Jesuits and other congregations are being confronted with difficult decisions about which institutions they can retain and which they should relinquish or close. At the Colegio San Ignacio, the youngest Jesuit was now sixty and the average age was seventy-five. The next ten or fifteen years will be difficult until the younger group of Jesuits are ready to take charge. Sister Casimira Gallego, the head of SECORVE, the umbrella organization of Venezuelan religious, told me that 50 percent of the members of most congregations were older than sixty, and that those between thirty and fifty were overloaded with responsibilities.

Understandably, said Suarez, the younger generation is more focused on the Jesuits as an institution than was his own. The current generation is more institutional because the times are more institutional. They are not necessarily more conservative, but they have recognized that institutions are necessary. "I would have liked to see religious life evolving in a different direction. I would have liked to see the congregations following their own special charism, but also becoming more integrated into society, breaking barriers. But I see them as trapped by the vocation shortage and by the pressure on us."

The question for the future is not simply quantitative (numbers of those entering religious life) but qualitative: is there a younger generation able to grasp the signs of the times and to respond to the new challenges of the twenty-first century?

Questions for Theologians

This book presents the concerns and issues I observed and detected while making inquiries among the churches of two Latin American cities during a period when people like Father Alfredo (Introduction) were finding themselves with fewer answers and more questions. I could not help wondering why the liberation theologians who insist that their method is one of "critical reflection on praxis" had not raised these issues long before I had.

To take only the most obvious point, the rise of pentecostal religion was invisible to most of the well-known theologians until very recently, and even now one sees little indication that their theological curiosity has been piqued. During my relatively short stay in Brazil and Venezuela, I had the distinct impression that I had learned more about the specific features of the major pentecostal churches than almost any Catholic with whom I spoke. Catholics seemed to have formed generic ideas of evangelical churches not from direct observation but from reading or lectures. I was astonished to find several people urging me to read *Os Demonios Descem do Norte* (The Devils Come Down from the North) by a Brazilian journalist who had recycled material from U.S. publications on the international activities of the religious right, but evidenced no insight into Brazilian pentecostalism.

A 1991 book on new challenges to liberation theology was symptomatic.[12] The editor had interviewed a number of theologians meeting in Sao Paulo.[13] The book consists of short sections, often of a hundred words or so, excerpted from the interviews and arranged so as to respond to a large number of questions, (for example, "Is there room for everyone in the church of the poor?"). Despite the title, both the questions and the answers repeat well worn ideas. Evangelicals, for example, are present only in passing references to the "sects."

Here I would like to indicate, rather unsystematically, a few areas for theological reflection arising out of the pastoral situations observed here. A first and obvious example is that of the situation of women in the church and in society. As indicated in Chapter 8, women of faith were responding to opportunities to reflect together on their lives, including—indeed, starting from—their bodies. Latin American feminist theologians frankly admit that they are behind North American feminists. Public discussion of reproductive matters is stifled, not because Latin American women are so different from European and North American women, but because of male power in society, buttressed by periodic ecclesiastical intervention. If there is a distinctive "Latin American perspective" on women's issues, it is difficult to discern, largely because Latin American women—poor and well off, scholars and barrio leaders, nuns and factory workers—are not free to express it. The voices heard in Chapter 8 suggest what might happen if women's voices were not suppressed.

Approximately twenty years ago, the major Latin American male theologians were at least forced to recognize sexism as a particular form of oppression. There is little evidence, however, that they have internalized the critique of patriarchy. In this respect they are little different from other Latin American male intellectuals who show few signs that they have been challenged by the feminist critique. It may be that women's ordination is not an issue in Latin America, but those who use their ecclesial power to thwart discussion are not in a position to know that. To his credit, Leonardo Boff over a decade ago offered his own opinion that there was no scriptural or theological impediment to the ordination of women. Some might argue that, given the reality of poverty, women's access to church office is a luxury, but only women could make such a determination.

As the multiple voices in Chapter 8 suggest, women were voicing some of the elements of a Latin American feminist theology; it would take into account women's experience, and in particular that of their bodily experience; their roles as nurturers, breadwinners, and community leaders; abuse against them from rape and domestic violence; their limited presence in public life; and their own meanings of God, cosmos, and human relationships. There were many constraints, however. Forces in society ranging from traditional elites, the military, and the Catholic hierarchy were largely successful in muzzling public discussion of reproductive issues. Most trained women theologians were either members of religious orders or worked in Catholic institutions, particularly universities, where they enjoyed nothing like the academic freedom found in Catholic universities elsewhere. Nevertheless, a Latin American feminist theology seems destined to be expressed more and more forcefully in the coming years.

A second area largely overlooked in liberation theology is the urban character of Latin American society. One could read dozens of volumes by liberation theologians without realizing that Latin America has made the "urban leap" in the last generation or so. It might be argued that the theologians are not writing about either rural or urban people as such, but in fact one of the volumes in the Theology and Liberation series is entitled "The Indian Face of God" and is composed of case studies of inculturation of Christian faith in indigenous societies. Another, entitled "Theology of Land," is a theological reflection of church involvement in the struggles of the landless, particularly in Brazil.[14] Surely the experience in urban shanty towns (people struggling to survive, to create a community and family life, to deal with social polarization and build base communities) could have been the source of important theological reflections.

Indeed, in *The God of Christians,* the Chilean theologian Ronaldo Munoz does reflect urban Latin America. For example, he outlines how the image of God changes when peasants migrate to the city, based no doubt on his own decades of experience in the shanty towns of Santiago.[15] Over a decade ago, Clodovis Boff published a theological journal on his pastoral work in the rubber gathering area in the state of Acre near the Bolivian border (where Chico Mendes later rose to fame and was murdered). Some of Ivone Gebara's essays reflect her life in Camaragibe (near Recife). What I am suggesting is that it is time for theologians to write out of experiences, such as those of Matias Camuñas. Pablo Richard has recently spoken of a "breakdown" in cities which "need to be cleansed of the poor. In several countries (e.g., Colombia) death squads maraud nightly, killing off street children, tramps, beggars, prostitutes, homosexuals, the unemployed, the homeless, etc." He goes on to say that the change in the situation of the poor—from being exploited to being excluded and regarded as redundant—challenges liberation theology "radically at every level—terminology and world view, commitment and pastoral practice, as well as moral and spiritual depth."[16]

A related matter is that of the emerging popular culture, which is urban and very much influenced by international (U.S.-led) consumer culture. Minutes after landing in Brazil (and for a few weeks afterward), I heard the piped-in voice of a current hit by Whitney Houston. One finds virtually no sensitivity to this culture in the major theologians, who are quite ready to endorse the need for "inculturation" vis-à-vis indigenous cultures (and those of African origin). Again, Comblin at least puts his finger on matters when he says that in the 1970s it was hoped that popular religiosity could be the link between base communities and the masses. In fact, however, "traditional Catholic religiosity, traditional Catholic customs and practices are also rapidly disappearing. The 1980s were decisive. During that decade television spread everywhere and has gone into almost every house. Today television takes up the time that used to be reserved for traditional culture, for religion, prayers, processions, saints' feasts, and so forth. What is left is a much fuzzier reservoir of religiosity, one almost without beliefs and with few religious practices. The new popular masses have abandoned or are abandoning the traditional ceremonies and religious customs. That is why they are predisposed to any other kind of new religion."[17]

If Comblin is even partly correct, these matters demand serious reflection. However, one might read a dozen volumes by liberation theologians without encountering the word "television," let alone a discussion of its implications for today. The same might be true of many North Atlantic systematic theologians, but they are less inclined to claim that their theology arises out of practice.

The foregoing observations are examples. My intent is not so much to chastise theologians for not having anticipated the matters raised in this book as to suggest that Latin American theologians and others must examine afresh the world in which we live.

Prospects for the "Restorationist" Program

The program of the papacy of John Paul II has been called in shorthand one of a "restoration" of the discipline, loyalty, and doctrinal and moral unity allegedly lost in the aftermath of Vatican II. Hence, the other side of the coin of the Vatican's attack on liberation theology and on the Latin American progressive church in general (as well as its disciplining of theologians and others regarded as unorthodox elsewhere in the world) is the promotion of a series of movements regarded as theologically and politically conservative: Opus Dei, Communion and Liberation, and the Charismatic Renewal (to which might be added in Latin America the Cursillos de Cristianidad and the neocatechumenate), and the ambitious project Evangelization 2000 and its media component Lumen 2000. In Latin America some refer to this tendency as "re-Romanization."

A certain amount of research has been done on the ideas and intentions of the leaders of such movements, even of the hermetically secretive Opus Dei, but less is known about what has actually been achieved. Although I could not make such movements a central concern, it seemed important to do at least some probing. Hence, in both Brazil and Venezuela I tried to get a sense of the Catholic charismatic movement, which unquestionably responds to the needs of some Catholics. However, besides Fr. Dougherty's rather expansive and unsubstantiated claim to have 3.5 to 5 million participants in Brazil, all other representatives of the movement told me that the figures were unavailable or were still being compiled. The figure for prayer groups in Sao Paulo suggested far more modest numbers (Chapter 7). Recall further that the stadium event scheduled in Caracas for the Saturday before Pentecost was canceled for lack of participants.

Similarly, I found no indication to justify the concerns that Evangelization 2000 would be mounting a vast conservative campaign. As of 1995 a non-profit organization was beginning to establish a Catholic cable TV network in Brazil, influenced but not dominated by charismatics, whose programming did not represent any single tendency in the church.

Communion and Liberation in Brazil seems to be of modest size. Judging from the writings of its founder, Fr. Luigi Giussani, Communion and Liberation is a humanistic, modern form of Catholicism, whose central focus is an emphasis on friendship between fellow members based on a personal encounter with Christ. Father Vando, the chaplain to the movement in Sao Paulo, said that there were probably 300 to 350 adults in Sao Paulo who had encountered the movement in the university and who were now professional people. (I stumbled across the movement when I met a woman member who was working at a small foundation.) At any given moment, the number of university student participants seems quite small. Despite the approbation it received from Cardinal Ratzinger and others, and its publications, (*30 Giorni, Litterae Communionis,* and the theological journal *Communio*) Communion and Liberation in Brazil did not seem destined to take possession of the church.

In short, contrary to sometimes expressed concerns or fears, none of the "movements" seems likely to be a spiritual juggernaut. Even though charismatic Catholics can assemble stadium crowds, the movement generates relatively small cadres of people truly devoted to it, while most of its adherents attend prayer groups for their own needs. It is conceivable that under the aegis of Evangelization 2000 or a similar movement the Catholic church may organize media events (perhaps combining use of TV programming, some door-to-door canvassing, and large mass events). Such campaigns might be proposed to mark the end of the millennium. Even if it were to be called a "new evangelization," such a massive effort would almost certainly have only a very temporary effect. Evangelicals themselves, it should be noted, now doubt that stadium campaigns yield significant numbers of conversions.

Leaders of the charismatic movement already claim that the majority of parish activists (readers, hymn leaders, and so forth) are charismatics even where the pastor is not. Given the Vatican's criteria for episcopal appointments, it is possible that over time many or most bishops may have ties to one or another of such movements.

Even if the influence of the Charismatic Renewal and other conservative "movements" continues to spread among the hierarchy and clergy, I believe that the "restoration" program will remain limited in its impact. Talk of a "new evangelization" notwithstanding, Vatican policy rewards docility, not creativity. For over a decade, bishops have been appointed not for their pastoral gifts and accomplishments, but for their good conduct. The "narrow way" is that of strict doctrinal and moral orthodoxy and the avoidance of controversy. Bishops can use their power to constrain public behavior and discourse, but they are unlikely to inspire creative innovation.

Of course, these assertions could always be disproved by facts. At some point a conservatively inspired Catholic movement might catch fire among masses of people, but so far that has not happened, and I would argue that it is unlikely.

A New Generation?

The crisis in pastoral work, if there was one, was not that the postconciliar and post-Medellin efforts had failed, but that the context was changing and presenting new challenges. The Medellin generation, which was now in its fifties and sixties, would continue to develop, but it would do so largely along the lines it has already laid down. Innovation was likely to be the work of a new generation. Was there such a generation waiting in the wings, I wondered.

"On the basis of my experience here," a seminary professor in Sao Paulo told me frankly, "this group is not going to build anything. The seminarians of the diocese are not going to build the church of the future. The quality of our 'manpower' [he used the English term] is very poor." Seminary students were typically from rural areas and, despite their good will, were unlikely to be very creative in dealing with the challenges of large cities.

Few candidates were coming from the cities, either from the middle classes or the *favelas* on the outskirts. One obvious reason was related to celibacy. In a society where sexuality is omnipresent it is very difficult "to present celibacy as a value for young people." The second reason, he said, was that today being a priest did not offer the same prospects as it once had, in part because of his own generation's demystifying of the priesthood by making the priest not a boss but one who serves. A third and related reason was that the priest had to be a "highly qualified professional," somewhat on the level of a university professor or a businessman, and was regarded as a trainer of leaders—and yet was expected to live on the equivalent of two minimum salaries (very roughly $120) a month. A "heroic saint" might manage this but, given human limitations, it was unrealistic to expect many people to do so. He was seeking to explain why urban youth scarcely considered becoming priests, not arguing that better pay would resolve the problem.

He may have been overstating for emphasis, but his observations were consistent with what I found repeatedly among those training priests and religious. Wagner Suarez contrasted the younger generation of Jesuits and other religious with his own generation. Today's religious were more turned inward and did not have the same sensitivity as his own; they were more institutional, but that was understandable given the pressures on the institution. He also said that current candidates for religious life were "intellectually less powerful" than those of a previous generation. They were not coming from Catholic schools but from marginal barrios, where schools were inferior and studying was difficult. Even in religious life, studying did not come easily. With their long years of training, the Jesuits might be able to remedy that lack of earlier preparation, but the concerns of the new generation of Jesuits were more pastoral than intellectual, and hence Suarez did not expect young priests to be on the forefront intellectually.

Kenneth Serbin has traced the developments in Brazilian seminaries during the post-conciliar period. As elsewhere, the late 1960s and early 1970s were a period of turmoil and experimentation. An estimated thirty-five hundred priests resigned, largely because of celibacy. The existing model of seminary education was abandoned and students majored in subjects other than philosophy in their university years. Seminaries were decentralized into small houses located in neighborhoods where students also did pastoral work. The "vocation crisis" bottomed out around 1975, and since then the numbers in seminaries have risen, although only slightly.

With the advent of John Paul II, however, the tendency has been toward the reimposition of discipline.[18] Serbin finds that the overall effect has been a kind of "synthesis," that is, some of the results of the period of experimentation have been retained, but greater control is being exercised. His statistics confirm the impression of seminary staff members that at the very time when Brazil was becoming more urban, seminarians were coming increasingly from rural areas. In 1960, 44.6 percent of seminarians had parents who were farmers; in 1982 the figure was 56.5 percent—even though the figure for the agricultural population had dropped from 53.9 percent to 31.5 percent. Few come from the working class and few from upper-class families.

Serbin warned of the consequences of lower academic standards. "The lack of intellectual preparation in seminaries could be harmful to the church as an organization that needs well trained cadres for the task of modernizing itself vis-à-vis Brazilian society." One indicator was that the Catholic church had no institution where priests could study for advanced degrees in the theological disciplines. For that they had to go to Europe.

Because seminary enrollment had rebounded slightly since the mid-1970s, bishops and religious superiors tended to believe that the vocation crisis had been surmounted. Even so, new ordinations were only roughly replacing losses of priests and religious; they were not keeping pace with population growth. Serbin warned against complacency and said that it was especially important to draw seminary students from wider segments of society.[19]

It could be objected that the foregoing discussion assumes that Catholicism depends on the clergy and religious and ignores the possibility of renewal through the laity. Especially in view of the major innovations by lay Catholics in the United States, both those closely connected to the institutional church and those who are working more independently, the approach here might seem quite clerical.

Certainly, it could happen that a new wave of innovation could arise from the laity somewhat independent of the hierarchy, clergy, and religious congregations, but such a development seems unlikely. It should be kept in mind that most Latin American lay people are not the sociological equals of middle-class Americans. The realms in which they can take initiatives are limited. Traditionally, poor people have organized little more than religious celebrations and sports leagues. During the past generation, the scope of their organizing has expanded, and can be seen in land invasions, soup kitchens, cooperatives, and so forth. In most cases, however, these initiatives are crucially dependent on "mediators," whether church personnel or development organizations, and on outside funding. In this respect the base community is no different: it is not an independent lay initiative, but the product of a pastoral strategy initiated by sisters or priests, who continue to play a central role. That indeed, is precisely the critique of Comblin (Chapter 5): unless base communities are allowed to develop their own independent lay structures, the whole movement is in danger of declining and even disappearing. While grace and novel developments can produce surprises, it is sociologically unrealistic to expect Latin American laity, primarily the urban poor, to be the source of renewal by themselves.

The church cannot be built "without the figure or role of the priest who presides over the eucharist, that man or woman who becomes the builder of the community," insisted the priest in seminary education who did not share the sanguine view of the bishops that the vocation crisis had been resolved. The celibate male model of priest is "gone forever." The problem was not the lack of vocations but the "filter" keeping people who had a vocation from reaching the priesthood. "I simply can't imagine the church meeting the challenges of the modern world without a competent clergy, and I simply can't imagine a future clergy that is not a married clergy" (meaning not that current priests should get married but that people in stable marriages could be ordained).

Why not have a twenty-year plan in which a thousand parishes would be preparing such people and having them ordained deacons, he wondered. They would be like evangelical pastors, that is, very similar to the people of the community. When it became possible, they could be ordained priests. Although in principle bishops could be doing so, the whole issue was "too hot to handle," and so they were vainly trying to fill their seminaries.

Crisis of Growth

In assessing the present state and future prospects for Catholicism, pastoral theologians implied that, even a generation after Vatican II, church renewal was just beginning. A pastoral advisor to the Brazilian bishops admitted that there were "no emerging models" for pastoral activity yet. A parish should be a "network of communities," understood as more than base communities. More than one person observed that the problem with base communities was that they had been absolutized.

Father Virgilio Leite Ochoa, a long time staff person at the Brazilian Bishops Conference, said that the church was discovering "its insufficiency vis-à-vis the urban society that is arising in Brazil." He singled out the "problem of the laity": despite many efforts, the kind of laity needed for a modern society had not been developed. He was thinking of the laypeople who had developed through the Catholic Action of the 1950s and early 1960s. No better pedagogy than that one—combining action and reflection—had yet been developed.

At its best, such Catholic Action led to the formation of small groups of people who were working in specific environments, such as the university, labor unions, or politics. In their meetings they would reflect on what they had done in specific real situations, whether their action had been inspired by the gospel, and whether that action had had an impact. This was in fact the source of the observe-judge-act method used in the base communities and the progressive church in general. Some of the major individual lay Christians in public life to this day in Brazil and elsewhere emerged from those groups, but now they are in their fifties and sixties. Although Ochoa did not say so explicitly, even the base communities did not produce the same kind of laity, people who could take major initiatives in society. The reason is not one of methodology but of culture: members of base communities are poor and their scope for initiative is limited. Even leaders of specific base communities are largely dependent on the sisters or priests in charge of the overall program.

A number of people stated that the Catholic church was ill-prepared to deal with the challenges of the city, since the church's structures and mindset are the product of a rural world now on the wane. Somewhat curiously, perhaps, the word "modernity" kept recurring in discussions of the prospects for the church. To a degree this may have been a spillover from a wider discussion of the need for Brazil to "modernize" technologically in order to have a place in the rapidly globalizing economy. These discussions tended to be conflated with discussions of postmodernity among intellectuals.[20] In the pastoral context, I had the impression that because the very terms "modernity" and "modernization" for years had borne the stigma of their association with the "dependent capitalism" that had to be overthrown, only recently were theologians finding it meaningful to discuss modernity.[21]

The 1995-1998 pastoral plan for the archdiocese of Sao Paulo (briefly cited in Chapter 1), drafted in the knowledge that it would probably be the last prepared under Cardinal Arns, represents an interesting effort to focus on the challenges of the present. The church must "have the courage to break with old forms and methods of pastoral action and to seek those suited to the needs of the city of Sao Paulo," entailing new kinds of engagement, and it must encourage new ministries for the urban situation. New local areas for evangelization outside of parishes must be created. The document envisions "pass-through" parishes, particularly those downtown (including the cathedral), whose ministry would be aimed at the large number of people present only during the day. Another possibility envisioned is the creation of spaces for evangelization in large public places such as commercial districts and railway and bus stations. One notable feature of the plan is that church activities are not divided into neat categories, such as liturgy and social ministry, but liturgy, bible study, catechesis, and so forth, are seen as dimensions of the church's one mission to the city. The four priority areas are work, health care, housing, and education. The parishes and other church entities are to renew their missionary ardor so that "inculturating themselves ever more in the urban environment, they might hear and respond to the cries of the people with solidary actions, and especially of those who are deprived of work, health care, housing, and education."[22]

Although Catholic pastoral theologians had begun to consider the specific requirements of an urban ministry in the 1960s the discussion was largely abandoned for two decades or more, perhaps because it seemed to reflect the assumptions of capitalist development. Urban ministry in Latin America was coming onto the agenda once again after a long hiatus.

As my interview with Father Dagoberto Boim, the rector of the Sao Paulo cathedral, was drawing to an close, he said, "My last point would be that this is a crisis of growth, and of questioning—not of weariness. The crisis is that of models that were regarded as unique and absolute. No pastoral model and no model of the church exhaustively represents the church and testifies to the Reign."

13
Coming of Age

Issues and Prospects for Protestants

THIS CHAPTER, LIKE THE PREVIOUS ONE, moves from observations on particular churches in two cities to reflections on issues within the Protestant and evangelical community. My own Catholic identity, however, no doubt colors my approach.

Differences That Matter

Latin American Catholics tend to divide Protestants into the historic churches, with which they may have ecumenical relations, and all the other churches which they continue to call "sects." Although Brazilian Catholics may be aware of Bishop Edir Macedo of the Universal Church because of his media notoriety, they have little sense of the other churches. Catholic pastors, for example, may know the location of a dozen or so churches in their parish but would be hard pressed to explain the differences between them.

To outsiders, poor evangelical churches may look much alike, but from within the evangelical community differences are significant. The clearest faultline is between pentecostal and non-pentecostal churches. The latter may be subdivided into the historic churches (they would be called mainstream denominations in the United States) which in these cities are largely represented by Presbyterians, Baptists, Methodists, and the churches that grew from faith missions (such as the Dios Admirable church in Caracas, Chapter 11). The pentecostal churches may be divided into those whose origins date from early in the century (Assemblies of God) and those of more recent formation (although, as Chapter 2 makes clear, such a division is not entirely appropriate for Brazil). Hence, the following serves as a rough categorization:

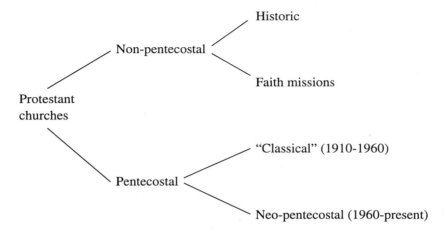

These differences are primarily a matter of church order, not doctrine. Indeed, the content of doctrine seems to be of little practical concern to pentecostal churches.

Differences within the broad pentecostal community are wider than might be supposed. The point of greatest division concerns what are commonly called "usages and customs," particularly in behavior and dress codes. At one extreme is the God is Love church whose manual, as has been noted, contains detailed prescriptions, each with a scriptural quotation, on behavior and particularly dress (down to what kinds of belts or eyeglasses are regarded as vain). Violation of each prescription entails a punishment. In most churches, such practices are primarily a matter of custom and of expectation. As Nancy Pereira discovered, evangelical women are proud that their loose, long-sleeved dresses make them stand out visibly. At least the more sophisticated church leaders have some awareness that such matters are not directly grounded in scripture but are the result of historical practice and that, for example, Protestants in some countries may enjoy tobacco or alcohol. Most behavioral matters are left to the discretion of the believer in the Las Acacias and Foursquare Gospel churches. In the spirit of its founder, Aimee Semple McPherson, the Foursquare Gospel church even holds dances. The Universal Church does not seem to enforce any such behavior code, at least at services intended primarily for the general public. The longstanding relaxed attitude of Las Acacias toward such practices has earned it anathemas from other evangelical churches and has been part of its appeal. It seems possible that a significant group of Latin Americans wish to be evangelical but are unwilling to submit to detailed behavioral prohibitions. Some pentecostal leaders, such as Ricardo

Gondim (Chapter 2) and Samuel Olson and Inesio Murillo (Chapter 11) believe that it is essential to relativize strict behavior codes; for others these codes are part of a church's very identity.

Differences over customs to some extent reflect differences of class and culture among the churches. All those attending the God is Love church were visibly poor, and I concluded that the entire church leadership was in tune with the culture of the poor. Although the Universal Church resembled God is Love in some respects—with its multiple services, cures, and exorcisms ("liberation"), cadres of preachers, and *caudillo* leader—it was clearly more multi-class in orientation (even if its center of gravity was lower middle class). Certain groups or churches were extremely class-specific (for example, ADHONEP, the Full Gospel Businessmen's Association).

Although pentecostal (and conservative) churches shun the word "ecumenical," they generally take a position toward other churches. The Christian Congregation and God is Love do not recognize other churches. Because the Assemblies of God is by far the largest church, it tends to act in a largely self-sufficient manner, but it acknowledges the legitimacy of some other pentecostal churches and on occasion will work with them in such activities as evangelism crusades, for example. Las Acacias cultivates relationships with other churches.[1]

Ministry provides another obvious point of comparison. Numerous independent churches are formed by lay preachers who discover their gifts in practice. Given this route to ministry, many pastors receive little or no formal training. In both Brazil and Venezuela, the Assemblies of God officials claimed that their ministers are required to receive seminary training (although the degree of compliance remained unclear). In both God is Love and the Universal Church, ministerial formation is very much in-house; becoming a minister is like being initiated into a guild.

In most churches, formal ministry is an exclusively male prerogative. A notable exception is the Foursquare Gospel church, 35 percent of whose ministers are women (Chapter 2). Paul Freston observes that 22 percent of the head pastors are women and in some cases the primary pastor is a woman and her husband is the auxiliary pastor. Furthermore, women have headed the Foursquare Biblical Institute in Brazil for almost its entire life. Freston goes on to say, "No historical church, no matter how progressive its language, comes anywhere close to these figures. While women priests in the Catholic church seem to be further and further away, and some historic Protestant churches are taking timid steps that do not seem to really meet what women are asking, the fact that a pentecostal church has developed a surprisingly egalitarian model without boasting to others or undergoing crisis ought to make us question certain stereotypes about the religious field." Bryan Froehle found that 7 percent of pastors in Caracas are women. Very often they are single mothers pastoring churches in very poor neighborhoods where many households are headed by women.[2]

Pentecostal churches vary in their political and social stances more than might be expected, given the common impression that they either shun all worldly activities or actively support right-wing candidates and parties. Some churches reject in principle any political involvement by their members (Christian Congregation and God is Love); an early contrary case was Brazil for Christ, some of whose members (with encouragement from its founder Manoel de Mello) were elected to national and lower level offices even in the early 1960s. For some years now, Latin American evangelicals have been moving toward more direct political and social involvement. In some cases the basis for such an approach was articulated in the statement of the Lausanne (Switzerland) Covenant, a key paragraph of which reads: "Although reconciliation with man [sic] is not reconciliation with God, nor is social action evangelism, nor is political liberation salvation, nevertheless, we affirm that evangelism and socio-political involvement are part of our Christian duty...The salvation we claim should be transforming us in the totality of our personal and social responsibilities." That text, which was the result of a great deal of discussion, and was a consensus position at the 1974 worldwide meeting of evangelicals, is a central expression of the theological justification for "holistic" mission, so much so that the word "Lausanne" is a kind of shorthand for a whole understanding of church mission. It should be recognized, however, that although some church leaders, such as Ricardo Gondim (Chapter 2) find it meaningful, others do not. The Las Acacias church and others associated with it agree with the sentiments of the Lausanne statement, whereas it is ignored by churches such as God is Love, the Universal Church, and the Christian Congregation.

The chart on page 172 may serve to illustrate schematically some of the differences. These differences, which reflect each church's history and circumstances, show clearly that pentecostal churches differ among themselves on important (at least to them) issues. One result is that individual churches can be oriented toward the tastes and needs of particular segments of the religious market (to use such terminology for a moment) ranging from the rigidity of God is Love, which perhaps offers some poor people a mooring in a hostile and threatening world, to the Renascer Youth services, where a rock concert format is intended to lead youths to personal acceptance of Christ.

	Assemblies of God	Christian Congregation	Foursquare Gospel	God is Love	Universal Church	Las Acacias
CUSTOMS	Relatively rigid	Rigid	Flexible	Strictly enforced	Not enforced	Left to discretion of believer
SOCIAL CLASS	Multi-class, primarily poor	Multi-class, often descendants of immigrants	Multi-class, lower middle class	Very poor	Multi-class, with aspirations to success	Multi-class, with middle-class feel
MINISTERIAL FORMATION	Often seminaries	All leadership lay, no formally trained ministers	Seminary	Internal	Closed in-group, under control of Bishop Macedo	Lay formation; interdenominational seminary closely connected to church
ATTITUDE TO OTHER CHURCHES	Accepts some other (pentecostal) churches	Does not accept others	Accepts others	Does not accept others	Claims to be all-embracing in ideas; open-door policy	Accepts others
POLITICAL AND SOCIAL STANCE	Large number of members (including ministers) in Brazilian congress in late 1980s	Shuns political involvement; social programs for members	Open	Shuns involvement	Bishop Macedo has supported politicians; operates social ministries	Church operates many social ministries; some influential people are members

A Protestant Community?

To what extent is it meaningful, however, to speak of a Protestant or evan-gelical community? A consciously ecumenical Protestant like Jaime Wright, who believes that the criterion for the church's authenticity is its contribu-tion to the whole of society, seems to have virtually nothing in common with anyone in the Universal Church where "liberation" means deliverance from evil spirits. Wright is more at home—theologically and spiritually—with Catholics who share his position than with most of his fellow Presby-terians. There is likewise a large—seemingly unbridgeable—gap between theological liberals and those whose interpretation is literal.

For decades Protestants have banded together to defend their inter-ests in a generally hostile environment. The AEV (Evangelical Association of Venezuela) was formed in the 1950s when Protestants in Venezuela were very few. In Brazil, even evangelicals who regarded the Universal Church as questionable were willing to band together to defend Bishop Edir Macedo's civil rights when he was accused of financial misdeeds. The concern was that he was perhaps being targeted unfairly because he was a flamboyant evangelical.

Another form of cooperation is the activity of the Bible Society, which in both Brazil and Venezuela manages to distribute large numbers of bibles as well as tracts with scriptural passages. The Bible Society scrupu-lously sidesteps taking any position on the divisions indicated above. Evangelical books and music cross denominational lines. Seminaries ac-cept students from more than one like-minded denomination. Churches work together to sponsor evangelistic campaigns, such as the week-long crusade preached by Alberto Motessi in the bull ring in Caracas.

Evangelicals increasingly believe that they still do not have a voice in society proportionate to their real weight; they believe that they deserve to be heard just as as much as the Catholic church is heard through a bish-ops conference and in other manners. They also believe that the secular media should take them more seriously. That concern is understandable since, as we have often noted, the number of active church-going Protes-tants approximates or may sometimes surpass that of Catholics.

One of the difficulties is the heterogeneity of Protestants noted above. Who speaks for them and by what authority? In Brazil the secular media have tended to give some attention to CONIC (Council of Christian Churches), which was recognized by the World Council of Churches. The half dozen Protestant churches in CONIC (along with the Catholic Church) do not have a large membership and most are centered in the far south of the country. The AEVB (Brazilian Association of Evangelicals), headed by the charismatic Presbyterian pastor Fabio Caio d'Araujo in Rio, which is certainly more representative of the evangelical mainstream, might eventually be the source of such a unified evangelical voice.

Coming of Age and Its Demands

It is perhaps worth recalling that until the middle of the present century the United States was a "Protestant" nation. All presidents (in addition to being white males) were Protestants of some sort until the 1960 election. To be a Catholic in the U.S.—other than in a few eastern cities with strongly ethnic neighborhoods—was to be consciously in the minority; anti-Catholicism was still a residual memory, despite the melting pot ideology and the "we're all American" feeling that came out of both world wars. The fears and prejudices triggered by the candidacy of John F. Kennedy were soon resolved by the candidate himself and by the liberalization that accompanied Vatican II. Moreover, during mid-century many Catholic families achieved middle-class status; they moved to the suburbs and their children began to graduate from universities and to enter professional and technical fields.

This recital of history is relevant if Protestants in Latin America are crossing an analogous threshold[3] likewise marked by political developments. In 1990 Jorge Serrano, a professing evangelical, was elected president of Guatemala. (The 1982-83 presidency of Efrain Rios Montt was less significant since it was the product of a military coup.) Evangelicals were a significant part of Alberto Fujimori's 1989 winning coalition in Peru. Remarkably, in the runoff election the Catholic bishops were supporting Mario Vargas Llosa, an unbeliever, against Fujimori, a practicing Catholic. In the 1986 election in Brazil, thirty-five evangelicals were elected to the national congress and the "evangelical bench" was the third-largest caucus.

This recent political visibility of evangelicals is a sign of acceptance or of coming-of-age, roughly analogous to what happened in the United States from the early to the mid-twentieth century. To be a Protestant no longer excludes one from public life and may even be an electoral plus: it may attract the votes of the "evangelical bloc" without sacrificing other votes. Indeed, the general Protestant reputation for probity is a selling point.

What is lacking to Protestants in politics, said Jochem Streiter, a Lutheran pastor in Caracas, is a "political project." Protestants entering politics have been distinguished only by their sense that their moment has arrived, and a claim that as evangelicals they are morally superior to other politicians, who are assumed to be corrupt. Without any larger purpose, however, they could easily fall into the patterns of traditional politicians, manipulating patron-client relationships (for the benefit of the churches, to be sure). Serrano's 1993 attempt to dissolve the Guatemalan congress, which backfired and sent him out of office, is illustrative.

The recent political visibility of Protestant politicians is likely to be a passing phase. Over time it will become clear that by itself being an evangelical does not make an individual a good public servant. To the extent that evangelicals as a whole realize that they have indeed come of age and are accepted by the larger population, defending evangelical interests may become less urgent. At that point the religion of a candidate or public office holder should become less relevant. Whether evangelicals will at some point have a distinctive contribution to make to politics and public life remains to be seen.[4]

Theological Education

Seventy to seventy-five percent of pastors heading churches in Latin America have never been able to study theology formally, said Jaime Rodriguez, the Venezuelan head of FLET (Latin American Faculty of Theological Studies), in his office at the First Presbyterian Church in downtown Caracas. That estimate seemed plausible to me from observation, particularly of the smaller churches at the neighborhood level. Churches vary widely in their attitude toward theological training. Until recently, explained Izes Calheiros, the director of AETAL (Evangelical Association for Theological Education in Latin America), what the Assemblies of God, for example, sought in a minister or church "worker" was outstanding behavior, experience in church leadership, and acknowledgment of that leadership by the church. Formal theological training was not given a high priority.

The historic churches have maintained seminaries and theological schools for years. The IMET (Methodist Institute of Theological Studies) in Sao Bernardo to the south of Sao Paulo is in fact a spacious, pleasant campus with full-time residential students. More typical, perhaps, is the Baptist Seminary a few blocks from where I was staying, where most students arrived in the evening after working during the day, attended classes until 9 P.M., and then rode buses to their neighborhoods where they could sleep a few hours and begin the routine once more. Several seminary educators expressed sympathy with their students (some of whom have trouble staying awake in class) but also indicated their own frustration, since students often fail to complete assignments. In relatively few cases can pastors (and their families) be full-time students for the three or four years needed to complete a seminary curriculum. Moreover, to do so might remove them from their own culture. On the other hand, an untrained pastor who knows nothing of biblical scholarship, church history, or systematic theology is likely to confuse his own improvisation with biblical revelation.

One response is that of FLET, which was set up to help those who are already church leaders but who cannot take time out to study full time. Rodriguez explained to me that students meet in groups, typically of five to seven participants, under a tutor (who may not be highly trained but has a teacher's manual) in courses organized into thirteen-week units. In addition to the weekly hour-and-a-half meeting, students are given workbook assignments that are expected to take several hours a week. The first level of FLET courses is accessible to people of very limited education. The second is at a high school level, and the third level looks like a seminary curriculum and includes courses in hermeneutics, church history, and pastoral counseling. After a year and a half in Venezuela, the program had thirteen hundred students from a variety of churches. In Colombia, seven thousand were participating. About 30 percent of the participants were pastors, and the others were church leaders.

At first glance, the method seemed to be open and to reflect "theological anthropology," that is, an approach to theological questions that takes as a starting point a profound reflection on human experience and human nature. The texts were graced with photos, and the margins were sprinkled with quotes (Helen Keller, Disraeli, Cardinal Wyszynski) and even cartoons. The course titles in level two were: "The God Whom We Adore," "The Person Who I Am," The Family to Which I Belong," "The Church in Which I Serve," "The Community in Which I Live," and "The World to Which God Has Sent Me." Pedagogically, the workbook method seemed to be aimed at making the student reflect and respond, and had exercises such as interviewing other people on their religious beliefs.

Upon closer examination, however, it was clear that the underlying conviction of biblical inerrancy cast a long shadow over the whole work. For example, the creation account in Genesis was contrasted directly with evolutionary science. As I examined FLET materials, I could not avoid the impression that despite the reader-friendly appearance, the overall thrust was one of indoctrination rather than opening to inquiry and wonder. When the challenge of theological education is regarded as that of multiplying seminaries or FLET-type extension courses, it is questionable whether the result will be pastors and church leaders able to think critically.

Basis for Economic Development

Some observers were celebrating the evangelical moment because of its implication for society at large. David Martin opened *Tongues of Fire* with a large but simple idea, namely that North and South America represent two contrasting types of civilization, the Anglo and the Iberian, and that the economic success of the one and the backwardness of the other derived largely from that difference. The present wave of Protestantism represents the advance of Anglo values which may accordingly serve as the cultural basis for economic development. Martin sees the connection between capitalism and Protestantism not so much in the sixteenth-century reformers but in early Methodism, whose exuberance was closer to today's pentecostals than to the churches that now bear the name Methodist.

It was no accident that Peter Berger wrote the foreword to Martin's book and that funding for Martin's research was provided by the Institute for the Study of Economic Culture headed by Peter Berger. Since publishing *Pyramids of Sacrifice* over twenty years ago, Berger has criticized structural explanations for underdevelopment (such as the dependency school). The welcome given to Martin's ideas is rather like the embrace of the theories of Hernando de Soto in the late 1980s. Scholars had been studying the "informal sector" for years, but his book *The Other Path* explicitly proposed that small business could be the driving force of a new kind of society, and proposed a way of thinking about development that was an explicit alternative to the left.[5]

Martin's proposal cannot be refuted in advance. If in fact evangelical Protestantism provides the basis for a major cultural shift, and if that shift is a crucial element in rapid and broadly shared economic growth, his prescience will be obvious. At this moment, however, it is plain that Martin's arguments are filled with hidden assumptions and are presented with utmost aplomb. The most important of those assumptions is that the personal and household attitudes and habits of a society's citizens are the key elements in determining whether that society will attain development.

Despite decades of accumulated experience and thousands of research projects, there is simply no consensus on what drives economic development, that is, why some nations remain poor while others become richer. The editors of one recent collection of articles find four groups of explanations: the "classic thesis" that the onset of industrialization leads to a temporary increase in inequality as an inevitable phase on the road to development; explanations that seek the root causes in culture (such as Martin); dependency and world-system explanations which posit the existence of a prosperous core of rich countries, a poorer semiperiphery, and a periphery; and finally, a series of explanations focusing on state policies. Each of these broad categories includes numerous approaches. The point here is not which of these approaches, or which combination of them, has the greatest explanatory power, but rather that any serious proposal for discussion of development should at least display some awareness of the ongoing discussion. As it stands, Martin's grand proposal that the shift from Iberian to Anglo culture through evangelical churches will at long last spur economic development is closer to curbstone philosophy than it is to scholarship.

Let us imagine a nation in which, let us say, 30 percent of the population becomes evangelical and actively so. Among these people alcoholism and marital infidelity largely disappear, and hard work, sobriety, and wise use of earnings become the norm. These believers are devoted to education, and they support one another at the congregational level. Evangelical business people prosper, not through bribes and deals, but by upholding standards of customer service and honesty. Even non-evangelicals find themselves forced to emulate such behavior. Upright conduct becomes an advantage for politicians. Over time, the whole society becomes less "Iberian" and more "Anglo."

Certainly such a change would be welcome, provided it indeed led to enhanced living conditions for the people. Suppose, however, the country's wealth and power were distributed as they are in Brazil. What assurances are there that the 5 percent of prosperous will not continue to use their power to assure for themselves a way of life equal to that of the well-off in the developed countries—as they did during the "Brazilian miracle" of 1968-73 (when growth was around 10 percent a year) and have done since then? Chile, for example, is currently touted as a model of a country that has unleashed the power of the market and has been successful in world trade. A closer look, however, reveals that perhaps 40 percent of the Chilean population has had little share in the recent boom, and that disparities of income distribution, which were once more equitable by Latin American standards, now rival those of Brazil. Chile's boom, moreover, is largely based on the export of its own summer fruit during the northern hemisphere's winter. What if the country in which the "Anglo-shift" occurs has no such competitive advantage, real or potential?

Is it not entirely possible that the very variety of evangelical churches might in the end provide a Christian justification for winners and losers in the development lottery? The winners may accept Christ as their personal savior with others of their own kind at gatherings like ADHONEP; relative have-nots who aspire to be haves may find a home, at least temporarily, in prosperity-oriented services such as those offered by the Universal Church; the desperately poor could accordingly find consolation at churches like God is Love. Nancy Pereira Cardoso interpreted the plain dress of evangelical women as a rejection of the consumer society by people who knew they were excluded not only from the levels of consumption but from the very society that continually sought to tantalize them with images of what they could never be.

If in recent decades the left may have been tempted by seemingly clear and compelling explanations for underdevelopment (and clues to what liberation might look like) views such as Martin's are likewise misleading despite their seemingly common-sense clarity. Far from being the solution promised by Martin and enthusiastically celebrated by *Forbes,* the positive effects of evangelical growth on Latin American culture can be at most an ingredient in economic growth and development.

AS WAS NOTED ABOVE, the very existence of a "Protestant community" may be questioned. Nevertheless, a qualitative change is occurring, and Protestants and evangelicals are, or are becoming, a critical mass, despite the slowness of secular society and the Roman Catholic church to acknowledge that development. The kinds of questions sketched here will continue to arise as evangelicals reflect on the political, economic, and social implications of their coming-of-age.

14
Across the Divide

FOLLOWING SOME OBSERVATIONS on the current situation and prospects for Latin American Catholicism and Protestantism, it seems fitting to conclude with reflections on their mutual relations. That has been my aim since I first felt the disquietude that led me to Brazil and Venezuela.

From a common-sense standpoint, the emerging relationship between evangelicals and Catholics in Latin America would seem to be one of competition. Bryan Froehle's study of the churches in Caracas assumes that such is the case despite the relatively low proportion of evangelicals. David Martin's sweeping claim is not only that evangelicals are winning the competition, but that their rise might signal a sea change in Latin American society, a shift from an "Iberian" to an "Anglo" culture. Despite his attention-grabbing title, David Stoll did not argue that Latin America was necessarily "turning Protestant," but rather that evangelical Protestantism was more important statistically—and qualitatively—than the much discussed Catholic initiatives taking inspiration from liberation theology. *Conflict and Competition* was the title of a collection of articles on the churches edited by Edward Cleary and Hannah Stewart-Gambino. In *Looking for God in Brazil,* John Burdick systematically compared a Catholic parish, an Assemblies of God congregation, and an Afro-Brazilian *umbanda* in the religious "arena."

At various points, I have noted that Catholics are loath to admit a situation of competition, let alone to explicitly do battle. To some extent this may be an unwillingness to face uncomfortable facts. Bishops in particular will understandably be slow to acknowledge the situation if to do so would encourage the press, government officials, and society to cease regarding Catholicism as "the" church. I suspect, however, that there is something else at work besides institutional interest, and that the reluctance to regard the situation as one of competition reflects something deeper in the nature of Catholicism.

In a variation on the competition theme, some speak of a religious "bazaar" or "supermarket" in Latin America. The emphasis falls on the fact that Latin Americans can choose from a wide variety of religious goods: Catholicism varying from papal-restorationist, through charismatic, to liberal, or liberationist, and including many religious expressions with African and indigenous roots, and Protestantism, from mainline denominations to faith missions and pentecostal churches, as well as a variety of new religious movements. To anthropologists—or even casual visitors—such a variety of religious expressions has long been obvious. The notion of a market also puts emphasis on the individual as a "consumer" who can choose from many products and who need not be permanently loyal to any single brand.

Despite the advantages of such an analogy—which is no more than a metaphor—I would prefer to search for some other way of understanding the current religious situation in Latin America.

What is new in the present situation, says sociologist Paul Freston, is that religious pluralism is becoming a reality for the first time. Although various religious expressions have co-existed with Catholicism, their practitioners have identified themselves as Catholics. Freston cites the behavior of the *pais-de-santo* (leaders of the Afro-Brazilian religion candomblé) in Bahia, who announced that they would suspend their activities during the 1991 papal visit to Brazil. Even though the pope himself might not regard candomblé as Catholic—and anthropologists might agree that it is a religion with its own beliefs and practices—these leaders were expressing deference to the one that they regarded as their ultimate superior on earth. Evangelicals, by contrast, are defiantly outside the tent of Roman Catholicism. Thus, during Pope John Paul II's 1991 visit to Brazil, Bishop Edir Macedo on a single day assembled an estimated total of four hundred thousand for Universal Church stadium rallies in Rio, Sao Paulo, and Salvador while the pope was saying mass for one hundred thousand in Brasilia.[1] A less flamboyant example of a public challenge was the three-day evangelistic campaign organized by the Assemblies of God that I observed during Holy Week in Sao Paulo (Chapter 2).

Edward Cleary argues that Protestant advances need not mean Catholic losses: the churches are ultimately "siblings" rather than rivals. He first relativizes claims for evangelical growth by noting that those who join evangelical churches often come from other evangelical churches. Evangelical growth is not inexorable and some who become evangelicals eventually return to the Catholic fold. Most important, the Protestant expansion is taking place alongside renewed vitality within Catholicism. The matter of gains and losses is more than numerical, however. Most of Cleary's essay is an exploration of the possibility of convergence between Latin American Catholics and evangelicals, and particularly the possibility of a meeting between pentecostalism and the Catholic Charismatic Renewal. In the same spirit, here I would like to explore further such possibilities.

At a retreat center in Panama in 1966, I was the only Catholic at a meeting of a dozen or fifteen church leaders, mainly American missionaries. At one point Kenneth Mahler voiced the idea that perhaps the mission of Protestants was not so much to plant and expand their own churches as to stimulate and aid the Catholic church to do its own work: to evangelize its people and enable them to grow and form a Christian community.

From a Lutheran minister this was a bold idea but not entirely surprising since it reflected the ecumenical rapprochement of the post-Vatican II era. Since that time, many in the historic churches have in fact lived by that insight. ISAL (Church and Society in Latin America) began as a Protestant initiative, but by 1970 Catholics were very much involved in its various activities. Protestants, especially from the southern cone countries, were prominent in the ferment of liberation theology. Theologians and biblical scholars have worked ecumenically for over two decades. Protestant church agencies in Europe and the United States have funded ecumenical and Catholic work in defense of human rights. Jaime Wright's collaboration with Cardinal Arns and the formation of the ecumenical group CONIC are other expressions of that redefined sense of mission. Mahler's insight has been embodied in many modest if real ways, at least by the historic denominations.

Is it possible that the reverse might also be true? That is, could it be that the Roman Catholic church (and the historic churches) might be called to aid the pentecostal churches in carrying out their mission? In this final chapter I would like to explore some admittedly hypothetical possibilities in that regard.

Same Space, Different Stances

Based on what I had observed in Central America and on what I had read, I expected to find in Sao Paulo and Caracas at least the beginnings of organized Catholic responses to evangelical growth. It seemed logical to me that Catholics could "fight back" by using the same methods: charismatic-type worship, televangelism, and organized systematic door-to-door campaigning by Catholics combined with ways of bringing people to accept Christ as their savior and become part of a faith community.

Such initiatives have been developed elsewhere, particularly in the form of SINE (Sistema Integral de Evangelización—Holistic Evangelization System), an entire pastoral "package" combining scripture groups, the charismatic movement, the traditional Catholic "mission," and door-to-door visiting devised by the Mexican priest Rafael Navarro. Contrary to my expectations, I found no such systematic response in Brazil and Venezuela, and I now suspect that no major effort to confront evangelical growth directly will be forthcoming. Although the reluctance to admit that evangelicals are serious contenders may be partly due to a fear of losing Catholic influence as "the" church, I believe that at a deeper level it reflects fundamental differences in the stances of the two traditions.

To Catholics it is "connatural" to feel related to, and responsible for, an entire society even when they are a minority. The actual form of Roman Catholicism—its liturgy, theology, and spirituality—took shape during christendom, the period roughly between the fourth and the sixteenth centuries, when church and society in Europe were coterminous. The central act of Catholicism, the eucharist, is the complex result of a classic fourth-century synthesis that evolved into the Roman (somewhat monastic) mass, and was codified and frozen in Latin at the Council of Trent. A generation ago the Roman liturgy was restored, although doing so entailed more than merely wiping off centuries of grime and candle smoke to reveal the masterpiece below. In any case, it is typically Catholic that the liturgy is not the creation of the celebrant, but a larger drama in which celebrant and people follow their scripts. In doing so they are not speaking only for themselves, but for the church, humankind, the entire cosmos. Or to vary the metaphor, it is like a vehicle or ship in which the celebrant is at most a driver or captain.

The Catholic church is multi-class. Even though the worshippers at any particular parish will be relatively homogeneous, they are members of a church spanning all classes in the particular society. Catholic territoriality is suggestive: every square meter of Sao Paulo or Caracas is under the authority of a pastor, who is responsible by canon law for those residing there (even if individual Catholics may go searching around the city for a church suited to their taste).

The reformation led to a repudiation of Catholic christendom and to numerous efforts to recreate a pure and primitive biblically based community. Unlike the Latin mass, which was like a vessel transporting all passengers and the pilot (priest), Protestant worship, even in its regimented pulpit-centered forms, depended on the intensity of pastor and worshippers. Although the mainline churches know that they have a history, pentecostal churches typically believe—or assume—that the word is as directed to them today as it was to Isaiah, Paul, or Jesus' group of disciples, and that they are in direct contact with God.

Based on his observation of a progressive Catholic parish and an Assemblies of God church on the outskirts of Rio, John Burdick argues that whereas evangelical Protestantism is a religion of abrupt conversion, Catholicism is one of a lifelong journey. Even when Catholics speak of conversion, they envision it as a never-ending process rather than a one-time event. Such a conversion is less likely to inspire the clean break with the past that becomes engraved in people's conscience and serves as the starting point for a dramatically changed life.[2]

These are matters of degree, of course. It seems to me, however, that such considerations are useful for understanding the attitudes I encountered and, more important, what may be expected of the two traditions.

During the week of the Motessi campaign in the bull ring (Chapter 11), the Venezuelan Catholic bishops and the Catholic university held a week long "National Encounter with Civil Society" at the Catholic university. Each morning a panel of respected Venezuelan intellectuals presented ideas on a given area: political life, economic policy, administration of justice, and education. The participants were chosen on the basis of work that they had already done, and reflected a spectrum of positions. The aim was not merely to air interesting ideas, but to move toward areas of consensus (as well as to demarcate areas of disagreement) and to make proposals for Venezuelan society.

Whatever the impact on Venezuelan public life, it was typically "Catholic" of the bishops to sponsor an effort to devise solutions based on the common good. Although it was only by coincidence that evangelicals were engaged in a major crusade to bring individuals to Christ during the same week, I believe the symbolism of the two events says much about the characteristic stances of the two church traditions toward society.

For the foreseeable future, in other words, the Catholic church will continue to operate as though it is the church of the entire society (even though only a small portion of Catholics attends mass with any regularity), while evangelical churches will strive to convert individuals. Within Catholicism some efforts may be made to lead people to an "evangelical" level of conviction, while Protestant churches may seek a public role of service to society as a whole.

Crossing the Threshold: What Catholics Might Learn

As indicated at various points in this book, many Catholics were ready to admit—at least abstractly—that their church could learn from evangelicals. Catholicism has been too one-sidedly rational and too doctrinal, they admitted. While encouraging people to become critical and analytical, base communities had overlooked the emotional and bodily aspects of life. Evangelicals were obviously tapping into popular culture.

Catholics who might say such things however, gave every evidence of being little intrigued by the evangelicals. In both Caracas and Sao Paulo, it seemed clear to me that in a couple of months of inquiry I had entered more deeply into the evangelical world than any Catholics with whom I talked except social scientists doing religious research. In Brazil, all were aware of the Universal Church because of the publicity surrounding Bishop Edir Macedo, but few seemed to care about the differences between the Christian Congregation, the Assemblies of God, and God is Love, for example. It was now "pastorally correct," as it were, to acknowledge some positive features in the churches that seemed to have something that satisfied the yearnings of the poor, but Catholics seemed content with secondhand learning gained at pastoral workshops or from reading.

Perhaps the first step for Catholics is some unlearning: to consider the possibility that a significant religious development is taking place and that it cannot be understood without firsthand experience.

The next step is simply to cross the threshold: to enter churches not only to observe worship services, but also to engage in discussion with church leaders and members. Priests, sisters, or lay leaders in a parish might inventory the churches in their own neighborhood and visit them. Or they might be more comfortable observing a similar selection of churches (Assemblies of God, God is Love, and so forth) in another area. They might choose to do so openly as fellow Christians who happen to be Catholics, or anonymously, primarily to expose themselves to a religious experience that many of the people around them are finding meaningful. The same would be true of bishops.[3]

A first thing Catholics might observe would be the intensity of prayer, particularly in pentecostal churches. Even when the proceedings have an air of showmanship, the people in the chairs or pews are often deep in prayer. The point would not be to borrow techniques but to consider how Catholic liturgies could encourage a deeper spirit of prayer.

The role of the pastor should also prompt reflection. As has been noted, there are already far more evangelical pastors than Catholic priests in Brazil. In some instances they may be pastoring only two or three dozen people, but in others congregations number two or three hundred. What is striking is that the pastors are from the ranks of the poor and, despite their suits and ties, remain like the people around them in their of ways of life and outlook. Catholicism simply has no figure like the pastor; ordained priests, even if originally from the poor, have become "intellectuals," and lay leaders of base communities enjoy nothing like the independence of the evangelical pastor. An evangelical pastor is, so to speak, a religious entrepreneur: he must keep himself in business by holding onto his congregation and serving them well. A Catholic priest is far more a representative of the corporation. Entrepreneurial abilities may be useful at the parish level, but they are not required for ecclesiastical advancement.

At one time it might have been possible for leaders of base communities to be recognized as a Catholic version of pastors and to be ordained priests—without having to leave their culture. That possibility now seems to have been lost. As it presently functions, the Catholic church could not absorb a figure similar to the Protestant pastor. Lay leaders, for example, are far more dependent on the official Catholic structure than pastors. Exposure to how evangelical churches operate might make Catholics aware that devising new models of ministry remains on the agenda.

The foregoing is not intended to idealize Protestant or evangelical ministers. The exclusion of women—with some exceptions—and hence the generally male culture is one distorting factor, as is the general tendency toward personalistic authority at the congregation level, where the minister may be only reproducing what he observes in caudillo-type leaders such as Edir Macedo and David Miranda.

Comblin, in the already cited essay raising questions about base communities, asks what Catholics can learn from Protestants.[4] After mentioning some qualities of pentecostals that attract Catholics, such as concern for individual persons, small communities, a new sense of self-worth that comes with conversion, and missionary outreach, he comes to the figure of the pastor. Catholics continue to pour resources into seminaries to produce a few priests, while tens of thousands of evangelical vocations proliferate on all sides. "The solution is to accept the pastors that God is sending us and to grant them their place in the Church." Catholic lay leaders are stifled, whereas evangelical pastors, despite the authoritarianism of their churches, feel free: "They have the entire world to save." Base-community leaders "never achieve this sense of freedom and responsibility." The fundamental relationship between clergy and base-community leaders is one of fear. "[T]he hierarchy and most of the priests are afraid. The fearfulness of the authorities generates fear on the part of the animators and of their communities. Fear feeds upon fear; it is a vicious circle. But the *crentes* ["believers" = evangelicals] are not afraid of anything. This is their great strength."

One can wonder, however, how closely Catholics could approximate pentecostal missionary zeal. Some participants in the Catholic Charismatic Renewal obviously believe that one is not a true Christian unless one has been baptized in the Holy Spirit and accepted Christ: only charismatics have truly experienced Christian conversion (although they might be reluctant to formulate matters so bluntly). Catholics who so believe may well devote themselves to outreach, and for them the Charismatic Renewal functions as the real church within the larger Catholic communion. Need-

less to say, such an attitude is hardly Catholic and will remain a minority
(and largely unstated) position.

I would nonetheless suggest that some kind of outreach might still
make sense and become part of Catholic practice. In the early years of the
base-community movement, it was often assumed that the process of community formation would continue until parishes were networks of base
communities. What has tended to happen, however, is that priests or sisters
initiating the work in an area soon reach a level at which much of the time
and energy that they have left after attending to such duties as routine
parish matters, classes, development projects, and catechetics are devoted
to servicing and sustaining a small number of communities.

In base-community work in the 1960s and 1970s the "basic course"
was often followed by a "cursillo" (partly borrowed from the Cursillo de
Cristiandad), which was structured to lead to a conversion experience (typically on Saturday night). This experience was then expected to lead to ongoing membership and life within the community. Inevitably, however, it
proved impossible to sustain the drive, and many of those who became involved dropped out or became only marginal or occasional members.

The Catholic church cannot literally copy or duplicate evangelical
forms of outreach. Part of the strength of evangelical conversion is that
one turns away from one's previous identity as a Catholic and enters a new
community. When making house-to-house visits, evangelicals are missionaries in alien territory, and most people will turn them away; but the effort
pays off if they encounter even one receptive person or household.
Catholics knocking on doors as representatives of the local parish will find
not only an immediate identity, but also a subtle resistance: how is the way
I live my Catholicism any business of yours?

Could Latin American Catholicism be inspired by evangelicals to engage in more outreach, but could it do so in a more "Catholic" form?

When outreach is identified with drawing new members into a particular movement, such as base communities or the Charismatic Renewal,
and keeping them there, success is identified with expansion. By the same
token, those who cease to be active members are seen as "fallen away,"
and may even feel that way. Suppose, however, that the aim of outreach
was primarily to provide individuals and families and groups with the opportunity to hear the gospel at a particular moment in their lives with no
uniform expectation of what they would do in response. It would be assumed that most people are navigating their way through life under difficult circumstances and that doing God's will should not be identified with
any single course of action. Some people might indeed opt to become active in the parish community or do so for a period of time; most participants in a retreat, youth group, or course would not do so, but would have

some guidance for living their lives. Consider, for example, a parish offering courses on sexuality, marriage, and lay spirituality for adolescents and adults. Success would not be measured by the number of Catholic marriages; the very course itself would be regarded as a moment of grace.

Urban parishes typically have twenty thousand or more people who identify themselves as Catholics but who have only rare contact with the church; several hundred who attend mass one or more times a month; and a smaller number who feel a strong personal commitment to the parish. A core group could be organized to engage in systematic outreach to the wider community in a variety of ways: by providing marriage counseling, courses, and youth activities; by visiting their neighbors to offer parish services; by providing families with bibles and New Testaments at subsidized prices; by organizing prayer and bible discussion groups; by inviting people to retreats.

The outreach being described would be Catholic as opposed to evangelical, that is, it would be animated by a characteristic Catholic sense that "grace is everywhere," that God is operative in people's lives, that the aim of the church is to be a sign and means of grace, but that whether, when, and how individuals (even those calling themselves Catholic) relate to the church, is best left to themselves and to God. This stance would be theologically different from that of those (typically evangelical, but including some Catholics) who identify a particular model of explicit personal acceptance of Christ as crucial for salvation or who measure the health of a parish or of the church by the number of people attending Sunday worship.

This might appear to be a repackaging of some existing pastoral practice, for example, the ten ministries and eight zones in Padre Ticão's parish (Chapter 4) or the general approach of the Petare Group (Chapter 10). A priest in Brazil told me that whenever he worked with base communities he continually insisted that they were to regard their purpose as serving the surrounding masses of people. In practice, however, priests and sisters easily become fully absorbed with the demands made upon them, and lay groups are similarly absorbed with tasks of maintenance. Outreach tends to be seen as the arduous and usually disappointing effort to bring in new members to a particular activity. Moreover, the preoccupation of religious orders with the authenticity of their "presence" (as "inserted" communities) tends to take the edge off the need for outreach (Chapter 12). The proposal here is that a parish core, well aware that it is and will remain a relatively small group, continually engage in outreach to other Catholics, not in order to convert them to particular movements, but rather to help them follow God's will in their own particular circumstances.

From their evangelical neighbors, Catholics could learn to make greater efforts at outreach. They would do so in a Catholic way, however. To some degree this is implied in the pastoral plans of the Sao Paulo archdiocese in which the church is continually seen in relation to its "mission to the city." From evangelicals, Catholics might learn a greater sense of urgency, and to actually engage in outreach in a more systematic and ongoing fashion.

Embracing History: What Evangelicals Might Learn from Catholics and Historic Protestantism

A professor at the Baptist Seminary in Sao Paulo walks into his first class in hermeneutics and looks over his students, poor men from around the city who are struggling to pastor churches. Laying on the table a bible like the ones they use in their churches, he states, "This is *not* the word of God."

Pausing to allow the enormity of the statement to sink in, he repeats what he has said, and then adds, slowly, "This is a *translation*... of the *best texts* we can assemble... of what we believe is the word of God." It takes the rest of the class—indeed, the rest of the course—to discuss and explain what he means.[5]

Such shock therapy is powerful pedagogy. That God did not address Moses in Portuguese may never have occurred to some of the students. Although the issues may be troubling, the net effect is undoubtedly positive. As these pastors prepare their sermons they will be less naive, more conscious that they are engaged in an act of interpretation and that they must continually endeavor to deepen their understanding of the original context of the bible in order to preach God's word in a very different contemporary context.

This professor from a historic church tradition is broadening the view of students from around Sao Paulo. He is challenging them and presenting the opportunity for growth. This simple example is perhaps a paradigm of what the historic Protestant churches and the Catholic church may offer Latin American evangelical, and especially pentecostal, churches in the areas of biblical interpretation, church history, and social responsibility.

Biblical inerrancy appears to be the great divide. For fundamentalists, it is the bedrock of Christian faith; for liberals, it distorts faith and prevents deeper understanding. The persistence of various kinds of fundamentalisms in the late twentieth century suggests that conservative evangelicals will not be marching in a straight line toward a more liberal interpretation. It is perhaps helpful to recall, however, that the pre-conciliar Catholic church had its own version of inerrancy, although its fundamentalism was more papal than scriptural.

Because pentecostal churches are centered on prayer and praise, rather than doctrine, it may prove easier for them to move away from fundamentalism toward a more adequate understanding of revelation.

The Catholic church's identity is intimately connected with its historicity, (consider, for example, the statues of popes surrounding the basilica of St. Peter in Rome). Pentecostal churches, by contrast, are tempted to imagine themselves as being in contact with God in the immediate present and to ignore the mediation of historic tradition. Although traditions can constrain churches, they are also sources of inspiration and renewal. From Catholics and the historic churches, evangelicals may be able to learn to draw on the vast accumulated experience of the churches for perspectives on the present. At a very minimum, such an understanding should enable them to recognize their kinship with other churches.

As noted in the previous chapter, evangelicals generally are beginning to express a greater sense of responsibility toward society. This sense is often expressed in terms quite similar to those of Catholicism a generation ago: the human being is not spirit alone, but body, soul, and spirit; God saves not only individual persons, but persons in community; ministry is to the whole person, to the city, to society. These themes are more likely to be articulated by theologians or by staff members of parachurch organizations than by the pastor of a storefront church, but they are gaining ground. As individual pastors and churches move toward holistic ministry, they could learn from the experience of the Catholic church and historic Protestant churches during the past generation.

Seeking to discern the "signs of the times" has become second nature to Catholic pastoral agents. A comparable idea in Protestant circles has been that of "contextualization," although it tends to be seen primarily in terms of effective preaching of the word. Catholic "social analysis" has been a useful pastoral discipline or tool, even if in retrospect the seeming clarity that it once provided turns out to have been more partial than was realized at the time. (As one priest said to me, "It's fine to say 'see-judge-act,' but what about what we don't see?") Nevertheless, the very exercise of consciously looking for "signs of the times" has helped Catholics and the historic churches avoid acting merely on their own instincts. On the other hand, certain signs may have been privileged (labor union or neighborhood organizing) while others may have been downplayed or ignored (specifically female experience, or growth of mass popular culture).

In the future, Catholics and evangelicals may help one another to discern God's will in present circumstances.

Learning, Witnessing, and Working Together?

To date the evangelical and Catholic communities are still at odds. Many evangelicals regard the Catholic church as less than Christian, while Catholics tend to ignore the "sects" or to regard them as pernicious and illegitimate. Events in Brazil in late 1995 underscore the latent possibility of conflict. In October, Bishop Sergio von Helder of the Universal Church appeared on television alongside a statue of Our Lady of Aparecida. Can God be compared to a "doll like this," he asked, "so ugly, so horrible, so wretched? There's nothing holy about this object and it can't do a thing for you!" He then proceeded to hit and kick it. That sight, repeated on TV and in magazines and newspapers, stirred outrage and controversy all over Brazil. Spokespersons for the Universal Church said that his action had occurred on the spur of the moment and admitted that it was insensitive to the feelings of Catholics. Many observers, however, were convinced that it was a calculated gesture, and an indication of the "religious war" mentality of the Universal Church. The Globo TV network then aired a miniseries called *Decadência* centered on an Edir Macedo-like charlatan preacher, prompting the Universal Church to portray itself as persecuted by the most powerful man in Brazil, Roberto Marinho, the head of the network (which is indeed the fourth largest in the world, after CBS, ABC, and NBC in the United States), working in league with the Catholic church. The controversy raged on for several months, and Brazilian authorities began to look into accusations against Bishop Macedo with renewed vigor.[6]

Given a "holy war" mindset, religious polarization is at least conceivable, although remote. The example of the Las Acacias church and some others suggests other possibilities. In closing, I would like to suggest a few thoughts on possible lines of rapprochement.

First, is it not possible for Catholics and evangelicals at least occasionally to come together to pray for their community, city, or nation? Is occasional common prayer, bible reading, or meditation possible at the neighborhood level?

Evangelicals are increasingly searching for a way to have a "voice" in society analogous to that of Catholic bishops and episcopal conferences. In the present and near future, they will probably strive to create and build up representative organizations and have them recognized as a voice, as in, for example, the case of AEVB in Brazil. Might there not be occasions, however, when a combined voice of the Catholic church and Protestants of all kinds might be desirable?

At various points, this book has noted the seeming tendency toward growing polarization in Latin American cities and societies, symbolized in the very architecture of the high-rise towers that isolate and protect the middle classes. This "social apartheid" seems to be growing more severe, as some of the pathologies of the inner cities of the rich world are reproduced in the poor neighborhoods. Could the churches, whose members come from both sides of the growing chasm, find a way of issuing a gospel critique of the social forces driving the split, and suggesting ways to reverse it? Can the churches symbolize the possibilities of a different kind of society?

Most observers will agree that there is a crisis of the family in Latin America. Increasing numbers of female-headed households are a reality—or are being noticed systematically for the first time. One of the signs that the churches could offer is that of a new model of family, and of masculinity and femininity. Is mutual learning possible? Could Catholics learn from, say, the Las Acacias lay-led ministries and heavy emphasis on counseling? Could evangelicals learn to critique their own naive reproduction of male dominance and its justification by scripture (which bears the marks of its patriarchal cultures)?

These are speculative possibilities, offered tentatively. Let us hope that in the near future Catholics, Protestants, and evangelicals will be crossing one another's thresholds regularly, learning from one another, and together giving witness.

Notes

Introduction

1. David Stoll, *Is Latin America Turning Protestant? The Politics of Evangelical Growth* (Berkeley: University of California Press, 1990).

2. David Martin, *Tongues of Fire: The Explosion of Protestantism in Latin America* (Oxford: Basil Blackwell, 1990).

3. John Marcom, Jr., "The Fire Down South," *Forbes,* October 15, 1990.

4. James Brooke, "Pragmatic Protestants Win Catholic Converts in Brazil," *The New York Times,* July 4, 1993.

5. Jon Sobrino, "Preface," and "Preface to the English Edition," *Mysterium Liberationis: Fundamental Concepts of Liberation Theology* (Maryknoll, NY: Orbis Books, 1993), pp. ix-xiv.

6. Researchers have begun to look at the various expressions of religion (Catholic, Protestant, Afro-Brazilian) in an area side by side. See in particular Rowan Ireland, *Kingdoms Come: Religion and Politics in Brazil* (Pittsburgh: University of Pittsburgh Press, 1991) and John Burdick, *Looking for God in Brazil* (Berkeley: University of California Press, 1993).

7. Alan Gilbert, *The Latin American City* (London: Latin America Bureau, 1994), p. 26.

8. The country was also preparing for a plebiscite in which voters would be able to decide whether to replace Brazil's presidential-style government with a parliamentary system similar to those in most European countries. Indeed, the ballot contained a choice between monarchy and representative government. The citizenry was being given the opportunity to democratically choose—or at least ratify—its form of government. After a dozen years of economic stagnation, however, the form of government was rather remote from most people's concerns.

9. In 1994 Fernando Henrique Cardoso, the finance minister, formulated a plan that halted the high inflation that had plagued Brazil for over a decade; that success catapulted him beyond Lula in the polls and into the presidency at the end of the year. Cardoso, it may be noted, was one of major figures of the "dependency" school of economic thinking embraced by the Latin American left in the 1960s. He entered politics in the 1970s and by the 1990s was a centrist whose economic thinking was congenial to the business sectors eager to accept the neoliberal agenda of opening Brazil to free trade and downsizing the role of government.

1. A Church for the Megacity

1. *Time,* January 11, 1993 (cover story on "Megacities," p. 36), gave the figure of 19.2 million inhabitants for the metropolitan region. The figure may have been based on earlier projections by U.N. agencies and by an extended definition of the urban region.

2. Department for Economic and Social Information and Policy Analysis, "Population Growth and Policies in Mega-Cities: Sao Paulo," New York, United Nations, p. 3.

3. Jorge Wilhelm, "Sao Paulo," *Cities,* November 1984.

4. This figure is from "Population Growth and Policies," p. 26.

5. Ana Flora Anderson, interviews February and March 1993. One of the Dominicans was Frei Betto whose letters from prison were published even before he was released. He later wrote a detailed account of Dominican activities and government repression, interrogation, and torture; the book, entitled *Batismo de Sangue,* became a best-seller in Brazil in the early 1980s. See Chapter 4.

6. Jaime Wright, "D. Paulo e os Direitos Humanos II," in *Paulo Evaristo Arns: Cardeal da Esperança e Pastor da Igreja de São Paulo* (Sao Paulo: Edições Paulinas, 1989), pp. 56ff., esp. 63-66. This book is a tribute to Cardinal Arns with comments from fellow bishops, priests, and others, and includes a bibliography of his works and works about him.

7. Interview with Jaime Wright, March 1993. See also Jaime Wright, "D. Paulo e os Direitos Humanos," in *Paulo Evaristo Arns: Cardeal da Esperança* as well as interviews with Ana Flora Anderson and Ana Dias, March 1993.

8. *Torture in Brazil* (New York: Vintage, 1986). Paul Freston in *Protestantes e Política no Brasil: da Constituinte ao Impeachement* (doctoral thesis, Campinas, Brazil, 1993, p. 1) notes that the original publication, *Brasil, Nunca Mais* (translated as *Torture in Brazil*) was the largest selling non-fiction book in Brazilian history. For an account of the publication project, see Laurence Weschler, *A Miracle, A Universe: Settling Accounts With Torturers* (New York: Pantheon, 1990).

9. José Pegorado, "Um só povo, muitos pastores? A divisão da arquidiocese de São Paulo," in *Paulo Evaristo Arns: Cardeal da Esperança,* presents a detailed account of the print media's coverage of the division of the archdiocese.

10. Interview with Bishop Decio Pereira, April 1993.

11. *Arquidiocese de São Paulo: 7a Plano de Pastoral—1995–1998* (Sao Paulo: 1995), p. 9, developed on pp. 47-48.

2. Windows into the Evangelical World

1. The ministries are not territorial, but reflect slight differences within the church. Some churches of the Rio-based Madureira Ministry are in Sao Paulo. All ministries belong to a single Convention.

2. According to the 1986 Anuario Pontificio of the Vatican, there were 386 diocesan priests and 658 religious priests in the Sao Paulo archdiocese (prior to its division). SIDEAT, *Hacia un Mapa Pastoral de América Latina* (Bogotá: CELAM, 1987).

3. As noted at the outset, most Latin American Protestants call themselves *evangélicos,* which does not necessarily have the same sense as the English "evangelicals," with its resonance of social conservatism and biblical literalism, although most Latin American Protestants are "evangelical" as understood in English.

4. Rubem Cesar Fernandes, "Censo Institucional Evangélico CIN 1991 1os. Comentários" (ISER: Rio de Janeiro, 1992), chart, p. 18.

5. Paul Freston, *Protestantes e Política no Brasil,* p. 66.

6. First name pronounced "Edi" (or "Eddie") since Brazilians add an "ee" sound after a final consonant.

7. For an an account of the founding and early decades of the Assemblies of God in Brazil, see W. J. Hollenweger, *The Pentecostals: The Charismatic Movement in the Churches* (Minneapolis: Augsburg Publishing House, 1972), pp. 75-84.

8. I estimated the crowd by counting a section of one hundred from an overhead bridge, and then used that to estimate the area occupied by one thousand people, thus arriving at a rough estimate of the total attendance.

9. The Christian Congregation is so resistant to a personality cult that it has not only not published a biography of Francescon, but is said to have burned the papers of someone who had begun to do so. (Interview with Key Yuassa, a Japanese-Brazilian pastor of the Holiness Church who was working on a biography.)

10. Reed Elliot Nelson, "Análise Organizacional de uma Igreja Brasileira: A Congregaçáo Cristã no Brasil," in *Revista Eclesiástica Brasileira* (Sept. 1984), pp. 544-58. Also Francisco Cartaxo Rolim, "Congregação Cristã no Brasil," in *Sinais dos Tempos: Igrejas e Seitas no Brasil,* Cadernos do ISER 21 (Rio de Janeiro: ISER, 1989), pp. 53-57.

11. Reed Elliot Nelson, "Análise Organizacional," pp. 555-56.

12. Antônio Gouvêa Mendonça, "Un Panorama do Protestantismo Atual," *Sinais dos Tempos Tradições Religiosas no Brasil* (Rio de Janeiro: ISER, 1989), p. 78.

13. See Harvey Cox, *Fire from Heaven: The Rise of Pentecostal Spirituality and the Reshaping of Religion in the Twenty-first Century* (Reading, MA: Addison-Wesley Publishing Company, 1995) for a recent sympathetic appreciation.

14. Mendonça, "Un Panorama do Protestantismo Atual."

15. Figures on September attendance from *Veja* October 17, 1990, reprinted in the dossier collected and published by CEDI (Centro Ecumênico de Documentação e Informação, *Alternativas dos desesperados: Como se pode ler o pentecostalismo autônomo* (Rio de Janeiro, 1991), p. 11.; drowning at baptism *Folha de Sao Paulo* September 26, 1990, in CEDI, *Alternativas,* p. 120.

16. Ricardo Mariano, interview, March, 1993.

17. Frei Gorgulho, Ana Flora Anderson interviews, March 1993.

18. Mariza Soares, "Guerra Santa no País do Sincretismo," in Leilah Landim (ed.) *Sinais dos Tempos: Diversidad e Religiosa no Brasil,* Cadernos do ISER (Rio de Janeiro: ISER, 1990), p. 86. Paul Freston gives a somewhat different schedule. Freston, *Protestantes e Politica,* p. 100.

19. Macedo interviews in *O Globo* (April 29, 1990), and *Isto É* (June 20, 1990) in CEDI *Alternativas,* pp. 89 and 109.

20. Bispo Macedo, *Vida com Abundância* (Rio de Janeiro: Editorial Gráfica Universal, Ltda., n.d.), p. 84.

21. Margarida Oliva, interview, Sao Paulo, February 1993.

22. Bispo Macedo, *A Libertação da Teologia* (Rio de Janeiro: Editorial Gráfica, Ltda., n.d.).

3. Effectiveness and Authenticity

1. Ricardo Gondim, interview, Sao Paulo, February 1993.

2. Personal correspondence with author, February 1996.

3. The ISER team searched records of denominations, the Bible Society, telephone books, the *Diario Oficial* of the State of Rio de Janeiro, and so forth. ISER Núcleo de Pesquisa, *Censo Institucional Evangélico CIN 1992 Primeiros Comentários* (Rubem Cesar Fernandes et al.)

4. Ibid., p. 25.

5. Handwritten conference notes of Rev. Ed Kivitz.

6. Christine Kraft, SEPAL, interview, April 1993.

7. Ricardo Mariano, interview, March 1993.

8. Eudes Martins, interview, March 1993; data from "Pesquisa ABEC – Ano 1991" (photocopy of fax).

9. Assuming that 85 percent of the 138,000 million inhabitants were Catholic.

10. Alves was initially associated with the liberation theologians (*A Theology of Human Hope,* Washington DC: Corpus Books, 1969) but by the early 1970s had moved in other directions (cf. *Tomorrow's Child: Imagination, Creativity, and the Rebirth of Culture* [New York: Harper & Row, 1972]), although he has continued to teach and write on religion.

11. As an example of how racism operates, Wright told of a black friend who was frequently stopped while driving because police suspected any black man driving a car. He would let them arrest him before revealing that he was a priest.

12. Paul Freston, "O Potencial Político das Comunidades Evangélicas ou (Quase) Tudo que a Esquerda Precisa Saber sobre os Evangélicos mas Nunca teve Coragem de Perguntar," in Freston, *Fé Biblica e Crise Brasileira: Posses e Política; Esttoerismo e Ecumenismo* (Sao Paulo: Abu Editoria, 1992), pp. 73-96. In this little book, addressed to the evangelical community, Freston combines sociological insight with a distinct theological stance.

4. Contending with Dragons

1. Ana Dias, interview, Santo Amaro, March 1993.

2. Frei Betto's legal but rarely used name is Carlos Alberto Libanio Christo. Among his works: *Against Principalities and Powers: Letters from a Brazilian Jail* (Maryknoll, NY: Orbis Books, 1977); *A Vida Suspeita do Subversivo Raul Parelo* (Rio de Janeiro: Civilização Brasileira, 1977) short stories; *Fidel and Religion* (New York: Simon & Schuster, 1985); and a four-volume *Catecismo Popular* (Sao Paulo: Editorial Atica, 1989).

3. *Batismo de Sangue: Os domincanos e a morte de Carlos Marighella* (Rio de Janeiro: Editora Civilização Brasileira, 1982).

4. Police had spread the rumor that Marighella had been betrayed by the Dominicans, hoping to sow division among the opposition.

5. *Fidel and Religion* (New York: Simon & Schuster, 1985). Castro reflected at some length on his childhood and upbringing and spoke positively of the role of the churches. Critics faulted Betto for avoiding hard questions and showing an adulatory attitude toward the interviewee.

6. People were to vote first on whether the country should be a monarchy or a republic. This was unfinished business from 1889 when there had been no formal vote to choose republican government after the abdication of the Emperor Pedro II. Assuming a ratification of republican government, voters in 1993 were then to choose whether to continue with the existing presidential system or to move to a parliamentary system such as those in most European countries. A parliamentary system, because it avoids the winner-take-all dynamic of a presidential system and provides better expression for minority currents among the public, was attractive to many intellectuals and political analysts. A common-sense argument against making the change was that Brazilian politicians under a parliamentary system would continue to be self-seeking and perhaps corrupt.

7. Working in *mutirões* (sing. *mutirão*), voluntary mutual aid construction crews (similar in spirit to barn raising groups in U.S. history) has been encouraged by the church in order both to economize and build community.

5. Questions about Base Communities

1. Phillip Berryman, *Stubborn Hope: Religion, Politics, and Revolution in Central America* (New York: The New Press and Maryknoll, NY: Orbis Books, 1994), p. 182-83.

2. Jose Comblin, "Algumas Questões da Prática das Comunidades Eclesiais de Base no Nordeste, *Revista Eclesiástica Brasileira,* vol. 50, No. 198 (June 1990); abridged translation, "Brasil: Base Communities in the Northeast," in Guillermo Cook (ed.), *New Face of the Church in Latin America* (Maryknoll, NY: Orbis Books, 1994).

3. Pedro Ribeiro de Oliveira, "CEBs: Estrutura ou Movimento?", *Revista Eclesiástica Brasileira,* Vol. 50, No. 200 (December 1990); Jorge Atilio Silva Iuliannelli, "Afinal a união faz o não faz a força?"; Roberto Van der Ploeg, "As CEBs na Fase da Adolescência (Reflexão sobre a Igreja dos pobres a partir do VII Encontro Intereclesial)"; Eduardo Hoonaert, "Futuro das CEBs"; latter three articles all in *Revista Eclesiástica Brasileira,* Vol. 51, No. 201 (March 1991).

4. See W. E. Hewitt, *Base Christian Communities and Social Change in Brazil* (Lincoln: University of Nebraska Press, 1991).

5. John Burdick, *Looking for God in Brazil: The Progressive Catholic Church in Urban Brazil's Religious Arena* (Berkeley: University of California Press, 1993).

6. It is particularly ironic when Catholics whose funding comes from abroad denounce as "foreign" pentecostal churches which subsist through their members' tithing.

7. Jean Daudelin, "Brazil's Progressive Church in Crisis: Institutional Weakness and Political Vulnerability" (Ottawa, August 1992, unpublished paper).

8. Ivone Gebara, taped interview, 1993.

6. Ministries to the Marginal

1. John Drexel, O.M.I., Leila Rentroia Iannone, *Criança e Miséria* (Sao Paulo: Editora Moderna, 1991); Drexel and Iannone, *Walking Together* (Sao Paulo: Mary Helen Drexel Association, 1991). It should be noted that recent research indicates that the numbers often cited for street children may have been substantially overestimated. Drexel himself insisted that most were "children *in* the street," and that the number of full-time street children was far less. On street children, see Gilberto Dimenstein, *Brazil: War on Children* (New York: Monthly Review Press, 1991) and several articles in *NACLA Report on the Americas,* "Disposable Children: The Hazards of Growing Up Poor in Latin America," Vol. XXVII, No. 6, May/June 1994.

2. Much later I learned that the eviction did take place. Because they were organized, the residents were able to find other places to live. About half of the residents moved into another unoccupied building.

7. Church within the Church?

1. For example, Penny Lernoux, *People of God: The Struggle for World Catholicism* (New York: Viking, 1989).

2. Soap operas, it should be noted, are shown at prime evening time, and are the most popular programs on Brazilian TV. They engage the Brazilian equivalent of the writers, actors, artists, and other talented people of the U.S. entertainment industry in Hollywood and New York.

3. From Paul Freston, personal correspondence, February 1996. By comparison, 1.8 percent said that they participated in Christian base communities, and a total of 13.5 percent participated in some "movement" in the Catholic church (including, besides these mentioned, Marriage Encounter, youth groups, and so forth). To put the figure on Catholic charismatics into perspective, it should be noted that it is considerably less than even a conservative estimate of the members of the Assemblies of God.

4. During the years of dictatorship, the annual Corpus Christi procession had been a rallying point for Catholic groups in Sao Paulo. A priest later told me that after military rule ended much less attention was given to organizing the observance. In 1995, however, after renewed emphasis, newspapers reported that 50,000 people had taken part.

5. In 1995 a Catholic network began to operate on cable TV with the approval of the bishops. It featured eclectic programming that was strongly influenced by

charismatics. The cost of cable subscriptions meant that it would be restricted to relatively well-to-do households.

6. The fact that tens of thousands attend the Pentecost celebration at the Morumbí stadium, however, makes it clear that influence of the movement extends beyond prayer group members. Paul Freston suggests that the Charismatic Renewal has a larger "mass" component than base communities, and that hence it is misleading to apply the same kind of measurement. In any case, accurate figures for the Charismatic Renewal remain elusive.

7. Development is described as the "transition from less human conditions to those which are more human," (*Populorum Progressio,* 20-21). The passage describes development as moving from overcoming material need and oppressive structures to developing knowledge, culture, and the will for peace, to acknowledgement of God, and ultimately to participation in God's life. At Medellin the bishops quoted the passage in full, and gave this notion of "integral development" a further theological warrant by likening it to God's delivery of Israel from Egypt (Introduction, 6).

8. "No, We Don't Accept..."

1. For interviews with Latin American theologians on women, see Elsa Tamez, *Against Machismo: Interviews* (Oak Park: Meyer-Stone Books, 1987). The exceptions among the major male theologians are Leonardo Boff, *The Maternal Face of God: The Feminine and its Religious Expressions* (San Francisco: Harper & Row, 1987) and Enrique Dussel, who incorporated "the erotic" (man-woman relations) and "the pedagogic" (parent-child relations) into his earliest work. See, for example, Enrique Dussel, *Philosophy of Liberation* (Maryknoll, NY: Orbis Books, 1985) which systematizes the framework he had been developing since the 1960s.

2. Scholars are finding that, despite the patriarchal ideology of evangelical churches and restriction of leadership to males, these churches often help women deal with problems of domestic violence and abuse. See, for example, Elizabeth Brusco, "The Reformation of Machismo: Asceticism and Masculinity Among Colombian Evangelicals," in Virginia Garrard-Burnett and David Stoll, *Rethinking Protestantism in Latin America* (Philadelphia: Temple University Press, 1993). John Burdick notes that the Catholic church is ill-equipped to deal with everyday domestic issues: small base communities grounded largely in family ties are loath to take sides in disputes and the progressive Catholic ideology is that such issues are only symptoms of structural ills. Priests are reluctant to intervene and their celibacy discredits them in the domestic realm. A woman does not find herself judged morally in Afro-Brazilian religion or Protestantism, because domestic problems are attributed to malevolent forces outside her. Cf. Burdick, "'I Struggle at Home Every Day': Women and Domestic Conflict in the Religious Arena," *Looking for God in Brazil,* Chapter 4.

3. Heidi Jarschel, interview, Santo Amaro, March 1983.

4. Along with dozens of party activists, I observed about two hours of this meeting on closed circuit TV at the PT assembly held at a hotel in Sao Paulo. Of

the fifteen or twenty delegates who spoke while I was present, only one defended her decision. It had been an uphill battle for women to bring the party to agree that a designated proportion of party officials (one third) should be women. No such proposal was even made in more traditional parties.

5. It should be noted that McDonnell and Kirkconnell sometimes gave biblical courses under diocesan sponsorship.

6. The Brazilian bishops have opposed abortion, but it has not been a major theme of their pronouncements.

7. Gebara's recent thinking may be found in *As a Deer Longs for Flowing Streams,* forthcoming 1997.

8. As it happened, she went to Brussels to study, and was allowed to return to Brazil after one year.

9. Crisis and Polarization

1. Figures vary considerably. Many speak confidently of 4 million in the metropolitan area but experts say the number is smaller, perhaps around 3.8 million (roughly on a par with greater Philadelphia).

2. He had not taken the money but had used it improperly for his own gain. In the public mind, however, it was as though he had taken it.

3. Interviews, Wagner Suarez and Pedro Trigo, May 1993.

4. Alberto Micheo, Luis Ugalde, "Apéndice I: Proceso historico de la Iglesia venezolana, La Iglesia en la Venezuela Republicana y Agraria (1810–1936)," in CEHILA *Historia General de la Iglesia en América Latina: Colombia y Venezuela* (Salamanca: Ediciones Sígueme, 1981), p. 613.

5. Ibid, p. 630

6. Cf. Brian Froehle, "The Catholic Church and Politics in Venezuela: Resource Limitations, Religious Competition, and Democracy," in Edward L. Cleary and Hannah Steward-Gambino, *Conflict and Competition: The Latin American Church in a Changing Environment* (Boulder: Lynne Rienner Publishers, 1992), and Bryan Thomas Froehle, "Religion and Social Transformation in Venezuela: Grassroots Religious Organizations in Contemporary Caracas" (Dissertation, University of Michigan, 1993).

10. Hope and Reality

1. The word *malandro* does not appear in standard Spanish dictionaries. In Rio de Janeiro it denotes a young male who lives by his wits on the edge of legality, if not in criminal activity itself. Thus the emphasis is on a style. Yves Pedrazzini, Magaly Sanchez, *Malandros, Bandas y Niños de la Calle: Cultura de Urgencia en la Metropoli Latinoamericana* (Valencia-Caracas: Vandell Hermanos Editores, 1992) is based on interviews with young people in the hillside barrios of Caracas. However, with its mixture of social science jargon and polemic, it ultimately delivers less than the title seems to promise.

2. The looting in Panama City and Colon during the 1989 U.S. invasion of Panama was a sign of this social breakdown, as were the fears of many in the middle class who bought guns and took shooting lessons.

3. Matias Camuñas was one of more than a dozen human rights activists brought to New York in December 1993 by Human Rights Watch. See *The New Yorker*, January 10, 1994, p. 70. The account here is based on several visits to the parish and two formal interviews with Camuñas.

4. Gustavo Gutierrez, *We Drink from Our Own Wells* (Maryknoll, NY: Orbis Books, 1984).

11. Preaching to the Tribe of Caracas

1. *Latin America Mission* (articles photocopied, no date).

2. The following chart gives some indication of the larger churches within Venezuela:

	Members	Churches
Asambleas de Dios	60,000	350
Iglesia Luz del Mundo	35,000	300
OVICE	20,710	269
Federacion de Iglesias Evangelicas Peniel	18,000	200
Convencion Nacional Bautista	16,500	287
Iglesia Presbiteriana de Venezuela	15,769	11
Iglesias Nativas de Venezuela	11,200	140
Plymouth Brethren	7,800	78

"Lista de Entidades Eclesiásticas de Venezuela," prepared by Amanacer (DAWN Ministries) Venezuela, n.d. (The low figure for Presbyterian churches is probably a typographical error.)

3. Data on the Assemblies of God could not be obtained. The Coalition of Evangelical Churches and DAWN ministry 1992 study did not list the Assemblies church under that name.

4. The survey defined the boundaries of Caracas in narrower terms than those sometimes used and hence the lower overall population figure.

5. Bryan Thomas Froehle, "Religion and Social Transformation in Venezuela: Grassroots Religious Organizations in Contemporary Caracas" (dissertation, University of Michigan, 1993).

6. M. Francisco Liévano, "Grupos Básicos de Discipulado Cristiano: Una alternativa que, combinada con muchas otras, puede contribuir a la evangelición de la ciudad."

7. When I asked Ursula Hahn to explain this, she said that the situation was "very relative." She distinguished between young troops and their officers, and also between the army and the police or other bodies, which she admitted are violent and attract violent people. These eighteen-year-olds are given a rifle and are placed in a

kill-or-be-killed situation. As valid as that point might be, I was troubled by the ease with which a major Las Acacias leader made the soldiers themselves "victims."

8. I could not but be reminded of the Catholic parish San Miguelito, on the outskirts of Panama City, where in the mid- to late 1960s hundreds of priests, sisters, and other observers visited each year in order to observe an impressive early example of base-community pastoral work.

9. Interview, Inesio Murillo, May 1993.

12. End of a Cycle or Crisis of Growth?

1. Rubem Cesar Fernandes, *Censo Institucional Evangélico CIN 1992, Primeiros Comentários.* During that period, 220 spiritist centers had also been founded.

2. Clodovis Boff, *Theology and Praxis: Epistemological Foundations* (Maryknoll, NY: Orbis Books, 1987); *Feet-on-the-Ground Theology* (Maryknoll, NY: Orbis Books, 1987).

3. Interview, Sao Paulo, April 1993.

4. "Opening Address of the Holy Father," par. 12, Alfred Nennelly, S.J. (ed.), *Santo Domingo and Beyond: Documents and Commentaries from the Historic Meeting of the Latin American Bishops Conference* (Maryknoll, NY: Orbis Books, 1993), p. 47.

5. Jesús Hortal, S.J., "Movimentos Religiosos Autônomos," in *Comunicado Mensal: Conferência Nacional dos Bispos do Brasil* (photocopy, n.d., approx. 1991).

6. Official at National Conference of Brazilian Bishops, April 1993.

7. Interview, Sao Paulo, February 1993.

8. Quoted by Jean Daudelin from a 1991 interview. Daudelin, "Brazil's Progressive Church in Crisis," p. 3, f.n. 2.

9. Jorge Castañeda, *Utopia Unarmed: The Latin American Left After the Cold War* (New York: Alfred A. Knopf, 1993), p. 3. Other assessments of the left: Barry Carr and Steve Ellner (eds.), *The Latin American Left: From the Fall of Allende to Perestroika* (Boulder: Westview, 1993); Susanne Jonas and Edward J. McCaughan, *Latin America Faces the Twenty-First Century: Reconstructing a Social Justice Agenda* (Boulder: Westview, 1994); Ruben Zamora, "Toward a Strategy of Resistance," *NACLA Report on the Americas* (July/August 1995).

10. Bryan Thomas Froehle, "The Catholic Church and Politics in Venezuela: Resource Limitations, Competition, and Democracy," in Edward Cleary and Hannah Stewart-Gambino, *Conflict and Competition,* p. 105.

11. *Anuario Pontificio Per l'Anno 1994* (Vatican City: Libreria Editrice Vaticana, 1994).

12. Faustino Luiz Couto Texeira (ed.) *Teologia da Libertação: Novos Desafios* (Sao Paulo: Edições Paulinas, 1991).

13. This was the 1989 meeting to discuss the Theology and Liberation series, which as visualized by its planners in the early 1980s was to be a fifty-volume series covering virtually every aspect of theology from a Latin American standpoint.

By the end of the decade the project was foundering, in part because sales were disappointing. Translations of several volumes have been published by Orbis Books, and Ignacio Ellacuria, Jon Sobrino (eds.) *Mysterium Salutis: Fundamental Concepts of Liberation Theology* (Maryknoll, NY: Orbis Books, 1993) captures something of the original comprehensive design (the two-volume Spanish original contains a few articles not found in the English).

14. Manual M. Marzal, et al. (eds.), *O Rostro Indio de Deus* (Sao Paulo, Vozes, 1989); Marcelo de Barros Souza, OSB, José L. Caravias, S.J., *Teologia da Terra* (Petropolis: Vozes, 1988).

15. Ronaldo Munoz, *The God of Christians* (Maryknoll, NY: Orbis Books, 1990).

16. Pablo Richard and Team, "Challenges to Liberation Theology in the Decade of the Nineties," in Guillermo Cook (ed.), *New Face of the Church in Latin America* (Maryknoll, NY: Orbis Books, 1994), p. 250.

17. Jose Comblin, "La Iglesia Latinoamericana desde Puebla a Santo Domingo," in Jose Comblin, et al. (eds.), *Cambio Social y Pensamiento Cristiano en América Latina* (Madrid: Trotta, 1993), pp. 38-39.

18. Early in the papacy, the Jesuit J. B. Libânio wrote *A Volta à Grande Disciplina* (Sao Paulo: Edições Paulinas, 1984) on the contours of the shift taking place.

19. Ken Serbin, "Os seminários: crise, experiências e síntese," in Pierre Sanchis (ed.), *Catolicismo: Modernidade e Tradição* (Sao Paulo: Edições Paulinas, 1992).

20. For a wide range of examples, see John Beverley, Michael Aronna, and José Oviedo, *The Postmodernism Debate in Latin America* (Durham and London: Duke University Press, 1995).

21. Jose Comblin "O Cristianismo e o Desafio da Modernidade," and Julio de Santa Ana, "Teologia e Modernidade," both in *América Latina: 500 Anos de Evangelização: Reflexões Teológico-Pastorais* (Sao Paulo: Edições Paulinas, 1990).

22. Arquidiocese de Sao Paulo, *7a Missão na Cidade: Plano de Pasotral 1995–1998,* p. 48.

13. Coming of Age

1. Samuel Olson had officiated at weddings with Catholic priests, and the Evangelical Seminary of Caracas, which was closely associated with Las Acacias, had made a point of stocking its library with books by Catholic authors.

2. Freston, *Protestantes e Política,* pp. 85-85. Froehle reached his figure by examining lists of pastors and churches (approximately two thousand pages) drawn up by a parachurch organization, whose results were never published. Private communication with Froehle, June 1996.

3. Cf. Daniel R. Miller (ed.), *Coming of Age: Protestantism in Contemporary Latin America* (Lanham, MD: University Press of America, 1994), which collects papers presented at a conference at Calvin College in 1993.

4. It is significant that the writers who are now claiming that the "evangelical moment" has arrived (for example, René Padilla, ed., *De la Marginación al Com-*

promiso [Quito: Latin American Theological Fraternity, 1990]) are typically not themselves pentecostals but members of relatively conservative churches (not the liberal historic churches) in the pietist tradition. They tend to be of an older generation, people who in their own lifetimes have seen Protestant churches grow from being a tiny fraction of the population to their present strength. Because they are themselves not pentecostals, however, they are somewhat marginal to the development that they are celebrating. In other words, the charismatic preachers and church leaders who are most responsible for the recent dynamic growth are devoted to their own churches and do not regard themselves as spokespersons for a larger evangelical movement.

5. David Martin, *Tongues of Fire,* esp. Chapters 1, 2, and 13; Peter L. Berger, *Pyramids of Sacrifice: Political Ethics and Social Change* (New York: Basic Books, 1975); Hernando de Soto, *The Other Path: The Invisible Revolution in the Third World* (New York: Harper & Row, 1989).

14. Across the Divide

1. Joseph Page, *The Brazilians* (Reading MA: Addison-Wesley Publishing Company, 1995), p. 380.

2. Burdick, *Looking for God in Brazil,* pp. 45-46.

3. In fact, it would seem only reasonable that church authorities should not make statements about other Christians based only on hearsay or reading without personal observation and contact.

4. José Comblin, "Brazil: Base Communities in the Northeast," pp. 202-25; reflections on pentecostals, pp. 217ff.

5. Donald Price, professor at the seminary, speaking of a colleague. Interview, Sao Paulo, March 1993.

6. Extensive reporting on the events was found in the Brazilian media for weeks. See, for example, *Isto É,* September 9, 1995.

Index